Get the eBook FREE!

(PDF, ePub, Kindle, and liveBook all included)

We believe that once you buy a book from us, you should be able to read it in any format we have available. To get electronic versions of this book at no additional cost to you, purchase and then register this book at the Manning website.

Go to https://www.manning.com/freebook and follow the instructions to complete your pBook registration.

That's it!
Thanks from Manning!

Learn SQL in
a Month of Lunches

JEFF IANNUCCI

MANNING
SHELTER ISLAND

For online information and ordering of this and other Manning books, please visit www.manning.com. The publisher offers discounts on this book when ordered in quantity.

For more information, please contact

> Special Sales Department
> Manning Publications Co.
> 20 Baldwin Road
> PO Box 761
> Shelter Island, NY 11964
> Email: orders@manning.com

Manning Publications Co.
20 Baldwin Road
PO Box 761
Shelter Island, NY 11964

Development editor:	Becky Whitney
Technical editor:	Mike Shepard
Review editor:	Kishor Rit
Production editor:	Deirdre Blanchfield-Hiam
Copy editor:	Keir Simpson
Proofreader:	Melody Dolab
Technical proofreader:	Trevoir Williams
Typesetter:	Tamara Švelić Sabljić
Cover designer:	Monica Kamswaag

ISBN 9781633438576
Printed in the United States of America

For you, dear reader.
May this book help you on your
journey through our data-driven world.

brief contents

contents

preface

My experience with the SQL language started in the late 20th century when I first worked with relational databases. I wasn't a software developer, and my programming skills were limited mostly to typing a few DOS commands on a home computer. Yet even though I was thrust into learning how to use SQL to perform my job, I quickly found how easy it was to write and execute scripts in this intuitive programming language.

In the years since, I've shared my knowledge of SQL with hundreds of colleagues. What I've found interesting is that most of these colleagues weren't software developers either; they were folks in other departments, such as finance, marketing, or sales, who needed to use SQL to directly access data that was vital to the organization. They didn't have time to learn concepts like third normal form and tuples. They just needed to learn a few basic commands to get started.

If you think about it, we learn a lot of things in life this way. Most of us didn't learn how to build a car before we learned how to drive. We didn't go to culinary school before we started cooking meals. We didn't learn how hard drives stored data and how processors managed CPU threads before we started using computers. Rather, we learned a few necessary concepts and methods to get going and continued learning more as we progressed.

This is the main reason why I was excited to write this book. As someone who has read several books in the Month of Lunches series, I appreciate the fact that one of the main goals is to help the reader become "immediately effective" with the subject. Like others in the series, this book was designed and written to help you start using SQL as quickly as possible. I hope that before you reach the end of chapter 2, you'll already be excited about writing queries in SQL, learning more about the language, and using it with almost any brand of relational database.

Although no single book can cover every concept in the SQL language, I believe that by the end of this book, you'll be able to query and manipulate data successfully for nearly any task required of you. That said, finishing this book should by no means be the end of your journey. I encourage you not only to seek out other books, blog posts, and videos to expand your knowledge of SQL, but also to attend regional events and local user groups to learn from others who use this popular language.

For now, though, enjoy the book. Take heart in the fact that a world full of data will soon be available to you!

acknowledgments

The process of creating this book was the most unexpected adventure of my life. I'd never considered writing a tech book, yet from the moment I was contacted by the folks at Manning Publications about this opportunity, I was excited to be encouraged by so many people. This book has my name on the front, but many others helped get it ready for you.

First, I'm eternally grateful to my development editors, Karen Miller and Becky Whitney, who patiently helped me create this book, as well as Mike Shepard for his outstanding technical reviews and recommendations. Mike is a solutions architect at Jack Henry and Associates who studied math and computer science at Missouri State University. In his 27-year IT career, he has been a developer, a DBA, a sysadmin, and a solutions architect. He specializes in process improvement with PowerShell and SQL Server. Many others behind the scenes helped immensely with organization and promotion, including Mike Stephens, Eleonor Gardner, Malena Selic, Aria Ducic, Paul Spratley, Matko Hrvatin, Adriano Sabo, Ana Romac, Susan Honeywell, and Stjepan Jurekovic. Thank you also to my project editor, Deirdre Blanchfield-Hiam; my copyeditor, Keir Simpson; and my proofer, Melody Dolab. I'm blessed to have worked with such an awesome group of folks!

Many thanks also to my friend Mike Walsh and all my colleagues at Straight Path Solutions for their support and encouragement while I was working on this book, as well as the wisdom of those who have mentored me over the years, including Martin Grant, Curt Johnson, Chris Rose, Chris Hinson, Andy Yun, Ginger Grant, Buck Woody, Grant Fritchey, and Kevin Kline.

Thanks to all the reviewers: Ali Shakiba, Andres Sacco, Cristian Antonioli, Dave Corun, Eder Andres Avila Niño, Foster Haines, Giampiero Granatella, Grant Colley, Greg Grimes, Harlan Brewer, Helen Mary Barrameda, Iyabo Sindiku, Jane Noesgaard

Larsen, José Alberto Reyes Quevedo, Malisa Middlebrooks, Mary Anne Thygesen, Matthias Lein, Mike Baran, Oliver Korten, Paolo Brunasti, Paul Love, Peter Schott, Rajeshkumar Muthaiah, Ravichandran Raja, Rohini Uppuluri, Simon Tschoeke, Sleiman Salameh, Steven Joseph Herrera Corrales, and Sveta Natu. Your suggestions helped make this book better.

Finally, I can't possibly thank my beautiful wife, Amy, enough. She not only helped with most of the formatting but also served as my "pre-editor," checking each chapter before I submitted it. She never complained as I locked myself in my office to write chapters, and she devoted countless hours to reviewing my messy drafts. There's no way that this book would have been finished without her. Thank you, Amy. I love you always.

about this book

Although the SQL programming language was created in the 1970s, our ever-increasing use of relational databases has grown exponentially since then. Now, organizations continually look for folks who can use this data in meaningful ways, and I'm not just talking about software developers.

It's amazing how knowing this one language can offer career opportunities to programmers and nonprogrammers alike. Because, if there's any prerequisite for learning SQL, it's proficiency in the English language. SQL was designed to be as close to English as possible, and for this reason, you should feel confident that nearly anyone can learn it.

This book contains examples that use the MySQL version of the SQL language, but don't think the content won't be relevant if you use SQL Server, PostgreSQL, or some other relational database. Most of the SQL shown in this book works with other relational database products, and I've done my best to note any exceptions for the most popular ones.

Who should read this book

Unlike most books about programming languages, *Learn SQL in a Month of Lunches* was written to make learning easy and accessible to all SQL beginners, regardless of their experience with programming languages. It emphasizes practical ways to use the language, helping you quickly learn the necessary skills to work with data in relational databases.

If you're a non-IT professional who needs to collect data for clients, supervisors, or anyone else who needs to make data-driven decisions, this book is for you. I've had the opportunity to work with colleagues in all sorts of professions who needed to use data, and I haven't met anyone who couldn't learn how to write functional SQL queries. I often say that if you've worked with spreadsheet products like Microsoft Excel and Google Sheets, you should have little difficulty working with relational databases and the SQL language.

That said, if you're a software developer or another type of IT professional who needs to learn the SQL language, this book still offers value to help you get up to speed quickly. Although the book is designed to help even absolute beginners, you shouldn't find it patronizing. I'm confident that the exceptions and warnings in each chapter will help make your SQL more effective and efficient than that of most others who use SQL.

How this book is organized: A road map

Learn SQL in a Month of Lunches is organized into 24 chapters, each of which builds on the keywords and concepts from previous chapters. You'll start with the most basic ways to retrieve data and move on to search for specific data, join multiple sets of data in different ways, change data, and even create database objects to store data and your SQL scripts.

Chapter 1 introduces the SQL language and shows why it's so vital for accessing data in relational databases. This chapter also helps you set up your first database using MySQL.

Chapter 2 jumps right into using SQL, guiding you through your first query and showing you how the language emulates spoken English.

Chapter 3 gets you started querying data in the most basic (and common) ways.

Chapter 4 shows you how to sort or limit the results of your queries and gets you started adding valuable comments to your SQL.

Chapters 5 to 7 delve into some of the most common elements of filtering the data you choose to see, providing helpful keywords and addressing the common misconceptions about null values.

Chapters 8 to 11 describe how to join sets of data, connecting them in different ways via the relationships designed in the database.

Chapter 12 walks you through grouping data to find basic arithmetic values such as the maximum, average, and count of values in a set of data.

Chapter 13 introduces variables—staples of nearly all programming languages that allow you to store values for later use in a script.

Chapters 14 and 15 cover functions, which are special keywords that perform repetitive tasks such as returning date and time values and changing the way data is displayed.

Chapters 16 and 17 help you manipulate data when you need to add, change, or remove values in a database.

Chapters 18 and 19 reveal how to store data in tables you create, as well as how to use constraints and indexes to improve data integrity.

Chapter 20 shows you how to reuse your SQL by saving it in database objects like stored procedures and views.

Chapter 21 provides ways to make decisions inside queries based on different conditions.

Chapter 22 describes how cursors evaluate data one value at a time and discusses alternatives to their use.

Chapter 23 gives you the chance to use everything you've learned by not only reading SQL scripts written by someone else but also considering ways to improve the scripts.

Chapter 24 wraps up the book by giving you encouragement and guidance on your next steps in growing your SQL knowledge.

About the code

This book contains many examples of source code, both in numbered listings and in line with normal text. In both cases, source code is formatted in a `fixed-width font like this` to separate it from ordinary text. Sometimes code is also **in bold** to highlight code that has changed from previous steps in the chapter, such as when a new feature adds to an existing line of code.

In many cases, the source code has been reformatted; we've added line breaks and reworked indentation to accommodate the available page space in the book. In rare cases, even this was not enough, and listings include line-continuation markers (➥). Additionally, comments in the source code have often been removed from the listings when the code is described in the text.

You can get executable snippets of code from the liveBook (online) version of this book at https://livebook.manning.com/book/learn-sql-in-a-month-of-lunches. The complete code for the examples in the book is available for download from the Manning website at https://www.manning.com/books/learn-sql-in-a-month-of-lunches and from GitHub at https://mng.bz/PNl8.

liveBook discussion forum

Purchase of *Learn SQL in a Month of Lunches* includes free access to liveBook, Manning's online reading platform. Using liveBook's exclusive discussion features, you can attach comments to the book globally or to specific sections or paragraphs. It's a snap to make notes for yourself, ask and answer technical questions, and receive help from the author and other users. To access the forum, go to https://livebook .manning.com/book/learn-sql-in-a-month-of-lunches/discussion. You can learn more about Manning's forums and the rules of conduct at https://livebook.manning.com/ discussion.

Manning's commitment to our readers is to provide a venue where meaningful dialogue between individual readers and between readers and the author can take place. It is not a commitment to any specific amount of participation on the part of the author, whose contribution to the forum remains voluntary (and unpaid). We suggest that you try asking the author some challenging questions lest their interest stray! The forum and the archives of previous discussions will be accessible on the publisher's website as long as the book is in print.

about the author

JEFF IANNUCCI is a senior consultant with Straight Path Solutions, specializing in relational database administration and SQL programming. He has used SQL to solve database puzzles for more than 20 years. He has shared his knowledge as a speaker at technology conferences and user-group meetings, as a writer for various technical sites, and as a Pluralsight content author.

Before you begin

Nearly every act of our lives generates data. Every purchase we make, every mile we travel, and every internet link we click adds to a colossal amount of ever-growing data, which for many organizations has become their most valued asset. This data is often stored in a relational database, which keeps the data secure, scalable, and available to be constantly read and modified by innumerable users.

But how exactly can these users work with the data in a relational database? More important, how can you read and write data that is critical to your organization? The answer, and the subject of this book, is *Structured Query Language*, more commonly known as *SQL*.

1.1 Why SQL matters

Now, you may be wondering whether SQL is important enough for you to invest an entire month of lunches in it. Be assured that learning this language is undoubtedly one of the best skills anyone who uses data can acquire. Even though much of the data of our modern lives is stored in relational databases from different brands, such as Oracle, Microsoft, and IBM, nearly all use SQL to work with data and have been using it for quite some time.

Although many application languages have a lifespan of only a few years, SQL has been the standard language for querying relational databases for decades and should continue to be so for the foreseeable future. This means the skills you'll learn and develop by reading this book and practicing the recommended exercises can potentially benefit you for your entire career.

1

Perhaps most important, SQL is very easy to learn because it was designed to be written like the English language. If you are familiar with English, the commands and syntax used in SQL will seem intuitive. If you need to work with your data to find the first and last names of customers in Canada, for example, you might use a SQL statement like this:

```
SELECT FirstName, LastName FROM Customers WHERE Country = 'Canada';
```

See how easy that is? Although you may not understand every bit of that statement, I assure you that within the first few chapters of this book, you will be able to write queries like this one.

1.2   Is this book for you?

There is no shortage of books, videos, courses, or websites that offer to teach you SQL, many of which are designed for an audience with software development experience. They frequently start with the history of a language, move on to a discussion of its many technical concepts, and follow with chapters grouped by showing what various commands do. Though nothing is inherently wrong with that approach, it ignores the many nontechnical folks who need to learn SQL—folks like me.

Despite using SQL for more than two decades now, I didn't begin my career in software development. My first experience with databases was in a position called data administrator, where I was responsible for importing data from various sources into a relational database. I needed to read that data to validate the success of the import process, and the only way to do that was by learning and using SQL.

Even though I had limited programming experience, I quickly grasped how to use SQL. If you understand how to write in English, I'm confident that you can do the same. As you will see throughout this book, most SQL commands and keywords are exactly what you would expect them to be in English.

1.2.1   The many uses for SQL

Data isn't just for the IT department, of course. If you are a business analyst, for example, you can use SQL to quickly retrieve and analyze data about operational trends to make smarter business decisions. If you are a marketing professional, you can use SQL to uncover actionable insights about recent ad campaigns that can help you grow your business. If you work in finance, you can use SQL to retrieve vital data that can help your company meet compliance requirements.

All this data is the lifeblood of any modern organization, and success depends on having members of nearly every department possess the skills to use relational data to make critical business decisions. This book is designed to help people like you learn SQL to build those skills. If your technical experience is limited to working with spreadsheets, you're at a great starting point.

Then again, if you are a software developer, database administrator, or data scientist, this book doesn't exclude you; it just takes a different approach to learning. Whereas most other SQL books begin with terminology and concepts, this book gets you using SQL quickly to solve practical problems while briefly sharing concepts and defining terminology along the way.

Conversely, this book isn't designed simply to teach you a bunch of SQL commands. Instead, it's designed to progressively show you how to apply components of the SQL language to do your job, regardless of your level of computer programming experience.

1.2.2 *The many flavors of SQL*

Although we will be using a MySQL database to learn about SQL, nearly all the SQL concepts and techniques will work with any relational database. This means that what you learn will apply to any of the following database management systems:

- IBM DB2
- MariaDB
- Microsoft SQL Server
- MySQL
- Oracle
- PostgreSQL

When you've developed a solid foundation for using SQL, you can easily work with data in any of these systems. Be aware, however, that there will be occasional exceptions for individual systems. These exceptions will be noted throughout this book so you can be proficient in whatever system you use to work with data.

1.2.3 *A word about AI and SQL*

With the advent of generative artificial intelligence (AI), you may be wondering why you should learn to use SQL instead of using a tool like ChatGPT to write any SQL you might need. Though AI seems like a handy way to avoid investing in learning SQL, you still need to have a good grasp of SQL to understand whether the code that any such tool provides will give you correct results. Moreover, to get a SQL statement from a generative AI source, you have to provide details about your database, which your organization may expressly prohibit.

That said, generative AI tools can be useful when you have a good understanding of a language such as SQL. As you become proficient and understand how to write SQL that does exactly what you intend, you can use these tools to quickly review your code for performance problems or explain what a query appears to be doing. You still need to possess SQL knowledge to interpret the recommendations or explanations, and this book can help you attain that knowledge.

1.3 *How to use this book*

The idea of this book is that you will read one chapter each day. You don't have to read during lunch, but most chapters should take about 40 minutes to read, leaving you about 20 minutes to practice what you've learned while you finish eating.

1.3.1   *The main chapters*

Chapters 1 and 2 help you get up to speed quickly, making you familiar not only with the idea of a table and how to think about querying it but also with the tools we will be using throughout this book. In some ways, they're the most important chapters of the book.

Chapters 3 through 22 represent the primary content, so you can expect to complete them in about a month—even a short month like February. Not every chapter will require a full hour, but it's important to follow the order because each chapter builds on the skills and commands demonstrated in previous chapters. Also, though you are certainly free to read multiple chapters per day, I recommend focusing on a single chapter daily and spending ample time practicing what you learned. Doing this will give your brain time to focus on a handful of concepts and examples, which should prove to be optimal in solidifying your knowledge quickly. As the great basketball coach John Wooden said, "Be quick, but don't hurry."

1.3.2   *Hands-on labs*

Nearly all chapters include a short lab exercise that helps you apply the concepts and commands you've learned. Don't think of these exercises as quizzes but as opportunities to apply and reinforce your new SQL skills. Though the answers to these labs appear at the end of each chapter, I can't stress enough how vital working through these labs will be in retaining your new knowledge.

1.3.3   *Further exploration*

Because this book is designed for those who are just starting to use SQL, it only scratches the surface of the ways you can use and manipulate relational data. For this reason, some chapters end with suggestions for further exploration of ways to use the concepts and commands. If you have the time and inclination, take a look at these resources to expand your ever-growing SQL skill set.

1.4   *Setting up your lab environment*

Your time is valuable, so let's get started with setting up your lab environment. This task won't be resource-intensive, and you can likely set it up on your own computer in a few minutes. We'll install only two pieces of free software and then execute some ready-made SQL scripts to give us some data to use.

1.4.1   *Installing MySQL and MySQL Workbench*

The first step is downloading MySQL and installing it on the computer of your choice. MySQL is not only freely available but also one of the most popular relational database applications in the world.

We'll also install MySQL Workbench, which is the tool we'll use to execute all the queries contained in this book. It also uses very few resources, so you shouldn't worry about installing it on a laptop.

The steps for downloading and installing both of these applications are available at my GitHub repository, located at https://mng.bz/PNl8. Because the MySQL software is frequently updated, the version numbers you see may be later than the ones shown in the documentation. Don't worry about that; nothing we do should be affected by newer versions.

1.4.2 Executing the lab scripts

Throughout this book, we'll rely on a single set of data for our queries. The data is based on a set of orders from a hypothetical publisher of SQL-based novels, using a database named sqlnovel for all our queries. We'll discuss this data more throughout the book, but for now, let's create the database and populate the sample data by executing a prepared SQL script.

The steps for setting up our sqlnovel database are also located at https://mng.bz/PNl8, and they're even simpler than the process for installing MySQL and MySQL Workbench. Although you are likely to simply execute the script, near the end of the book, we will review parts of the script to examine what it does. By that point, you should be able to create your own sets of data!

1.5 Online resources

Throughout the book, I'll give you examples and exercises to try. I encourage you to type all scripts on your own and even to write SQL in a different style from the one I present in this book if you prefer. When you type the SQL, you may encounter an error that you don't understand. For this reason, the online resources also contain every SQL script presented in this book. Please try to use them only for troubleshooting because typing the SQL yourself will help you learn faster than simply copying scripts.

1.6 Being immediately effective with SQL

As with every other book in the Month of Lunches series, the primary goal of this book is to make you immediately effective. Nearly every chapter that follows presents a particular part of the SQL language and discusses it briefly, though most of any given chapter focuses on how to apply what you've learned using real-world scenarios. Furthermore, at the end of every chapter, you get hands-on practice by completing exercises in a lab environment.

As stated earlier, if you are looking for a deep dive into relational database theory and history, many other books can guide you down that path. Although many parts of this book discuss details and nuances, every chapter is driven by the goal of making you immediately effective at accomplishing real tasks.

OK, that's enough about this book. Let's start using SQL!

Your first SQL query

2

Chapter 1 ended with a word about being immediately effective, and so now we're going to do just that. We're going to start looking at some data as it might be stored in a relational database, and we're going to examine the way that data is structured. Doing this will help you better understand some terms to describe the data, which we will use throughout the book. Don't worry, though: you'll see just a handful of terms, and they are all words you have seen and used in conversation. I'm just defining them in the context of data stored in relational databases.

Also, you'll get started with your first query. In case you didn't know, a *query* refers to executing some SQL to retrieve data. As you progress through this book, you'll execute quite a few queries to level up your SQL skills. If you haven't already completed the installations of MySQL and the MySQL Workbench (see chapter 1) and executed the `Create_SQLNovel_database.sql` script to create our sample database, please do those things now so that you'll be ready to query data. Before you begin querying, though, let's look at some data.

2.1 You know tables if you already know spreadsheets

Although it's not a prerequisite for learning SQL in this book, it will be helpful if you have experience working with Microsoft Excel or some other spreadsheet program. You may not realize it, but spreadsheets are structured similarly to the most fundamental objects in any database. We'll also introduce a few terms in this section to help make sense of the way data is stored in a relational database—more accurately known as a relational database management system (RDBMS).

Now, we don't just gather data and dump it into an RDBMS; rather, we organize and store it in objects based on the nature of the data. These objects are known as *tables*. We typically organize data in tables relating to elements, such as orders, customers, or payments. Tables are the building blocks of any RDBMS and are structured quite a bit like spreadsheets, so looking at a spreadsheet will help you understand the associated terms in this chapter and throughout the book.

If you don't know the basic terms used to describe a spreadsheet, take a look at the typical spreadsheet in figure 2.1, which contains information about some extraordinary fictional books. Consider this information a set of data, commonly known as a *data set*. Seems easy enough, right? The data set is stored in a spreadsheet, but had this data been stored in a table, it would have essentially the same structure.

	A	B	C	D	E
1	Title	Price	Advance	Royalty	Publication Date
2	Pride and Predicates	$ 9.95	$ 5,000.00	15%	4/30/2015
3	The Join Luck Club	$ 9.95	$ 6,000.00	12%	2/6/2016
4	The Catcher in the Try	$ 8.95	$ 5,000.00	10%	4/3/2017
5	Anne of Fact Table	$ 12.95	$ 10,000.00	15%	1/12/2018
6	The DateTime Machine	$ 7.95	$ 5,500.00	15%	2/4/2019
7	The Great GroupBy	$ 10.95	$ -	20%	12/23/2019
8	The Call of the While	$ 8.95	$ 2,500.00	15%	3/14/2020
9	The Sum Also Rises	$ 7.95	$ 5,000.00	12%	11/12/2021

Books +

Figure 2.1 **A spreadsheet with five columns (A through E) of values for several fictional books. The spreadsheet is organized similarly to a table in a database.**

I've said that I don't want to overload you with jargon, but you need to understand three simple but critical terms related to tables before you start using SQL to read and manipulate any data contained in tables. As I noted at the beginning of the chapter, you've likely heard these words before:

- Column
- Row
- Value

A table, at its most basic level, is a construct of one or more *columns* of data. Columns run vertically, like columns in architecture. In figure 2.2, we see columns for Title, Price, Advance, Royalty, and Publication Date, with Title highlighted. You may see or hear the term *field* used to refer to a column, but *field* isn't a term in the SQL language.

Another term we need to consider is *row*, which refers to a horizontal collection of data in the table. Each row represents a single item of whatever the element of the table is, which in this case is the title of a book. In figure 2.3, we can see that each row has the same structure and follows the same order of columns—a requirement because each row must include a representation of all columns in the table.

	A	B	C	D	E
1	Title	Price	Advance	Royalty	Publication Date
2	Pride and Predicates	$ 9.95	$ 5,000.00	15%	4/30/2015
3	The Join Luck Club	$ 9.95	$ 6,000.00	12%	2/6/2016
4	The Catcher in the Try	$ 8.95	$ 5,000.00	10%	4/3/2017
5	Anne of Fact Table	$ 12.95	$ 10,000.00	15%	1/12/2018
6	The DateTime Machine	$ 7.95	$ 5,500.00	15%	2/4/2019
7	The Great GroupBy	$ 10.95	$ -	20%	12/23/2019
8	The Call of the While	$ 8.95	$ 2,500.00	15%	3/14/2020
9	The Sum Also Rises	$ 7.95	$ 5,000.00	12%	11/12/2021

Figure 2.2   The spreadsheet of book titles, with the Title column highlighted to show the vertical nature of columns

These rows are also enumerated in the left sidebar, but in any given table, the designer may not include explicit identifiers for each row. It's worth noting that the terms *row* and *record* are often used interchangeably because certain applications refer to rows as *records,* but for tables in most RDBMSes, the correct term is *row.*

	A	B	C	D	E
1	Title	Price	Advance	Royalty	Publication Date
2	Pride and Predicates	$ 9.95	$ 5,000.00	15%	4/30/2015
3	The Join Luck Club	$ 9.95	$ 6,000.00	12%	2/6/2016
4	The Catcher in the Try	$ 8.95	$ 5,000.00	10%	4/3/2017
5	Anne of Fact Table	$ 12.95	$ 10,000.00	15%	1/12/2018
6	The DateTime Machine	$ 7.95	$ 5,500.00	15%	2/4/2019
7	The Great GroupBy	$ 10.95	$ -	20%	12/23/2019
8	The Call of the While	$ 8.95	$ 2,500.00	15%	3/14/2020
9	The Sum Also Rises	$ 7.95	$ 5,000.00	12%	11/12/2021

Figure 2.3   The spreadsheet of books, with the first horizontal collection of data highlighted to show the horizontal nature of rows

The last term, at least for now, is *value,* which represents the distinct pieces of information described by the columns of the data set. Every row contains one value for each column. In figure 2.4, the value of Title in the last row of our data set is The Sum Also Rises, and the value of Price in that row is $7.95. It's worth noting that even though all columns are required for all rows, the values for the columns can be empty, such as the Advance value for the row with the Title value The Great GroupBy.

	A	B	C	D	E
1	**Title**	**Price**	**Advance**	**Royalty**	**Publication Date**
2	Pride and Predicates	$ 9.95	$ 5,000.00	15%	4/30/2015
3	The Join Luck Club	$ 9.95	$ 6,000.00	12%	2/6/2016
4	The Catcher in the Try	$ 8.95	$ 5,000.00	10%	4/3/2017
5	Anne of Fact Table	$ 12.95	$ 10,000.00	15%	1/12/2018
6	The DateTime Machine	$ 7.95	$ 5,500.00	15%	2/4/2019
7	The Great GroupBy	$ 10.95	$　　-	20%	12/23/2019
8	The Call of the While	$ 8.95	$ 2,500.00	15%	3/14/2020
9	The Sum Also Rises	$ 7.95	$ 5,000.00	12%	11/12/2021

Figure 2.4　The value of Price in the row with the title The Sum Also Rises highlighted to indicate a value. This value is just one of many.

OK, that's enough terminology about tables for now. Let's start talking about how to use this information to query a table.

2.2　*Learning SQL is like taking an English class*

A common question many people have is how to pronounce *SQL;* some folks say "ess-cue-ell," whereas others say "sequel." Considering that the earliest version of SQL was called Structured English Query Language and was abbreviated as SEQUEL, you can see how the latter pronunciation became commonplace. For what it's worth, there was already a trademark on SEQUEL, so the creators dropped the word *English* from the name and shortened the abbreviation to SQL.

This brings us to another reason for the popularity of SQL: unlike many other programming languages, it's designed to resemble the English language. You see, SQL is a *declarative* language, meaning that you specify what data you want and not how you want to get it, which is something that the RDBMS you are using will figure out.

We can take this concept of SQL being a declarative language a step further, using simple verbal declarations to say what we want to do with the data. This may seem unusual, but you'll soon see that many basic SQL statements are similar to a verbal declaration for a simple request. Let's walk through an example. Suppose that you have a table of vegetables named vegetables, like the one shown in figure 2.5, and you want to know the names of all the vegetables. If you want to declare this request verbally, you might say something like this: "I would like all the names of the vegetables." SQL isn't intuitive enough for that to work, but it isn't too far off. To accomplish this hypothetical query, you need to include in your declaration the two most basic keywords used in SQL. A *keyword* is any word in the SQL language that helps you do . . . well, anything. The first keyword to learn is SELECT, which, when it comes to databases, will be your new

VegetableID	Name
1	Artichoke
2	Asparagus
3	Beet
4	Bok Choy
5	Broccoli

Figure 2.5　A vegetables table with two columns and five rows. We're going to learn how to create a query that shows the names of all the vegetables.

best friend. Believe me—you and SELECT will work together a lot. Why? Simply put, SELECT is the keyword used to define what you want to see and how you want to see it: "I would like to SELECT all the names of the vegetables."

All right, we're on our way to forming an actual SQL query, but we need to add something else: the FROM keyword. The FROM keyword specifies which data set we want to look at, which in this case is the vegetables table: "I would like to SELECT all the names FROM the vegetables table."

That's better, but when we specify a data set using FROM, we don't explicitly say that it's a table. Even though tables are one of several kinds of data sets you can query, your RDBMS can determine the kind of data set based on the name of the data set: "I would like to SELECT all the names FROM vegetables."

We're getting closer. Now let's consider "SELECT all the names" for a moment. If we want to select all the names, we're in good shape because that is the default for this type of query. Nothing here specifies that we want any particular names, so we don't need to state that we want them all: "I would like to SELECT names FROM vegetables."

This part is tricky because we'll need to look at the table in figure 2.5. We can see that the name of the column with the data we want is called Name, not Names. As you query more data, you'll probably find that a column name is hardly ever plural because the value in each column rarely has more than one value for each row. Let's adjust our verbal declaration a bit: "I would like to SELECT Name FROM vegetables."

We're almost there. The last modification is to remove the "I would like to . . ." text because we start queries with a keyword, which in this case is SELECT. Also, that part is kind of wordy, don't you think?

One more thing: we need to add a semicolon to the end of the declaration. The semicolon tells the RDBMS that this is the end of what we're declaring and that anything else after it is another query:

```
SELECT Name FROM vegetables;
```

There you go! This is the correct way to query the names of all the vegetables. Next, let's go from designing a query for hypothetical data to writing and executing a query on actual data.

2.3   *Writing your first SQL query*

For the first bit of actual SQL you're going to write and execute, simply seek the outcome of your first query. As noted previously, we can start by declaring a sentence in English that defines what we want: "I would like the outcome of my first query."

Fortunately for us, the data to be queried already exists in a table named MyFirstQuery, and the values are in a column named Outcome. Convenient, right? Using what we learned about SQL syntax in section 2.2, we can easily craft a simple query to accomplish our goal:

```
SELECT Outcome from MyFirstQuery;
```

As you can see, the query ends with a semicolon. To add a little more to what I said earlier, in SQL, a semicolon is used as a *statement terminator*. We don't need to go deep into this subject; just know that a semicolon effectively means we're done with this statement and anything that comes after it is another SQL statement. Doing this prevents confusion for the database engine (especially when we get into more complicated statements later), so we'll use semicolons as statement terminators in all our SQL queries.

You may wonder what the difference is between a *statement* and a *query* and whether these terms are interchangeable. Well, statements and queries aren't the same things, but they're related. Think of a query as a special kind of statement for retrieving data. As you advance your SQL skills, you'll find yourself using statements beyond queries. For now, though, queries are the only SQL statements you'll use.

> **NOTE** Depending on which RDBMS you're using, a semicolon may not be required as a statement terminator. Although the RDBMS you use may not require it, it's good to develop the habit of ending all SQL statements with a semicolon—even statements as simple as your first SQL statement.

Before we go any further into the weeds on statements, let's get back to our query. Now that we have our query, the next thing we need to do is open MySQL Workbench so that we can execute the query. *Executing* is like clicking Send in your instructions to the RDBMS, which will figure out the best way to complete your query and then return the results to you. Those results are displayed in a different window in MySQL Workbench.

Try it now

Open MySQL Workbench, and click to open the Month of Lunches connection we created in chapter 1. Alternatively, right-click Month of Lunches, and choose Open Connection from the pop-up menu. You should see something like figure 2.6, with Query 1 highlighted. That represents the top of the Query panel, including the number 1 in the panel. That number indicates the first line of any query we enter here.

I'd like to point out a few things in MySQL Workbench. The first item is the tab at the top that says *Month of Lunches*. This tab tells us the context of our connection, which we set up in chapter 1 for the lunch user. We're not going to change that context for any exercise right now, but if you find yourself working with MySQL beyond the scope of this book, you'll always want to pay attention to the connection you're using when querying data.

The second item I want to focus on is the left side. You can see the Administration panel, but the tab next to that one, named Schemas, is more important to us. Click the word *Schemas*, and notice the sqlnovel database here. This database was created in the scripts we executed in chapter 1, and we want to set it as the default database for all our queries. To do this, right-click sqlnovel and choose Set as Default Schema from the pop-up menu. Your MySQL Workbench screen should look like the one in figure 2.7.

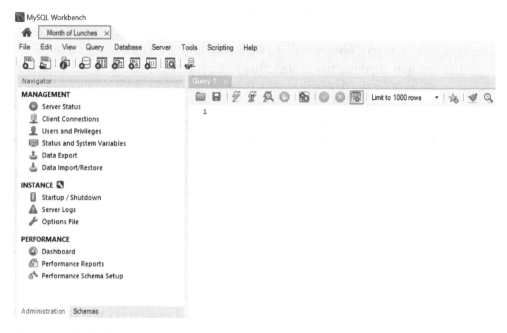

Figure 2.6   The MySQL Workbench open with our Month of Lunches connection, with administration information shown in the Navigator panel. We enter queries like the one we just wrote in the Query panel.

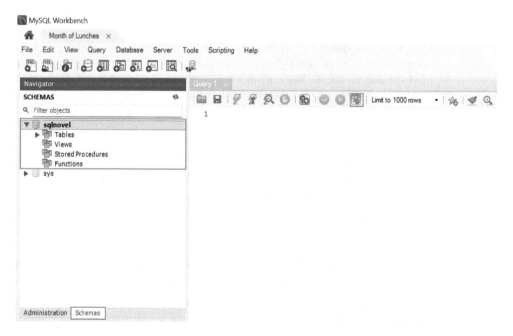

Figure 2.7   The Month of Lunches connection again, now with the Schemas information in the Navigator panel and the sqlnovel database shown in bold text, indicating that it's the default database

As we progress through the book, I'll take time to point out more information that is contained in MySQL Workbench. For now, though, verifying the connection and the database we'll be using is enough. Let's get back to the query:

```
SELECT Outcome FROM MyFirstQuery;
```

Try it now

Move the cursor to the Query panel, and click to the right of the 1 and the blue dot. Enter your first SQL query here by typing the query that precedes this sidebar. It should look like figure 2.8.

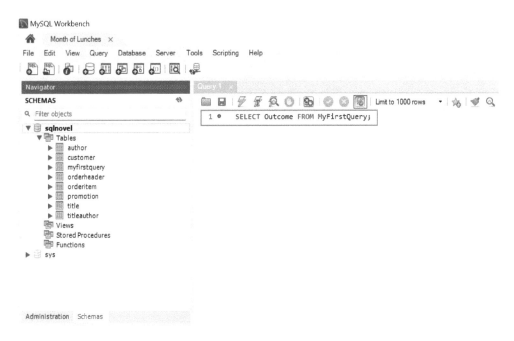

Figure 2.8   The query entered in the Query panel, ready to execute

I know your anticipation is building, so let me assure you we're almost done. We can execute the query in one of several ways. First, we can select Execute All or Execute Current Statement from the Query menu at the top. For this single query, both commands do the same thing because we have only one statement in the Query panel.

As you may have noticed, the Query menu has a few hotkeys we could use to execute the query. Pressing Ctrl+Enter on your keyboard will execute the part we selected, and pressing Ctrl+Shift+Enter will execute the contents of the entire panel. Again, because we have only one line, these shortcuts effectively do the same thing for this particular query.

Finally, you may notice some buttons directly above the first line of the Query panel. Several of them look like lightning bolts, but let's focus on the first one on the left. That plain lightning bolt, highlighted in figure 2.9, does the same thing as pressing Ctrl+Enter: it executes the selected part of the Query panel.

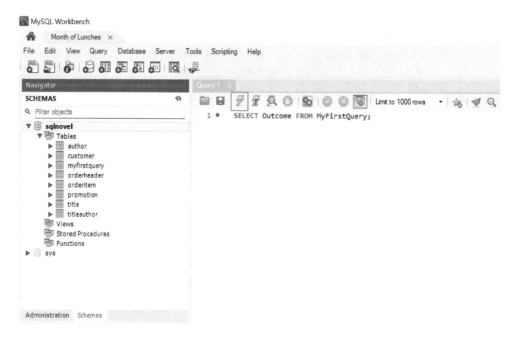

Figure 2.9   The highlighted plain lightning bolt in the Query panel. Clicking the plain lightning bolt executes the selected part of the Query panel, which does the same thing as pressing Ctrl+Enter on your keyboard.

Try it now

Make sure that you place the cursor at the end of the SQL statement before you choose your method of execution. Go ahead—do it!

After executing the query, you should see information in two new panels below the query. Your Workbench screen should look like figure 2.10.

Below the Query panel is the Result panel, and as you see, the result of the first query is "Hello, World!" If you aren't a computer programmer, you may not know that one tradition in learning a computing language is to first learn how to get "Hello, world!" as output in that language. SQL may not be like most programming languages, but we're still going to be respectful of traditions.

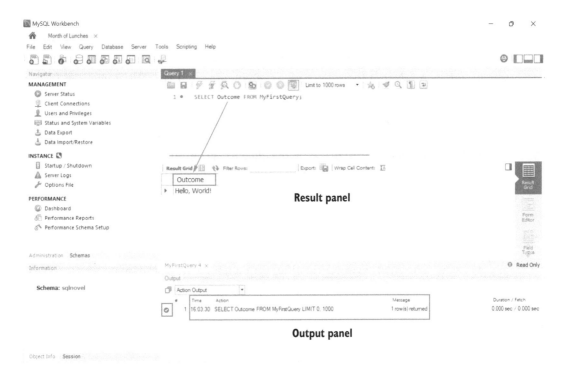

Figure 2.10 **The result of query execution. In the Result panel, we see the result is "Hello, World!" In the Output panel, a circle with a check mark (which appears green onscreen) indicates the query executed successfully, and other information shows the time it was executed, what the query was, how many rows it returned, and the duration of query execution.**

Look at what's immediately above "Hello, World!," though. It's the word *Outcome*, which indicates the column that we selected to query. This result, as small as it is, is still considered a data set. It's one column and one row, but it's not a table. We queried a table named MyFirstQuery, but the result of the query is a separate data set all by itself.

One final thing to notice about our execution is the Output panel below the Result panel. This panel provides several bits of information, such as the time when our query was executed, what the query was, how many rows were returned, and how long it took to execute the query. Most important is the circle with a check mark (green onscreen), which indicates that the query executed successfully. If our query hadn't executed successfully, we would have seen a circle with an X (red onscreen) to indicate an error. Ideally, we won't see many circles with an X as we work through this book.

2.4 Key terms and keywords

In this chapter, we've covered a handful of simple terms and a few keywords to get you on your way to querying data. Because these concepts and commands are the building blocks of SQL, let's take a moment to review them:

- *Data set*—A *data set* is a logical grouping of data that can be contained in a database, a spreadsheet, or any number of other places. As far as we're concerned, we're going to use SQL to query data in an RDBMS.
- *Table*—A *table* is a logical construct of columns that contains a data set. It's the most fundamental way to store data sets in an RDBMS.
- *Column*—A *column* is the vertical grouping of attributes for every row in a table.
- *Row*—A *row* is the representation of related data in a table.
- *Value*—A *value* represents the actual data for a column in a row.
- *Statement*—A *statement* is a way to declare to the RDBMS that we want to do something.
- *Query*—A *query* is a special kind of statement used to retrieve data.
- SELECT—The SELECT keyword starts queries. The next few chapters of this book delve deeper into ways to use the SELECT keyword.
- FROM—The FROM keyword identifies the data set that we want to query.
- *Semicolon*—Don't forget to end your queries with a *semicolon!*

2.5   *Lab*

Throughout the rest of the book, I will end each chapter with one or more lab exercises to put into practice what we have learned. These exercises are intended to emulate the practical use of SQL, simulating scenarios you would encounter using other people's data. Because this lab is the first, though, we'll start off easy with a few simple mental exercises to get a little more familiar with tables and their structure.

Considering what we've learned about using the second SELECT statement, or even considering the example in figure 2.1 to be a table, take a moment to ponder the following conceptual questions:

1 Imagine that spreadsheet in figure 2.1 is a table with several columns. Also, note that the table used in our second SELECT statement has at least one column. Is it possible for a table to have no columns?

2 Now imagine that either of these data sets has no rows that contain data. Is it possible for a table to have zero rows?

3 In figure 2.1, one cell in the Advance column does not have a value. If this figure were a table, do you think it would be required to have a value?

4 Assuming that we have a vegetable table in our sqlnovel database with a column named Name, what do you think would happen if we combined the two queries we discussed in this chapter and executed them at the same time? Think about the result of a query such as the following:

```
SELECT Name FROM vegetable;
SELECT Outcome FROM MyFirstQuery;
```

Do you think that this SQL would execute successfully?

2.6   *Lab answers*

1   No, it isn't possible to have a table with no columns. This is why I mentioned earlier that you can think of a table as a collection of columns. There must always be at least one column; otherwise, there's nowhere to put the values of data.

2   Yes, you can have tables without rows. Every time a table is created, it starts with no rows.

3   This question is a bit tricky because the answer depends on the way the table was set up. We can have rows of valid data that don't have values for particular columns. Think of a column for Middle Name in a table of people. Not everyone has a middle name, so we have to be able to accommodate that lack of data for rows with people who have no middle name. That said, designers can put restrictions on tables to require all rows to have a value for particular columns, such as a column that captures a last name for all rows in that same table of people.

4   These queries will execute, resulting in two separate data sets being returned. This is the very reason why we put those semicolons at the end of our queries: to tell the RDBMS that we have to separate the queries we're executing.

All right, let's move on to chapter 3 and learn more fun ways to query using the SELECT keyword!

Querying data 3

In chapter 2, we looked at a spreadsheet of fictional books to better understand some core concepts about tables in a relational database management system (RDBMS). With that spreadsheet in mind, we're going to work with a table that looks a lot like that spreadsheet and see some of the ways we can retrieve data using the SELECT command.

First, though, let's take a deeper look at your first query. Although it was simple, it had all the minimum components for a query. Let's briefly examine those components as well as some potential problems regarding formatting and the use of certain words.

3.1 Rules for the SELECT statement

Chapters 1 and 2 discussed the conversational way to think about writing a query, so let's take a moment to consider the technical aspects and requirements as well. Recall your first query, which looked like this:

```
SELECT Outcome FROM MyFirstQuery;
```

This statement has four components, each represented by a single word. Technically, the semicolon is a component as well, serving as the statement terminator, but we've already discussed the fact that it may not be required, so we won't count it.

3.1.1 SELECT requirements

The words "Outcome" and "MyFirstQuery" reflect the data we want to select. These words are crucial because they provide the minimum information the database needs to retrieve data from a table. These requirements are

- What data is to be selected
- Where the data is to be selected

In this case, the data to be selected is the Outcome column, and the location where the data is to be selected is the MyFirstQuery table. Both of those words follow specific keywords that are included in the SQL catalog of commands: SELECT and FROM, each of which represents a *clause* in your SQL statement. All SQL statements are made up of various clauses, but to retrieve data from a table, we're required to use at least these two. We commonly refer to clauses by the keywords used in them, so these two would be called the SELECT clause and the FROM clause.

> **NOTE** We always identify the data we want to select immediately after the SELECT keyword, and we always indicate the location where we want to select data after the FROM keyword.

It's important to note the order in which these clauses are used in SQL. Throughout the book, you'll learn several more clauses, and they must always be used in a particular order for a query to execute. As an example, we couldn't successfully switch the order of clauses in your first query:

```
FROM MyFirstQuery SELECT Outcome;
```

Attempting to execute this query would result in a syntax error because the SELECT clause must always come before the FROM clause.

3.1.2 Keywords and reserved words

Keywords such as SELECT and FROM are a subset of *reserved words* in the SQL language used by each RDBMS. When the RDBMS you're using finds those reserved words in a query, it presumes that you want it to complete a specific action associated with the reserved word. Numerous reserved words are universal, but some reserved words are specific to the RDBMS you're using.

As you progress in your SQL knowledge, take note of reserved words you use as commands so that you'll know not to use them as table names or column names.

> **TIP** If you want to know all the reserved words, you can find them in the documentation on the site where you downloaded MySQL and MySQL Workbench. Every major RDBMS has online documentation that catalogs its specific reserved words. As a general rule, if you're working in a development interface like MySQL Workbench, you'll see reserved words in a different color from the rest of your SQL.

Using reserved words for object names results in avoidable headaches caused by syntax errors because the RDBMS will be confused about what you want to do. Suppose that the MyFirstQuery table had a column named Select, and you wanted to execute the following query:

```
SELECT Select FROM MyFirstQuery;
```

> **Try it now**
>
> Type this SQL in your Month of Lunches connection in MySQL Workbench. You'll see the word `Select` in a different color from `MyFirstQuery`, which is your first clue that `Select` is a reserved word. As noted earlier, each RDBMS has dozens or even hundreds of reserved words, so when you see the color indicated for a reserved word, take caution before executing your query.

If you execute the preceding query, you'll get the error message that says, "You have an error in your SQL syntax." The MySQL database engine saw the reserved word `Select` consecutively, which won't work because you never said what you wanted to select after the first time you said `SELECT`.

3.1.3   *Case insensitivity*

While we're looking at this query that won't execute, notice that both `SELECT` and `Select` are identified as reserved words, even though they're in a different case. Keywords aren't case-sensitive, so each of the following queries will successfully execute and return the same result:

```
SELECT Outcome FROM MyFirstQuery;
Select Outcome From MyFirstQuery;
select Outcome from MyFirstQuery;
SeLeCt Outcome fRoM MyFirstQuery;
```

Just because you can use any kind of case with your keywords, however, doesn't mean you should. To write reusable SQL, many developers prefer typing keywords in uppercase to make code more readable and therefore make it easier to debug errors. For this reason, the examples throughout this book will continue to show keywords in uppercase.

> **WARNING**   Although SQL keywords can be used without regard to case sensitivity, the information relating to data may be case-sensitive, depending on the settings of your RDBMS. Be careful when specifying table, column, or value names in your queries because they may be case-sensitive.

3.1.4   *Formatting and whitespace*

One other thing to note about queries is the flexibility you have when using whitespace. Your RDBMS doesn't care much about it, so you can format your query in a nearly

infinite number of ways with spaces, tabs, and carriage returns. Your first query was written on a single line, but it would work the same way if it were separated into several lines.
All three of the following queries, for example, will execute and return the same result.

Query 1

```
SELECT Outcome
FROM MyFirstQuery;
```

Query 2

```
SELECT
Outcome
FROM
MyFirstQuery;
```

Query 3

```
SELECT
        Outcome
FROM
        MyFirstQuery;
```

Although there are no universal best practices in formatting, the best advice I can give
you is to be consistent. The goal of adjusting the format is to make the query more
readable, so if you find a particular way of formatting that's easy for you to work with,
use it and stick with it.

I think we've gotten all we can out of your first query. It's time to move on to querying
data that may be a bit more comparable to the kind you'll need to work with.

3.2 Retrieving data from a table

For the rest of this chapter, we're going to examine the title table in our sqlnovel database. Unlike the MyFirstQuery table, the title table has several columns and multiple
rows of data.

Unless you examined the scripts used
to create this database, you probably don't
know the names of the columns in the title
table. Fortunately, we can find this information easily by using MySQL Workbench.
Look at the top-left corner of the Navigator
panel, and notice the triangles next to sqlnovel and Tables. The triangle next to sqlnovel points down, which indicates that it
has been expanded. This expansion allows
us to see Tables, Views, Stored Procedures,
and Functions, as shown in figure 3.1.

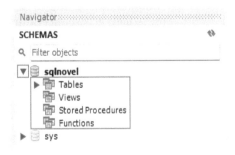

**Figure 3.1   The database name has been
expanded to show Tables, View, Stored
Procedures, and Functions.**

The triangle next to Tables points right, which means that the view of the contents below Tables has been collapsed. To see the columns in the title table or any other table, we need to click that triangle to expand the list of Tables. Then we'll need to find the title table, click the triangle next to it to expand further, and click the triangle next to Columns to expand it as well. When we complete all those clicks, we see the names of all columns in the title table, as shown in figure 3.2.

3.2.1 *Retrieving an individual column*

Now that we know the column names, we can start querying the table. Let's begin with a simple query of the TitleName column from the title table. Because we're going to be increasing the length and complexity of our queries, we'll start formatting our queries with the FROM clause on a separate line to make it a little more readable:

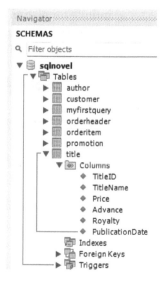

Figure 3.2   The Navigator panel, where Tables has been expanded to show individual table names and the title table has been expanded to show all columns in that table

```
SELECT TitleName
FROM title;
```

Try it now

Write and execute the preceding query. Consider this query your second one (not that anyone is counting).

Executing the query results in the eight rows shown in figure 3.3. If you happen to see the same eight rows in a different order, don't be alarmed. There is no implicit guarantee of ordering the results of a query.

WARNING I'm going to say it again because many SQL users have a misconception: there is no implicit guarantee of the order of results of a SQL query. You shouldn't be surprised when you execute the same query at different times and get the same results in a different order. This can occur due to any number of factors, from modifications in the values of the tables being queried to changes in the settings of the server with regard to your database. Remember that SQL is a declarative language: if your RDBMS isn't explicitly told how to order the results, the rows can appear in random order. That said, if you've peeked ahead in this book, you already know that we're going to discuss how to order results in chapter 4.

Figure 3.3   The values of the TitleName column in the title table are returned in no particular order.

Something else to note is that the name of the column in the query is TitleName. You may wonder why it isn't just Name. The main reason is that lots of columns in databases contain data with values for names of things or people, and TitleName is specific to this table. Another reason relates to what I said earlier about reserved words: the word Name is one of those reserved words.

Try it now

If you executed the previous query, take a moment now to click near `TitleName` and delete the letters in the Title prefix, leaving only `Name`. Did you notice that `Name` now appears in the same color as `SELECT` and `FROM`? That's because in MySQL, the word `Name` is a reserved word.

Name isn't a keyword command like SELECT or FROM, but it's a reserved word relating to a specific action that is done in this RDBMS. For this reason, avoid using the word *Name* for a column name.

TIP   Here's a neat trick that can save you some typing in the future: delete "Name" from your query as well, leaving a couple of spaces between SELECT and FROM. Now move the cursor to the Navigator panel. Click and hold Title-Name in the Columns list; then move the cursor to the space between SELECT and FROM. When you release the click, you should see *TitleName* appear as before without doing any typing. This shortcut is great to use, especially when you're dealing with long column names, and it works for objects such as table names too.

3.2.2   *Retrieving multiple columns*

Until now, we've selected only one column of data, but you'll want to write SQL queries that select multiple columns. Let's think about declaring a statement as we did in chapter 2: "I would like all the TitleNames and Prices of the titles."

We already know how to convert most of this statement into a query, so all we need to do now is consider replacing the word *and* with a comma. Because we have multiple column names, let's change the formatting a bit to make multiple column names more readable. Our query will look like this:

```
SELECT
    TitleName,
    Price
FROM title;
```

The comma tells the RDBMS that our query will request another column, just as the word *and* does in the English language. When speaking, we wouldn't end a set of words with *and*. We wouldn't say, "I would like all the TitleNames and Prices and of the titles" because the listener would think, "And what?" They'd know that something else should be included, but it's not clear what that something would be. For the same reason, don't put a comma after the last column in your SELECT statement. Doing so will result in a syntax error.

Also note that column order output is completely up to you, the SQL query writer. Just because the columns are in a certain order in the table doesn't mean that they can't be rearranged like this:

```
SELECT
    Price,
    TitleName
FROM title;
```

We can even include the same column multiple times if we want, like this:

```
SELECT
    TitleName,
    TitleName,
    Price
FROM title;
```

Having two columns with the same name does introduce a bit of confusion, though. Is there a better way to manage multiple columns with the same name? Why, yes, there is!

3.2.3   *Renaming output columns using aliases*

Although your SELECT query can't change the names of the columns in the tables you are querying, you can easily change the name of the output column to whatever you want. Let's declare a statement again: "I would like all the TitleNames as BookNames of the titles."

Just as you'd use the word *as* in your declarative statement, you use the word AS in your SQL statement to declare the new column name:

```
SELECT
    TitleName AS BookName
FROM title;
```

Now your output should show show BookName as the column name instead of TitleName, as in figure 3.4.

What we've done here is use an *alias*, which is a simple method of renaming the output column from its original column name. We can use column aliases to prevent confusion from similarly titled columns by giving the output columns unique names:

```
SELECT
    TitleName AS BookName,
    TitleName AS AlsoBookName,
    Price
FROM title;
```

Figure 3.4   The values of TitleName are now returned with the column header of BookName.

You don't need to use the word AS to use an alias, however. You can put the *alias name* after the query, although this format makes your column aliases a little less obvious:

```
SELECT
    TitleName BookName,
    TitleName AlsoBookName,
    Price
FROM title;
```

Column aliases can be wonderful tools for making column names more effective. Just remember to avoid using reserved words as your aliases.

3.2.4   *Retrieving all columns*

We've seen how to select a single column and multiple columns of data from a table. Often, you'll find that you need all the columns of data in a table to be meaningful, and you want to retrieve them all. Perhaps you need to write a detailed report that includes the maximum amount of sales data, or maybe auditors have asked you to supply every bit of customer data. Whatever the case, you have three ways to do this.

The first way is to type out all the column names, separating them with commas. Unless the column names are short and you're very proficient at typing, this approach is the hardest one.

The second way involves much less typing. Select the first column in a table in the Navigator panel, click it, hold down the Shift key, and click the last column. You should see all those columns highlighted, as they are in figure 3.5.

Now click and hold any of the highlighted columns, drag the cursor between SELECT and FROM in the Query panel, and release. You should see all the column names listed in your query, as they are in figure 3.6.

Figure 3.5   The column names in the title table, highlighted after selecting the first column name, holding down the Shift key, and clicking the last column name

Figure 3.6 The columns of the title table after they've been pasted into the Query panel

> **Try it now**
>
> Execute this query, and you'll see the values of all the columns in the table. If the right side of the query is blocked by another panel, you should be able to remove it by choosing View > Panel > Hide Secondary Sidebar.

The third method is probably the most common, as it involves less typing and clicking. You can see all columns in a table by using an asterisk in place of column names, commonly referred to verbally as "select star." This method is also called "select all," although less commonly:

```
SELECT
    *
FROM title;
```

This method gives you the same results as the preceding query, and I'm sure you can see why it's so popular. You can easily see the values for all columns with less effort than it takes to type a single column name!

Aside from minimal effort, the other benefit of this method is it allows us to see all the column names in a table quickly without using the Navigator panel. There are two significant reasons to be careful with SELECT *, however:

- You're selecting all the data, which means that the RDBMS has to read more data and send it across some network to you as output. It may seem that resources are infinite, but in my experience, the use of SELECT * on very large tables uses so much of the system resources that it causes performance problems for other queries. Be very careful when using this method.
- The second hazard of using SELECT * is that because it doesn't specify any column order, it should never be used in reusable queries. Suppose that you write a SQL query for a report that expects five output columns from a table. If one or more columns are added to or removed from the table later, your report may no longer work because the number of columns will be different.

WARNING   For the reasons noted earlier, you should use the SELECT * method only in ad hoc queries and sparingly even then. As shown in the second method, it's not difficult to click and drag the column names you want to use in a query.

3.3   *Lab*

1   Another table in the sqlnovel database is named author. What two methods could you use to find the names of columns in this table?
2   You need to write a query that returns all the first and last names from the author table. How would you write that query?

3 What do you think would happen if you forgot to put a comma between column names? Do you think this query will work, and if so, what would the output be?

```
SELECT
    TitleName
    Price
FROM title;
```

4 What would happen if you try to use the SELECT * method with an alias, as in the following query?

```
SELECT
    * AS Everything
FROM title;
```

3.4 Lab answers

1 The best method would be to expand the columns folder under the author table in the Navigator panel. If you're using an interface that doesn't allow you to do that, you can use the SELECT * method in the following query:

```
SELECT
    *
FROM author;
```

2 The answer is

```
SELECT
    FirstName,
    LastName
FROM author;
```

3 This query will execute, but the results won't be what you expect. Because the comma is no longer between TitleName and Price, the word "Price" is now considered to be a column alias for TitleName. Only one column with an aliased name of Price will be returned, but the values will be from the TitleName column.

4 This query won't execute because you can't alias column names with SELECT *. If you try this query, your first indication of a problem will be the red square with a white X on the line with the alias. This red square means the Workbench application found that your query has incorrect syntax.

Sorting, skipping, and commenting data

In chapter 3, I noted that your relational database management system (RDBMS) won't return results in a predictable order. This is by design, as any given request may or may not need the data to be ordered, and the RDBMS is simply taking the most efficient way of returning the data requested. The results may appear in some sort of order, such as the order in which the rows were added to a table, but there are no implicit guarantees about how the data in the results of a query will be ordered. If we want to be certain of the order of results, we need to say so explicitly in our SQL query.

Some fun features associated with ordering data allow us to manipulate the number of rows returned in our result set. These features can be useful if we have millions or billions of rows and need to see only the most recent entries or the entries with the smallest or largest values.

Because you're just starting to write SQL, this chapter also discusses how to use comments in SQL. Comments are indispensable tools for you and anyone else who may read your SQL, and if you're going to write queries properly, you should start building the habit of using comments today.

4.1 Sorting data

Everywhere we go, we find things sorted in some order. Books in a library are sorted by author name, floors in a building are sorted by number, and events in a daily planner are sorted by date and time. All kinds of things in our lives are organized for ease of use and readability, and the data we use should be no different.

4.1.1 Sorting by one column

To see how we do this in SQL, let's go back to a declarative sentence from chapter 3: "I would like all the TitleNames and Prices of the titles." The SQL for this request is as follows:

```
SELECT
    TitleName,
    Price
FROM title;
```

TitleName	Price
Pride and Predicates	9.95
The Join Luck Club	9.95
Catcher in the Try	8.95
Anne of Fact Tables	12.95
The DateTime Machine	7.95
The Great GroupBy	10.95
The Call of the While	8.95
The Sum Also Rises	7.95

Figure 4.1 The results of the query of TitleName and Price from the title table. The results are not ordered by either TitleName or Price.

As we can see in figure 4.1, this query won't return the data in a particular way.

Let's declare that we want the same results, this time ordered by the title name: "I would like all the TitleNames and Prices of the titles, and I would like the results ordered by TitleName." As before, the SQL we will use is very similar to what we just said. To fulfill the new request, we will add a new clause using the ORDER BY keyword:

```
SELECT
    TitleName,
    Price
FROM title
ORDER BY
    TitleName;
```

TitleName	Price
Anne of Fact Tables	12.95
Catcher in the Try	8.95
Pride and Predicates	9.95
The Call of the While	8.95
The DateTime Machine	7.95
The Great GroupBy	10.95
The Join Luck Club	9.95
The Sum Also Rises	7.95

Figure 4.2 The results of the preceding query, with the results now sorted alphabetically by TitleName

When we execute this command, we see that the rows returned are the same as before, but now they are ordered as requested, as shown in figure 4.2.

When it's used, the ORDER BY clause should almost always be the last clause in a SQL statement. With only one exception (which we'll get to later in this chapter), specifying any other clause after the ORDER BY clause in a query will result in a syntax error.

This should be easy to remember if you consider that data ordering will be the last operation the RDBMS will perform on your data. This point is often misunderstood; too many people use SQL thinking that ORDER BY indicates how the data will be read. In reality, the RDBMS has to complete the operations for the rest of your SQL statement first; then, after getting your result set, it organizes the data the way your query requests in the ORDER BY clause.

> **WARNING** The additional work that ORDER BY requires of the RDBMS is minimal for the queries in this book because the result sets are only a handful of rows. When you start querying data sets with millions or even billions of rows, however, adding an ORDER BY can be catastrophic for query performance. Even more problematic is the fact that ordering data for very large data sets can require large amounts of resources from the computer's processor and

memory, resulting in degraded performance for queries that other users are running. Always be careful with your use of ORDER BY.

When you consider that your RDBMS has to gather the entire result set before sorting the results, it should make sense that you can even use a column alias in the ORDER BY clause. The column aliases are applied when your result set has been created and before it has been ordered, so SQL logic like the following also works for sorting data, as shown in figure 4.3:

NameOfTheBook	Price
Anne of Fact Tables	12.95
Catcher in the Try	8.95
Pride and Predicates	9.95
The Call of the While	8.95
The DateTime Machine	7.95
The Great GroupBy	10.95
The Join Luck Club	9.95
The Sum Also Rises	7.95

Figure 4.3 **After you use an ORDER BY, the results of the preceding query are ordered by TitleName, which has been aliased as NameOfTheBook.**

```
SELECT
    TitleName AS NameOfTheBook,
    Price
FROM title
ORDER BY
    NameOfTheBook;
```

4.1.2 *Sorting by multiple columns*

ORDER BY isn't limited to a single column, of course. We can use commas in the ORDER BY clause similarly to the way we use them in the SELECT clause to specify ordering by multiple columns. Consider the following query:

```
SELECT
    TitleName,
    Advance,
    Royalty
FROM title
ORDER BY
    Advance,
    Royalty;
```

TitleName	Advance	Royalty
The Great GroupBy	0.00	20.00
The Call of the While	2500.00	15.00
Catcher in the Try	5000.00	10.00
The Sum Also Rises	5000.00	12.00
Pride and Predicates	5000.00	15.00
The DateTime Machine	5500.00	15.00
The Join Luck Club	6000.00	12.00
Anne of Fact Tables	10000.00	15.00

Figure 4.4 **The results of a query ordered by the Advance column and then by the Royalty column, both from highest value to lowest**

As figure 4.4 shows, the results of our query are ordered primarily by the Advance column, from lowest to highest. But when the values in Advance are the same—as they are for the third, fourth, and fifth rows, all with a value of 5000.00—the Royalty column is used to order those three rows.

Try it now

Now that you've seen a few ways to sort data in the title table, try using ORDER BY as shown in the examples, or try sorting on other columns, such as Price or PublicationDate.

4.1.3 Specifying sort direction

When we sort data with ORDER BY, there is an implicit direction of sorting, either alphabetically from A to Z or numerically from lowest to highest value. This direction is known as *ascending* data order. We can also sort results in the other direction, from Z to A or from highest to lowest values. This direction is known as *descending* order, and we must state it explicitly by adding DESC after the column name in the ORDER BY clause. Here's an example of the previous query data sorted by Advance values in descending order:

```
SELECT
    TitleName,
    Advance,
    Royalty
FROM title
ORDER BY
    Advance DESC,
Royalty;
```

The results in figure 4.5 show that the results are now ordered by Advance values from largest to smallest. But take a closer look at the fourth, fifth, and sixth rows: they are still sorted in value from smallest to largest Royalty. Royalty is still sorted in ascending order because no order was specified for this column.

For clarity, we can explicitly state the sort order for the Royalty column as well by adding ASC for ascending sort order to the ORDER BY clause, like this:

TitleName	Advance	Royalty
Anne of Fact Tables	10000.00	15.00
The Join Luck Club	6000.00	12.00
The DateTime Machine	5500.00	15.00
Catcher in the Try	5000.00	10.00
The Sum Also Rises	5000.00	12.00
Pride and Predicates	5000.00	15.00
The Call of the While	2500.00	15.00
The Great GroupBy	0.00	20.00

Figure 4.5   **The results are now sorted by Advance descending and Royalty ascending.**

```
SELECT
    TitleName,
    Advance,
Royalty
FROM title
ORDER BY
    Advance DESC,
    Royalty ASC;
```

TIP   The implicit nature of ascending order in an ORDER BY column can be confusing, so when you're writing SQL that other people will read, get into the habit of explicitly stating the direction of ordering, even though you don't need to for ascending order. As noted earlier, you should always try to make your SQL as clear and easy to understand as possible.

4.1.4 Sorting by hidden columns

You may encounter a certain scenario in which you want to order the results by a column that you don't want returned in the result set. This scenario is possible because you can order your results by one or more columns that aren't seen. Suppose that you revise the preceding query to return only the TitleName but still order the results by the Advance (descending) and Royalty (ascending) columns:

```
SELECT
    TitleName
FROM title
ORDER BY
    Advance DESC,
    Royalty ASC;
```

TitleName
Anne of Fact Tables
The Join Luck Club
The DateTime Machine
Catcher in the Try
The Sum Also Rises
Pride and Predicates
The Call of the While
The Great GroupBy

Figure 4.6   Only the TitleName values are in the results, but the rows are still sorted by Advance descending and Royalty ascending.

The results in figure 4.6 are the same as for the preceding query except that the Advance and Royalty columns aren't returned.

How can we sort by data that isn't included in our SELECT? The RDBMS accomplishes this little bit of magic by adding Advance and Royalty to the result set before it's returned to you, then organizing the data as requested, and finally returning only the columns requested in the SELECT clause. As you can imagine, this process is an extra bit of work, so be careful when you use this technique with very large data sets.

4.1.5   *Sorting by position*

If column names seem too long to type, you have a quicker way to specify sort order: list the *numerical column position* in the SELECT clause instead of the column name. Think of the numerical order of the columns in the SELECT clause, TitleName (1), Advance (2), and Royalty (3):

```
SELECT
    TitleName,
    Advance,
    Royalty
FROM title
ORDER BY
    2 DESC,
    3 ASC;
```

Now the sort order is listed as Advance descending and Royalty ascending. We know this because we can determine that Advance is the second column, represented by the 2 value in the ORDER BY, and Royalty is the third column, represented by the 3 value.

> **WARNING**   This kind of shorthand notation in the ORDER BY may be useful when you're writing SQL quickly for ad hoc queries, but because the readability is inferior to explicitly naming columns to be sorted, you should avoid this technique in any reusable SQL you write. As you can imagine, if the columns in the SELECT change, ordering by position would use different columns.

4.2   Skipping data

The result set of every query we've run includes all the data in the table. What if you don't want all the data returned? On some occasions, you want only a handful of rows to survey or maybe just one, skipping most of the result set. You may need to look at a table of data you're unfamiliar with to see how the data is formatted, for example. You can certainly do this in SQL.

4.2.1   Using LIMIT to reduce results

Let's use our declarative English language first to state our intentions of finding just three published books: "I would like all the TitleNames and PublicationDates, but limit the results to the first three rows." The new keyword here is LIMIT, which will be used to reduce the result set to a specified number of rows. We can accomplish this by using LIMIT like this:

```
SELECT
    TitleName,
    PublicationDate
FROM title
LIMIT 3;
```

The RDBMS grabs the first three rows it can find, so your results should look something like figure 4.7.

Using LIMIT with a result set returns only three rows instead of all eight in the table. Although this command may not seem useful, it can be incredibly helpful if you want to quickly sample the column names and types of values they contain.

TitleName	PublicationDate
Pride and Predicates	2015-04-30 00:00:00
The Join Luck Club	2016-02-06 00:00:00
Catcher in the Try	2017-04-03 00:00:00

Figure 4.7   The results of using LIMIT to return only three rows

Try it now

Using SELECT * and LIMIT, write a query that allows you to quickly sample some rows in the title table. You may or may not get rows with the three titles shown in figure 4.7, but that's because you didn't specify any sort order.

Because the preceding query would be used to sample data, the results can be imprecise. Let's use our declarative English language first to state our intentions of finding something more precise, namely the three most recently published books: "I would like all the TitleNames and PublicationDates, but limit the results to the three most recent PublicationDates."

To execute this query, we'll bring back ORDER BY, sorting by PublicationDate descending to give us rows with the most recent (latest) date values:

```
SELECT
    TitleName,
    PublicationDate
FROM title
ORDER BY PublicationDate DESC
LIMIT 3;
```

Note the order of the clauses here: the `LIMIT` clause is after the `ORDER BY`. The `LIMIT` clause is the only clause that should ever follow the `ORDER BY` clause, and if it's included, it's always the last clause in a SQL query. Placing the `LIMIT` clause anywhere else will result in a syntax error. Figure 4.8 shows the results of this query, which returns the three most recent TitleName values and their PublicationDate values.

TitleName	PublicationDate
The Sum Also Rises	2021-11-12 00:00:00
The Call of the While	2020-03-14 00:00:00
The Great GroupBy	2019-12-23 00:00:00

Figure 4.8 The three most recently published TitleNames and their PublicationDates when you use `ORDER BY` on PublicationDate and `LIMIT` the results to three rows

> **TIP** Although you're not required to do so, you'll almost always want to use `ORDER BY` whenever you use the `LIMIT` clause. Why? You'll likely intend to read a limited sample of rows based on their being the oldest, newest, largest, smallest, or some other order. As noted, using `LIMIT` without specifying the order can return random and unpredictable results.

4.2.2 Using OFFSET to select a different limited set

The scenario of writing a SQL statement to find the most recent data is not uncommon, but at times, you may want to skip certain rows other than the most or least. In those cases, you can use another feature of the `LIMIT` clause. The way to do this is to use an additional option in the clause: `OFFSET`. `OFFSET` can't be executed without `LIMIT`, but it can direct the RDBMS to ignore a specified number of rows before it starts returning the rows indicated by the `LIMIT` clause. Let's rerun the preceding query but use `OFFSET` to skip the first row that would be returned:

```
SELECT
    TitleName,
    PublicationDate
FROM title
ORDER BY PublicationDate DESC
LIMIT 3 OFFSET 1;
```

Figure 4.9 shows that the row with TitleName "The Sum Also Rises" has been skipped, and the results include a different row with Title-Name "The DateTime Machine," which has an older PublicationDate.

TitleName	PublicationDate
The Call of the While	2020-03-14 00:00:00
The Great GroupBy	2019-12-23 00:00:00
The DateTime Machine	2019-02-04 00:00:00

Figure 4.9 The most recent three TitleName and PublicationDate values after you use `OFFSET` to skip the first row

4.2.3 *Limiting data in another RDBMS*

Chapter 1 discussed the fact that each RDBMS has its own variation for certain commands. Unfortunately, the LIMIT clause is one of those commands.

> **WARNING** The LIMIT clause works with many popular RDBMSs, including MySQL, MariaDB, PostgreSQL, and SQL Lite, but it doesn't work with DB2, Oracle, or SQL Server. Those RDBMSes use other proprietary commands instead of LIMIT.

4.3 *Commenting data*

Throughout this chapter, we've been discussing ways to sort and skip rows in your queries. I've provided some explanation of each query in terms of its purpose and considerations for executions, but if someone else read only the SQL we've used, would they understand why the queries were written the way they were? Probably not, which is why now is a good time to talk about comments. *Comments* allow you to include text in your query that isn't considered for execution. Typically, this text includes some kind of note to indicate the query author's intentions, as well as their identity and the date when the query was written or modified. Essentially, a comment can be any kind of information you want to include above and beyond the SQL you wrote.

Why would you want to use comments? RDBMSes aren't the only entities that are going to read your query; people will read it as well. These people could be colleagues who use the script, or the person who replaces you after you use your ever-expanding knowledge of SQL to secure a better job. Your comments can be as simple as your name and the date when you made your SQL script or as detailed as line-by-line descriptions of what each bit of SQL is meant to accomplish.

The downside of not using comments is ambiguity. Other people may look at your SQL and need to spend hours trying to figure out your intentions. Worse, you may look at some SQL you wrote weeks, months, or even years ago and be confused by what your former self wrote.

Writing descriptive, helpful comments is the mark of any well-respected SQL developer. Other people will have greater appreciation for your work because the extra seconds or minutes you spend writing clear comments will save them (and your future self) hours of confusion.

You have a few ways to write comments. First, you can *comment out* a particular line by using two consecutive hyphens:

```
-- This query returns three random rows
SELECT
    TitleName,
    PublicationDate
FROM title
LIMIT 3;
```

The use of two hyphens allows you to comment a single line of code up to the next carriage return. This type of comment is called an *inline comment*. In MySQL, you can also achieve an inline comment with the number sign (#):

```
# This query returns the three rows with the most recent PublicationDate
SELECT
    TitleName,
    PublicationDate
FROM title
ORDER BY PublicationDate DESC
LIMIT 3;
```

This type of comment isn't as common, so be aware that another RDBMS may not recognize it as a comment.

A third way to use comments is to surround your comment with /* and */, encompassing your comment between those symbols, which allows for a multiline comment. You can comment out more than one line, as in the following example:

```
/* This query returns 3 TitleNames
...with the most recent PublicationDate
...excluding the single most recent TitleName */
SELECT
    TitleName,
    PublicationDate
FROM title
ORDER BY PublicationDate DESC
LIMIT 3 OFFSET 1;
```

> **TIP** Because they have greater functionality, multiline comments (using /* and */) are the preferred method for use in reusable code. They can be especially useful when you want to comment out entire sections of SQL. You may want to do this to indicate a section of your SQL that doesn't execute as intended or to indicate a previous version of a query that you may want to reference later.

You can put multiple-line comments around single-line comments as well. You might have made a one-line comment about a particular SQL statement but later decided to comment out the entire statement with multiple-line comments, replacing it with different SQL. You could indicate this in the following way:

```
/*
# This query returns 3 random titles, but it wasn't what we needed
SELECT
    TitleName,
    PublicationDate
FROM title
LIMIT 3;
*/

-- This is the updated query, now ordered by most recent PublicationDate
```

```
SELECT
    TitleName,
    PublicationDate
FROM title
ORDER BY PublicationDate DESC
LIMIT 3;
```

Comments can be invaluable when you write a query, save it, and then come back to it weeks, months, or even years later to review it. I've been writing SQL for a few decades, and there have been innumerable times when I had to review the comments of an old query to determine the goal of that query. There have also been plenty of times when I looked at a query someone else wrote that had no comments, which led to many hours of trying to figure out what the writer intended the query to do.

Do yourself a favor: start developing the habit of carefully commenting any SQL you write, no matter how simple. Commenting takes only a few seconds, but as I mentioned, it could save you or someone else who reviews your code much more time. For this reason, all the SQL in this book's supplemental scripts has been commented to help you understand the purpose of each query.

4.4 Lab

1 You need a list of all authors, but you need that list to be in alphabetical order. Write a query to return the FirstName and LastName of all authors, sorted by LastName and then FirstName.

2 You need to write a query that returns all columns in the title table for only the highest-priced title. What does that query look like?

3 Suppose that you have the following SQL statement, which gets all the carriage returns stripped out by the application executing it, and that this query ends up on a single line. What will the result of this query be?

```
-- Retrieve the book titles
SELECT TitleName
FROM title;
```

4.5 Lab answers

1 The answer is

```
SELECT
    FirstName,
    LastName
FROM author
ORDER BY
    LastName,
    FirstName;
```

2 The answer is

```
SELECT
    TitleID,
    TitleName,
    Price,
    Advance,
    Royalty,
    PublicationDate
FROM title
ORDER By
    Price DESC
LIMIT 1;
```

Alternatively, you could use SELECT * instead of listing all the column names.

3 Because the entire query is now on a single line preceded by two hyphens, the entire query executes as a comment. Although it won't result in an error, it also won't return the results that the query intended. This situation is one of several reasons why I advise you to use /* and */ for comments in reusable code; both the beginning and end of the commented line or lines are clearly marked.

Filtering on specific values

So far, you've been writing mostly queries that return an entire set of data, but as you write more purposeful SQL using larger sets of data, you'll find that you need only a subset of the data instead of all the rows. You did work a bit in chapter 4 to reduce the number of rows returned using LIMIT and OFFSET, but those commands aren't helpful for finding specific rows.

You may want only a report of sales for the past month, a list of orders with pending status, or a list of customers in New Hampshire, for example. All these scenarios have *conditions* for specific data being returned, and we apply those conditions using filtering. *Filtering* means taking the broader results of your data set and applying one or more conditions to restrict the data being returned. To do this, you primarily use a different clause: the WHERE clause.

It's highly likely that most of the SQL you'll write in your career will include a WHERE clause because there's a nearly infinite number of ways you may need to find data that meets specific criteria. The WHERE clause is incredibly powerful, with so many ways to filter data that it will take a few chapters to review them. Let's get started!

5.1 Filtering on a single condition

The most basic methods for filtering data are relatively intuitive and easy to learn. The main variations involve the type of data you're querying. As you may have noticed, there are different types of data—such as names, numbers, and dates—and each type has slightly different rules for filtering. We'll look at them all in this section, starting with filtering by using a condition with a numeric value.

5.1.1   *Filtering on numeric values*

Suppose that we want to know the TitleName of any Titles for which the Advance for the author was $10,000. Let's start by declaring a sentence: "I would like the title name of the title where the advance is 10,000 dollars."

Notice that grammatically, we not only use the word *where* for our filtering but also place our filtering condition toward the end of the sentence. In SQL, we're going to do the same thing, and we could write a query for this request like this:

```
SELECT TitleName
FROM title
WHERE Advance = 10000.00;
```

Let's take a closer look at that WHERE clause and examine the rules that govern it:

- As in the preceding SQL query, the WHERE clause comes after the FROM clause, as it naturally would in English.
- Notice that we use an equal sign (=) instead of the word *is*. The use of the equal sign indicates equality, which means that our filtering condition is looking for values equal to a specific value. In this case, the use of the equal sign makes a lot of sense.
- Note that we have no dollar sign or comma in 10000.00. Although we use commas to make numeric values more readable and use dollar signs to indicate currency, this data is typically stored as a number, and the computer that runs your relational database management system (RDBMS) doesn't care about a specific currency type or the readability of the numbers. Using dollar signs and commas in this case would be problematic.

> **WARNING**   When you start filtering for large numeric values, such as orders above $1 million, it can be tempting to put commas in the numeric values to make the data more readable. After all, it can be easy to mistakenly type 1000000 as 100000 or 10000000. Unfortunately, including commas in numeric values will cause syntax errors for your query.

Although currency types and commas can't be used with numeric values, decimals can often be added or removed without changing the results of the data. This is possible because numeric values can be equal, even if they don't have the same precision. *Precision* refers to the mathematical specificity of a value, and how precise the data is depends on how that data is stored and how you're querying it.

As an example, 1.00 is more precise than 1. We can increment 1.00 up to 1.01, but the next incremental value after 1 is 2. For this reason, the latter is less precise. For querying, though, even though 1.00 is more precise, it's mathematically the same as 1.

In the case of the Advance value we just used to filter, let's take a quick look at the value of the data shown with the following query (results shown in figure 5.1):

```
SELECT
    TitleName,
    Advance
FROM title
WHERE Advance = 10000.00;
```

TitleName	Advance
Anne of Fact Tables	10000.00

Figure 5.1 Only one row meets the filter criteria for an Advance value of 10000.00.

In terms of precision, $10,000.00 is more precise than $10,000, but numerically, the numbers are the same value. For this reason, we can write a query without the decimal values used to represent cents and still get the results shown in figure 5.1:

```
SELECT TitleName, Advance
FROM title
WHERE Advance = 10000;
```

> **Try it now**
>
> Use the previous two queries to test the WHERE clause; see how the results are the same. Also try using an even more precise value in your filter condition, such as 10000.0000. All the results should be the same.

5.1.2 *Filtering on string values*

So far, our queries have filtered on numeric conditions, but filtering on non-numeric conditions is a bit different. Instead of looking for a TitleName for a specific Advance, let's reverse that approach and query for the Advance of a specific TitleName (results shown in figure 5.2):

```
SELECT Advance
FROM title
WHERE TitleName = 'Anne of Fact Tables';
```

Advance
10000.00

Figure 5.2 The result of a query for the Advance from the title table where the TitleName is Anne of Fact Tables

Now the filter condition isn't a numeric value but a group of words. To the RDBMS, this group of words is a set of characters known as a *string value*, and any time we filter on a string, we need to place single quotes around the value. If we don't, our query will result in a syntax error.

> **WARNING**   Not all single quotes work. You must use the single quote on the same keyboard key as the double quotes for this query to work. If you use the tick mark next to the 1/! key on most keyboards, you'll get a syntax error. Also, if you copy and paste code from a document other than a SQL script, you may get incorrectly formatted single quotes like the ones in figure 5.3.

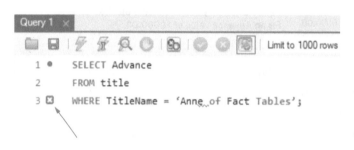

Figure 5.3   Incorrect single quotes, copied from a Microsoft Word document. Workbench is letting you know this with the square (red onscreen) with an X to the left of the line.

The value of the string used in our WHERE clause must be an exact match, as the slightest variation will prevent us from getting the intended results. If we forgot the letter *s* in Tables as in the following query, we won't get any results:

```
SELECT Advance
FROM title
WHERE TitleName = 'Anne of Fact Table';
```

> **NOTE**   Forgetting a character such as that last *s* may seem like a clear mistake, but subtle mistakes involving characters that don't seem like characters—such as extra spaces, tabs, and carriage returns—can lead to incorrect results. Although the RDBMS ignores the use of those characters in the format of SQL queries, it treats them as extra characters in your string values.

5.1.3   *Filtering on date values*

Date values have their own considerations in filtering because they're used as a kind of hybrid of numeric and string values. Like string values, date and time values must also be enclosed in single quotes. If you want to find the TitleName with a PublicationDate of March 14, 2020, for example, use the following SQL:

```
SELECT
    TitleName,
    PublicationDate
FROM title
WHERE PublicationDate = '2020-03-14 00:00:00';
```

The default format is year-month-day and then hours:minutes:seconds. The use of single quotes here may seem obvious because this value contains non-numeric characters, such as dashes and colons. But what if I told you that the RDBMS you're using is storing date and time values as numeric values? It's true. Storing those values this way is more efficient than storing them as a string of characters.

What this means for us and our use of SQL is that the rules of precision that apply to numeric values also apply to date and time values. Consider that the `00:00:00` in the filtering value represents hours:minutes:seconds—specifically, the exact second of midnight at the start of a day. If no time is provided, these zeroes are included in the default value for a date, as they are in the results of the most recent query (figure 5.4).

Now, given that we know 10,000.00 is numerically the same as 10,000, we can conclude that 2020-03-14 00:00:00 is also the same as 2020-03-14. Because the value of the data in the table has all zeroes for hours, minutes, and seconds, we can be confident that we'll get the results shown in figure 5.4 by writing the query without consideration of time, like this:

TitleName	PublicationDate
The Call of the While	2020-03-14 00:00:00

Figure 5.4 The TitleName and PublicationDate for a title published March 14, 2020. The time values are the equivalent of midnight at the start of the day.

```
SELECT
    TitleName,
    PublicationDate
FROM title
WHERE PublicationDate = '2020-03-14';
```

TIP   As your SQL skills progress, it will be helpful to be aware of the kind of data included in the tables you're going to query. It's easy to see that all the values for publication date in the title table have no precision for hours, minutes, or seconds and that we can safely query that data without including that level of time precision. But if a single value has so much as a second of precision, it would be better to write queries that account for the time as well.

5.2   *Filtering on multiple conditions*

So far, you've filtered on only a single condition, but in real-world queries, you often need to filter on multiple conditions. Imagine that you have to find a customer whose first name is Jeff and whose last name is Iannucci, or an Order that's number 1001 and an Item that's Product X. For queries like these, the WHERE clause allows filtering on multiple conditions using an intuitive method.

5.2.1   *Filtering that requires all conditions*

Suppose that we want to query the title table for Title Names for which the Advance is $5,000 and the Royalty is 15%. We would verbally declare our request like this: "I would like the TitleNames from title where the Advance is 5,000 dollars and the Royalty is 15 percent."

The use of the word AND to add to our filtering criteria is intuitively included in our SQL (results shown in figure 5.5):

TitleName	Advance	Royalty
Pride and Predicates	5000.00	15.00

Figure 5.5   Although multiple rows in the title table have a Price value of 5000.00, adding a second filter condition for a Royalty of 15.00 (%) reduces the result set to one row.

```
SELECT
    TitleName,
    Advance,
    Royalty
FROM title
WHERE Advance = 5000
    AND Royalty = 15;
```

In this context, the keyword AND is considered an *operator*, which means that it's a keyword that performs a specific operation in SQL. In the case of AND, the operation is to join multiple filter conditions within the WHERE clause. AND is the first of several operators we'll discuss.

The use of AND allows us to add as many filter conditions as we need for a given query, even beyond the example in the preceding query. Even though the result of the previous query is only one row, theoretically, we could refine the filter with additional criteria by putting another AND filter condition in the WHERE clause:

```
SELECT
    TitleName,
    Advance,
    Royalty,
    PublicationDate
FROM title
WHERE Advance = 5000
    AND Royalty = 15
    AND PublicationDate = '2015-04-30';
```

Try it now

Use the preceding two queries to test the WHERE clause; see how the results change with each filter. Try filtering first with a condition where the Royalty is 12; then add another filter condition where Advance is 6000. The rows in the result set should reduce from two rows in your first query to one row in the second.

Although there's no specific limit to how many filter conditions you can include in your WHERE clause, understand that for rows to be included in your result set, they must meet *every* one of the filter conditions. Failure to meet any single condition will exclude the rows from the results.

5.2.2   *Filtering that requires any one of many conditions*

Although the AND operator allows us to filter on multiple conditions that all rows must meet, sometimes we want to apply multiple filter conditions and get results that simply meet *one or more* of the conditions.

What if we want to find any book that has either an Advance of $5,000 or a Royalty of 15%? We could verbally declare the request like this: "I would like the TitleNames from title where the Advance is 5000 dollars or the Royalty is 15 percent." The word *or* has replaced *and* in our sentence, and it will do the same in our SQL:

```
SELECT
    TitleName,
    Advance,
    Royalty
FROM title
WHERE Advance = 5000
    OR Royalty = 15;
```

If this query is executed, we'll get very different results from the previous query, which used the AND operator instead of the OR operator. Now we have six rows returned instead of one (figure 5.6) because rows in the results need to meet either condition to be included—not both.

TitleName	Advance	Royalty
Pride and Predicates	5000.00	15.00
Catcher in the Try	5000.00	10.00
Anne of Fact Tables	10000.00	15.00
The DateTime Machine	5500.00	15.00
The Call of the While	2500.00	15.00
The Sum Also Rises	5000.00	12.00

Figure 5.6 The results for any rows in the title table that have either an Advance of 5000.00 or a Royalty of 15.00 (%)

We can use the OR operator the same way as the AND operator, in that we can add as many filter conditions as our query requires. Note that for each AND operator we add, a result set could get smaller as the conditions become more restrictive, whereas each OR operator could result in larger result sets as the conditions become more inclusive.

We can increase the result set from six rows to seven by adding an OR operator for Price and the Price column to the result set like this because any given row included in the results in figure 5.7 needs to meet only one of three filter conditions to be included:

```
SELECT
    TitleName,
    Advance,
    Royalty,
    Price
FROM title
WHERE Advance = 5000
    OR Royalty = 15
    OR Price = 9.95;
```

TitleName	Advance	Royalty	Price
Pride and Predicates	5000.00	15.00	9.95
The Join Luck Club	6000.00	12.00	9.95
Catcher in the Try	5000.00	10.00	8.95
Anne of Fact Tables	10000.00	15.00	12.95
The DateTime Machine	5500.00	15.00	7.95
The Call of the While	2500.00	15.00	8.95
The Sum Also Rises	5000.00	12.00	7.95

Figure 5.7 The seven rows that can match any of the three conditions of an Advance of 5000.00, a Royalty of 15.00 (%), or a Price of 9.95

We can go on and on adding filter conditions with multiple OR statements. Each time, we'll get as many rows as the time before—or more rows as the filter conditions become more inclusive.

5.2.3   *Controlling the order of multiple filters*

In some situations, we need to filter in a way that requires using both AND and OR in the WHERE clause. But we need to be very careful about how we do this.

Suppose that we need to find a list of TitleNames with a Price of $9.95 and either a PublicationDate of February 6, 2016 or an Advance of $5,000. To find this data, we might try writing a query like this:

```
SELECT
    TitleName,
    Price,
    PublicationDate,
    Advance
FROM title
WHERE Price = 9.95
    AND PublicationDate = '2016-02-06'
    OR Advance = 5000;
```

This query looks correct, but if we execute it, we'll find that the results don't match our intended logic. The RDBMS reads this query differently from what we intended, as shown in figure 5.8. This happens because the RDBMS prioritizes AND conditions over OR conditions, regardless of our intentions.

TitleName	Price	PublicationDate	Advance
Pride and Predicates	9.95	2015-04-30 00:00:00	5000.00
The Join Luck Club	9.95	2016-02-06 00:00:00	6000.00
Catcher in the Try	8.95	2017-04-03 00:00:00	5000.00
The Sum Also Rises	7.95	2021-11-12 00:00:00	5000.00

Figure 5.8   **The rows returned by the query don't match our intended filter conditions for TitleNames with a Price of 9.95 and a PublicationDate of 2016-02-06 or an Advance of 5000.00.**

Let's list the logic of our intended filtering conditions, either of which needed to be met:

- A Price of 9.95 and a PublicationDate of 2016-02-06
- A Price of 9.95 and an Advance of 5000.00

Because the RDBMS places a higher priority on AND conditions than on OR conditions, it determines the written filtering conditions differently from what we intended. To the RDBMS, our SQL is requesting rows that meet either of these conditions:

- A Price of 9.95 and a PublicationDate of 2016-02-06
- An Advance of 5000.00

The results in figure 5.8 show the only title that met the first condition (The Join Luck Club) and three others that met the second condition.

Getting this logic correct can be one of the most confusing problems for SQL beginners, but ironically, the solution is simple: all you need to do is use parentheses to explicitly prioritize your logic over the default SQL logic. Anything inside the parentheses is evaluated before anything outside the parentheses. To get the results we intended, we'd use parentheses in the preceding query like this:

```
SELECT
    TitleName,
    Price,
    PublicationDate,
    Advance
FROM title
WHERE Price = 9.95
    AND (PublicationDate = '2016-02-06'
    OR Advance = 5000);
```

Now this query will evaluate the values as intended, evaluating the OR condition before the AND condition. Executing this query returns a result set like the one shown in figure 5.9.

TitleName	Price	PublicationDate	Advance
Pride and Predicates	9.95	2015-04-30 00:00:00	5000.00
The Join Luck Club	9.95	2016-02-06 00:00:00	6000.00

Figure 5.9   With the parenthetical notation, the query returns data that has a Price of 9.95 and either a PublicationDate of 2016-02-06 or an Advance of 5000.00.

TIP   Whenever you write any SQL that uses both AND and OR operators in your WHERE clause, always use parentheses to explicitly control the evaluation. This approach not only helps the RDBMS figure out your intentions but also reduces guesswork for anyone else who will be evaluating your code.

5.2.4   *Filtering and using ORDER BY*

As you've gone through this chapter, you may have wondered what happened to the ORDER BY clause from chapter 4 and how it fits in with the WHERE clause in this chapter. When you use both WHERE and ORDER BY clauses in your SQL, you need to write the ORDER BY clause *after* the WHERE clause.

We can use a query from earlier in the chapter that returned four rows. Figure 5.7 shows the rows returned in no particular order, but if we wanted the results to be sorted by TitleName, we could easily add an ORDER BY clause like this (results shown in figure 5.10):

```
SELECT
    TitleName,
    Price,
    PublicationDate,
    Advance
FROM title
WHERE Price = 9.95
```

```
    AND PublicationDate = '2016-02-06'
  OR Advance = 5000
ORDER BY TitleName;
```

TitleName	Price	PublicationDate	Advance
Catcher in the Try	8.95	2017-04-03 00:00:00	5000.00
Pride and Predicates	9.95	2015-04-30 00:00:00	5000.00
The Join Luck Club	9.95	2016-02-06 00:00:00	6000.00
The Sum Also Rises	7.95	2021-11-12 00:00:00	5000.00

Figure 5.10 The four rows that match any of three conditions—a Price of 9.95, a PublicationDate of 2016-02-06, or an Advance of 5000.00—with the results sorted alphabetically by TitleName

We've covered a lot of examples of basic filtering today. It's time to use our new skills!

5.3   Lab

1 If we don't place single quotes around a non-numeric string value in our filter condition, we know that we'll get a syntax error. Try placing single quotes around a numeric value like Price in a filter condition and executing a query. What happens?

2 Why does the following query return no results?

```
SELECT
    TitleName,
    Price
FROM Title
WHERE TitleName = 'Anne of Fact Tables ';
```

3 What will the result of the following query be?

```
SELECT TitleName
FROM Title
ORDER BY TitleName ASC
WHERE Price = 9.95;
```

4 Write a query using the author table that returns rows with either a Payment-Method of Check and a FirstName of Jorge or a PaymentMethod of Check and a LastName of Miller. Include the columns FirstName, LastName, and Payment-Method in your result set.

5.4   Lab answers

1 The query executes as expected, although behind the scenes, the RDBMS has made the data match. It had to convert either the value in quotes to a number or all the values in the Price column to a string, which could negatively affect the duration of the query if we were using a larger set of data. For this reason, avoid putting single quotes around numeric values.

2 The query returns no values because there is an extra space after the word `Tables` in the `WHERE` clause. For a string used in a filter to be correct, it needs to be exactly like the values in the table, including unseen characters such as spaces, tabs, and carriage returns.

3 The query will result in a syntax error because the `ORDER BY` can't come before the `WHERE` clause.

4 This query is similar to the one in section 5.2.3. Because it uses `AND` and `OR` and parentheses, the query should return two rows and should look something like this:

```
SELECT
    FirstName,
    LastName,
    PaymentMethod
FROM author
WHERE PaymentMethod = 'Check'
AND (FirstName = 'Jorge'
    OR LastName = 'Miller');
```

6

Filtering with multiple values, ranges, and exclusions

As we saw in chapter 5, the WHERE clause offers many useful options for filtering results based on specific conditions. We looked at several examples of filtering on a single value using the AND and OR operators. Now we'll expand that concept to filter on even more values, including a list of specific values or ranges of unspecified values.

These are examples of *positive searches*, in which we try to match values that we want to see in the results of our queries. Because often, we'll want to do the opposite and see all the values except some specific filter conditions, we'll also see how to negate any of the conditions we've covered. Let's start by looking at a new operator for the WHERE clause.

6.1 Filtering on specific values

Previously, we looked at a basic search, finding the TitleNames for titles that had a certain Price. If we want to query titles that had a Price of $10.95, for example, we'd write our SQL like this:

```
SELECT
    TitleName,
    Price
FROM title
WHERE Price = 10.95;
```

But what if we want to find the titles with a Price of either $10.95 or $12.95? Now we know that we can write SQL to do this using the OR operator, so we could write a SQL query like this (output shown in figure 6.1):

TitleName	Price
Anne of Fact Tables	12.95
The Great GroupBy	10.95

Figure 6.1   The results of a query with filter conditions for a Price of 10.95 or 12.95

```
SELECT
    TitleName,
    Price
FROM title
WHERE Price = 10.95
    OR Price = 12.95;
```

This query will give us the results we want for our two filter condition values, but it could lead to some wordy SQL if we have a list of conditions that grows much longer. We don't want to use an OR operator if we have 3, 10, or even more filter condition values for a single column.

To resolve this problem, SQL has the IN operator, which allows us to consolidate our filter conditions into a single operator. The IN operator has three requirements:

- The list of values must be comma-delimited.
- The list of values must be enclosed in parentheses.
- The requirement of single quotes is the same as in any other filter condition.

As an example, we can rewrite the preceding query with an IN operator, like this:

```
SELECT
    TitleName,
    Price
FROM title
WHERE Price IN (10.95, 12.95);
```

Executing this query yields the results shown in figure 6.1 but in a more compact form of SQL. As I mentioned earlier, the use of single quotes is the same as what we used in queries that filtered for filter conditions with string or date values.

Try it now

Using the IN operator, execute a query looking for TitleName and Price from titles where Price is $7.95, $8.95, or $9.95.

If we want to search for titles with a specific PublicationDate, we need to use single quotes with our filter conditions because we're using data values instead of numeric values. We'd write our SQL like this (results shown in figure 6.2):

```
SELECT
    TitleName,
    PublicationDate
```

```
FROM title
WHERE PublicationDate IN ('2015-04-30', '2016-02-06');
```

NOTE As far as the relational database management system (RDBMS) is concerned, the order of values used with the IN operator is irrelevant. As with any query that doesn't involve an ORDER BY clause, the rows in the result set aren't guaranteed to be returned in any particular order. That said, as I've noted several times in this book, you should follow best practices to make your SQL more human-readable whenever possible. For this reason, it's best to list values in the filter conditions of the IN operator in numerical, alphabetical, or chronological order.

TitleName	PublicationDate
Pride and Predicates	2015-04-30 00:00:00
The Join Luck Club	2016-02-06 00:00:00

Figure 6.2   The results for titles with a PublicationDate of 2015-04-30 or 2016-02-06

6.2   Filtering on a range of values

Filtering on a list of specific values with the IN operator is useful if you know all the specific values you want to match, but not when you don't know all the specific values. Often, you need to find values with a range, such as any values higher than a certain amount or older than a certain date. You can use *comparison operators* in SQL, which compare two values to see whether they meet specific criteria, to find the desired results.

6.2.1   Filtering on an open-ended range

Assuming that you've worked with basic math, you're familiar with the *less-than* (<) and *greater-than* (>) signs. (On a typical keyboard, they share the same keys as the comma and the period, respectively.) Like the equal sign (=), these signs are commonly used comparison operators. Unlike the equal sign, the less-than and greater-than signs can be used to find an open-ended range of values.

In a query earlier in this chapter, we looked for any title that had a Price of $10.95 or $12.95. In our title table, these titles are the ones with the highest prices. We can find these same two titles by writing a query using the > sign. Let's also include an ORDER BY clause to see the Price values in order, recalling that the default is to order the results by ascending values. Figure 6.3 shows the output of this query:

```
SELECT
    TitleName,
    Price
FROM title
WHERE Price > 9.95
ORDER BY Price ASC;
```

TitleName	Price
The Great GroupBy	10.95
Anne of Fact Tables	12.95

Figure 6.3   The titles that have a Price greater than 9.95, ordered by Price ascending

We can use the < sign to do the opposite: find any titles that have a Price of less than $9.95. For this query, we'll sort by descending Price values to show the prices closest to $9.95 at the top of the results (shown in figure 6.4):

```
SELECT
    TitleName,
    Price
FROM title
WHERE Price < 9.95
ORDER BY Price DESC;
```

TitleName	Price
Catcher in the Try	8.95
The Call of the While	8.95
The DateTime Machine	7.95
The Sum Also Rises	7.95

Figure 6.4 The titles that have a Price less than 9.95, ordered by Price descending

You've probably noticed that neither of these result sets includes any titles that match the Price of $9.95. Certainly, you'll sometimes want to query a range of values including those that match the filter conditions, so SQL also includes the comparison operators *less-than or equal-to* (<=) and *greater-than or equal-to* (>=). Using one of these operators, we can query any title with a Price greater than or equal to a filter condition of 9.95 and get the results shown in figure 6.5:

TitleName	Price
Pride and Predicates	9.95
The Join Luck Club	9.95
The Great GroupBy	10.95
Anne of Fact Tables	12.95

Figure 6.5 The titles that have a Price greater than or equal to 9.95, ordered by Price ascending

```
SELECT
    TitleName,
    Price
FROM title
WHERE Price >= 9.95
ORDER BY Price ASC;
```

NOTE You can see how we can search for values greater than or less than a particular numeric or date value. Although the use cases are less common, you can also use these operators with string values. The values are typically returned with respect to precedence in the alphabet. Be careful when using these operators with string values, however: the way that the numeric, symbol, and case values are filtered is based on the collation settings in your RDBMS. *Collation* determines sorting rules based on character qualities such as the character set, letter case, and accent use; therefore, different collations return characters in a different order.

6.2.2 Filtering a defined range

The operators in section 6.2.1 are *open-ended*—that is, they could include an infinite number of values greater than or less than a value. If we want to find values greater than some value but lesser than another value, we have a couple of options.

You may have already thought of the first option, which is to use both > and < in the WHERE clause. If you're trying to find titles with a price between $8.95 and $10.95, you can write a SQL query like the following. Again, you'll use an ORDER BY in the query to organize the results so that you can see the maximum and minimum values returned by your filter conditions in figure 6.6:

TitleName	Price
Pride and Predicates	9.95
The Join Luck Club	9.95

Figure 6.6   The titles with Price values between the search conditions of 8.95 and 10.95

```
SELECT
    TitleName,
    Price
FROM title
WHERE Price > 8.95
    AND Price < 10.95
ORDER BY Price ASC;
```

We can see that the only Price value that matches the range of our filter conditions is 9.95. If we want to change the filter conditions to *include* the values we've specified, we need to use >= and <= in the WHERE clause like this:

```
SELECT
    TitleName,
    Price
FROM title
WHERE Price >= 8.95
    AND Price <= 10.95
ORDER BY Price ASC;
```

As figure 6.7 shows, now the result set includes titles that match the Price values used in the filter conditions.

We also have another way to search a range of values: instead of using >= and <=, we can use the BETWEEN operator to perform the same function. The rules for using BETWEEN are

TitleName	Price
Catcher in the Try	8.95
The Call of the While	8.95
Pride and Predicates	9.95
The Join Luck Club	9.95
The Great GroupBy	10.95

Figure 6.7   The titles with Price values between the filter conditions of 8.95 and 10.95 when the values used in the filter condition are included

- The column being searched is mentioned only once.
- Only two filter conditions can be supplied.
- The first value represents the low end of the range, and the second value represents the high end of the range.
- The filter conditions must be separated by the word AND.
- Any values matching either condition are included in the results.

We can write the previous query using the BETWEEN operator like this:

```
SELECT
    TitleName,
    Price
FROM title
WHERE Price BETWEEN 8.95 AND 10.95
ORDER BY Price ASC;
```

Even though we used one less line of SQL, the results of this query should be identical to the results shown in figure 6.7.

> **WARNING** I should mention again that when you're using BETWEEN, the first value represents the low end of the range, and the second represents the high end of the range. If you use BETWEEN, and the first value of the filter conditions of the range is higher than the second value, your query will return no results. The SQL query WHERE Price BETWEEN 10.95 and 8.95, for example, won't return any rows, regardless of other filter conditions. Logically, no values are both higher than 10.95 and lower than 8.95.

6.3 Negating filter conditions

So far, we've used the WHERE clause to specify filter conditions that match specific values or ranges of data. These conditions are known as *inclusive* because the results include rows with values that match the values we used in our filter conditions. The opposite conditions are known as *exclusive*; we want all values *except* the ones specified in the filter conditions. In a way, this is a bit like the way we used OFFSET in chapter 4 to exclude a specific number of rows, but we're being much more specific about what we're excluding.

6.3.1 Negating a specific value

In chapter 5, we learned to filter on specific values using the equal sign (=). Mathematically, we can represent the opposite using the *not-equal sign* (<>), which combines the < and > signs.

If we want to list all titles that don't have a Price of $7.95, we could use <> like this, with the ordered results shown in figure 6.8:

TitleName	Price
Catcher in the Try	8.95
The Call of the While	8.95
Pride and Predicates	9.95
The Join Luck Club	9.95
The Great GroupBy	10.95
Anne of Fact Tables	12.95

Figure 6.8 All titles, excluding the two that have a Price of 7.95

```
SELECT
    TitleName,
    Price
FROM title
WHERE Price <> 7.95
ORDER BY Price ASC;
```

Even though we've used <> for mathematical comparisons, we can use it with date and string values as well. If we want all titles *except* those published on February 6, 2016, we can use single quotes with <> to get the results shown in figure 6.9:

TitleName	PublicationDate
Pride and Predicates	2015-04-30 00:00:00
Catcher in the Try	2017-04-03 00:00:00
Anne of Fact Tables	2018-01-12 00:00:00
The DateTime Machine	2019-02-04 00:00:00
The Great GroupBy	2019-12-23 00:00:00
The Call of the While	2020-03-14 00:00:00
The Sum Also Rises	2021-11-12 00:00:00

Figure 6.9 All titles, excluding the one ("The Join Luck Club") that has a PublicationDate of 2016-02-06

```
SELECT
    TitleName,
    PublicationDate
```

```
FROM title
WHERE PublicationDate <> '2016-02-06'
ORDER BY PublicationDate ASC;
```

> **NOTE**   The RDBMS you use may offer the option to use != instead of <>. Both options perform the same function of negating a single condition. But I advise you to develop the habit of using <> in your SQL because not every RDBMS supports the != option.

6.3.2   *Negating any filter condition*

Although <> enables us to exclude a single value in a filter condition, one operator excludes an entire filter condition. This operator, NOT, turns any inclusive filter condition into an exclusive condition.

In the preceding query, for example, we used <> to exclude any title that has a PublicationDate of February 6, 2016. We can use the opposite of <>, which is =, with the NOT operator to achieve the same results. The following query produces the results shown in figure 6.9, with the results ordered by PublicationDate:

```
SELECT
    TitleName,
    PublicationDate
FROM title
WHERE NOT PublicationDate = '2016-02-06'
ORDER BY PublicationDate ASC;
```

In this case, the NOT operator immediately follows the word WHERE. You can use the NOT operator after the start of any filter condition to negate it, which means you could also use it immediately after conditions that begin with the AND or OR operator.

> **Try it now**
> Execute the two preceding queries to see how to use <> and NOT to exclude specific values.

You shouldn't use the negative NOT operator with > or < because you can logically use their positive opposites (<= and >=, respectively) to get the same results with simpler syntax. it's not uncommon, however, to use NOT with the IN operator mentioned in section 6.1.

Recall that we used a single condition with the IN operator to query all titles with a Price of $10.95 or $12.95 to replace two conditions using the OR operator. We can use NOT to negate this filter condition with the IN operator, returning all titles *except* those that match the conditions of a Price of $10.95 or $12.95, with the results sorted by Price (figure 6.10):

```
SELECT
    TitleName,
    Price
FROM title
WHERE NOT Price IN (10.95, 12.95)
ORDER BY Price ASC;
```

TitleName	Price
The DateTime Machine	7.95
The Sum Also Rises	7.95
Catcher in the Try	8.95
The Call of the While	8.95
Pride and Predicates	9.95
The Join Luck Club	9.95

Figure 6.10 All titles, excluding those with a Price of 10.95 or 12.95

You may have noticed the condition WHERE NOT Price IN in the preceding query, which sounds a bit clumsy to English-speaking people. There's a better and more common way to get the same results in SQL. There is a separate NOT IN operator, so we can also place NOT before the IN in our filter condition to make it more readable, like this:

```
SELECT TitleName, Price
FROM title
WHERE Price NOT IN (10.95, 12.95)
ORDER BY Price ASC;
```

This query also returns the results shown in figure 6.10. When we want to use an exclusionary list of values, as in the preceding example, NOT IN is more commonly used.

6.4 *Combining types of filter conditions*

This chapter has shown you several new ways to filter your data with inclusive and exclusive filter conditions. One last point to make is that you can (and will) combine both kinds of filter conditions in your queries. You could write a query, for example, to find any title that has an Advance value > 5000 but a Royalty <> 12%, with the results shown in figure 6.11:

TitleName	Advance	Royalty
Anne of Fact Tables	10000.00	15.00
The DateTime Machine	5500.00	15.00

Figure 6.11 The titles that have an Advance greater than 5000 with a Royalty that is not 12 (%)

```
SELECT
    TitleName,
    Advance,
    Royalty
FROM title
WHERE Advance > 5000
    AND Royalty <> 12;
```

With all the operators discussed in this chapter and chapter 5, you can begin to write some relatively complex filter conditions. If you want to include the preceding results (any title that has an Advance > 5000 but a Royalty <> 12 [%]) and also any titles published after January 1, 2020, you can easily do that by using the SQL for inclusive and exclusive queries and controlling the logic with parentheses. If you tried this approach, your SQL query might look something like the following, with the results shown in figure 6.12:

```
SELECT
    TitleName,
    Advance,
    Royalty,
    PublicationDate
FROM title
WHERE (Advance > 5000
    AND Royalty <> 12)
    OR (PublicationDate > '2020-01-01');
```

TitleName	Advance	Royalty	PublicationDate
Anne of Fact Tables	10000.00	15.00	2018-01-12 00:00:00
The DateTime Machine	5500.00	15.00	2019-02-04 00:00:00
The Call of the While	2500.00	15.00	2020-03-14 00:00:00
The Sum Also Rises	5000.00	12.00	2021-11-12 00:00:00

Figure 6.12　The titles with an Advance of 5000 that don't have a Royalty of 12 (%) or any title published after 2020-01-01

TIP　Although you can use exclusive filter conditions to achieve the same results as inclusive filter conditions, it's preferable to use inclusive filter conditions whenever possible. Generally, inclusive conditions are easier for others who read your SQL to comprehend and are processed more efficiently by the RDBMS. An exception would occur if you had only one exclusion or a few exclusions to filter, in which case it would likely be better to use exclusive filters instead of an inclusive filter with a vast number of inclusive conditions or values.

You're only a few chapters into this book, but already, you can search data in meaningful, accurate ways. You've used mostly filter conditions with numeric and date values so far. But chapter 7 discusses another series of tools you can use in the WHERE clause to perform advanced searches for data in string values.

6.5　Reviewing comparison operators

This chapter covered more than a dozen comparison operators that you can use for filtering in the WHERE clause. You may have been taking lots of notes, but in case you didn't, table 6.1 presents a list of what you used.

Table 6.1　Review of WHERE clause comparison operators

Operator	Description
=	Equality
<>	Inequality
!=	Inequality*
<	Less than
>	Greater than
!<	Not less than*
!>	Not greater than*

Table 6.1   Review of WHERE clause comparison operators (*continued*)

Operator	Description
<=	Less than or equal to
>=	Greater than or equal to
BETWEEN	Between two values, including those values
IN	Equality to a list of multiple values
NOT IN	Inequality to a list of multiple values
NOT	Inequality to stated condition

*May not be supported by every RDBMS

6.6   Lab

You have only one lab assignment today, but it is a challenge that uses your creativity. This chapter and chapter 5 covered quite a few ways to include and exclude data, so consider all that you've learned about using the WHERE clause for filtering.

TitleName	Price
The DateTime Machine	7.95
The Sum Also Rises	7.95
Catcher in the Try	8.95
The Call of the While	8.95
The Great GroupBy	10.95
Anne of Fact Tables	12.95

Figure 6.13   The titles with a Price that is not 9.95, ordered by Price ascending

For this exercise, think of as many ways as possible to use the WHERE clause to return the TitleName and Price for all rows in the title table that don't have a price of 9.95. The results of each query should include only the rows shown in figure 6.13, ordered by Price.

6.7   Lab answers

These are some of the many ways you can write the WHERE clause to exclude titles with a Price of $9.95:

- WHERE Price <> 9.95
- WHERE NOT Price = 9.95
- WHERE Price < 9.95 OR Price > 9.95
- WHERE PRICE NOT IN (9.95)
- WHERE Price IN (7.95, 8.95, 10.95, 12.95)
- WHERE Price BETWEEN 7.95 AND 8.95 OR Price BETWEEN 10.95 and 12.95
- WHERE NOT Price BETWEEN 9.95 and 9.95

That last answer may be a bit unexpected because it effectively negates a range of values that include only a single value. I show it here only to demonstrate that a range with the same high and low end can be executed.

7
Filtering with wildcards and null values

The preceding chapters are filled with different ways to filter the data returned by your queries using numerous comparison operators. We've worked with many methods for filtering on one or more values of equality or inequality using known values or ranges of values. Let's take one more chapter to examine some interesting ways to search for less specific data.

We'll look at how to filter data when we don't know the exact values to be searched. Instead of searching for specific values, we'll search for *patterns of values*. This approach can be incredibly useful when we want to look for a list of products that have specific text like *tomato* or *cable* in the name, or when we want a list of all customers whose last name starts with the letter *A*.

We'll also look at the trickiest value to search on: null. Null values are commonly misunderstood, and as such, they often lead to incorrect query results. We'll examine what a null value is (and isn't) and how to query for null values.

7.1 Filtering with wildcards

In chapter 6, you learned how to search ranges of numeric or date values. Even though you may not know all the specific values you want from a range, you know how to query the correct results using operators such as >, <, and BETWEEN.

Interestingly, we can use those same operators to search for string values. If we want to find all the first and last names of authors with a last name that starts with *S*, for example, we could write SQL using >= and < to get the result shown in figure 7.1:

```
SELECT
    FirstName,
    LastName
FROM author
WHERE LastName >= 'S'
    AND LastName < 'T';
```

FirstName	LastName
Jen	Strong
Gail	Shawn

Figure 7.1 The results of searching the author table for a range of last names that start with S

NOTE From here on out, we won't sort results unless sorting is necessary. As I stated in chapter 4, sorting data with ORDER BY increases the work required to process any query, so avoid doing that if possible. Just remember that without ORDER BY, it's always possible to get the same results in a different order for any given query.

This method of searching for string values in a range works most of the time, but not always. As briefly noted in chapter 6, depending on the collation settings, the character case (upper or lower), and characters used (such as letters with tildes or umlauts), you may not get consistent results using this method to filter on string values.

Also, it just looks weird to write a query this way, and we certainly wouldn't verbally declare how we want to filter results this way. We want a list of last names that start with *S*, not a list of names between *S* and *T*. In this case, a wildcard makes more sense.

A *wildcard* is a special character that can be substituted for any number of characters in a string. Using a wildcard allows us to search for specific patterns of values instead of being restricted to a range, as in the preceding query.

7.1.1 *Filtering with the percent sign*

The first wildcard we'll use is %, the percent sign. When used as a wildcard, % matches any string, including an empty string with no characters. Here's how we'd use it to find the names of authors with a last name that starts with *S*:

```
SELECT
    FirstName,
    LastName
FROM author
WHERE LastName LIKE 'S%';
```

Notice that we're using a new operator, LIKE. LIKE is the operator we'll always use when searching with a wildcard because in the SQL language, it indicates that we're searching for a pattern, not for precise conditional values. If we tried to use some other conditional operator (such as = or >) in this query instead of LIKE, we'd get no results.

Try it now

Execute the preceding query; then try using the = operator instead of LIKE.

Even though we know how the query ends, let's take a moment to compare it with how we might verbally declare this query: "I would like the first name and last name from the author table where the last names start with *S*."

I can assure you that SQL has no STARTS WITH operator, and although it might be useful for our query, it wouldn't be very flexible. We'd also need hypothetical operators for other queries, such as ENDS WITH and maybe even HAS IN THE MIDDLE. These operators would be excessively wordy, if not a bit ridiculous.

In SQL, the % operator is not only shorter but also has the same functionality as all those other hypothetical operators. The easiest way to remember how to use it is to think of the % wildcard as the word *something*. The *something* pattern we're looking for could be 0 characters or 100. Here's a verbal way to say what we're doing with the query: "I would like the first name and last name from the author table where the last names are like *S* and then *something*."

This statement is fairly close to what our new query looks like, and the results will be the same as those shown in figure 7.1. As I just mentioned, the % wildcard can be used anywhere in a string of characters, which means that if we want to search for all last names that end in *N*, we could verbally declare a query like this: "I would like the first name and last name from the author table where the last names are like *something* and then *N*."

As you can imagine, our query would be very similar to the verbal declaration. Here it is, with the results shown in figure 7.2:

FirstName	LastName
Robert	Davidson
Gail	Shawn
Andy	Melkin
Deepthi	Mahadevan

```
SELECT
    FirstName,
    LastName
FROM author
WHERE LastName LIKE '%N';
```

Figure 7.2   Authors who have a last name that ends with *N*

If we wanted to refine this search to include only the last names that not only end with *N* but also start with *M*, like the results shown in figure 7.3, we can certainly do that as well:

FirstName	LastName
Andy	Melkin
Deepthi	Mahadevan

```
SELECT
    FirstName,
    LastName
FROM author
WHERE LastName LIKE 'M%N';
```

Figure 7.3   Authors who have a last name that starts with *M* and ends with *N*

We can also use the % operator both before and after a character or string of characters to find a pattern in the middle of our data. Here's an example of searching for authors with the string "de" anywhere in their last name, with the results shown in figure 7.4:

FirstName	LastName
Buck	Fernandez
Deepthi	Mahadevan

Figure 7.4   Authors who have a last name that contains "DE"

```
SELECT
    FirstName,
```

```
    LastName
FROM author
WHERE LastName LIKE '%DE%';
```

This technique can be useful for searching a column of comments or other freely entered text. If you want to find any comments that include the word *good*, for example, you'd search for column values `LIKE '%good%'`. As I noted in chapter 3, most relational database management systems (RDBMSes) aren't case-sensitive, so you should be able to return values including "Good" and "GOOD." Then again, you might also get string values like "not very good" and "goodbye" in your results because they also match the pattern.

> **WARNING** Although the `LIKE` operator isn't case-sensitive in the default collations of MySQL, Microsoft SQL Server, and SQLite databases, it can be case-sensitive in the default collations of PostgreSQL and Oracle databases.

As helpful as the `%` wildcard can be for finding patterns of characters, it lacks precision. If we want to search values at a particular position, we can use a different wildcard.

7.1.2 Filtering with an underscore

Whereas the `%` wildcard matches any string of characters (including zero characters), the `_` wildcard, an *underscore*, looks only for any single character. What's more, we can combine `_` with `%` in our search patterns if necessary.

> **WARNING** The `_` wildcard is not supported in DB2.

If we want to find the first and last names of any author with a first name that starts with *R* and has *b* as the third letter, as shown in figure 7.5, we can use `_` and `%` to find them:

FirstName	LastName
Robert	Davidson
Rebecca	Miller

Figure 7.5 Authors who have a first name that starts with *R* and has *b* as the third letter

```
SELECT
    FirstName,
    LastName
FROM author
WHERE FirstName LIKE 'R_b%';
```

Although the `_` wildcard is generally used less often than the `%` wildcard, you can still face scenarios of searching for patterns at one specific position, such as if you need to find items with a color value of gray, which could be spelled *gray* or *grey*. To find all matching values, you could search `WHERE color LIKE 'gr_y'`.

You can also search for values or locations that have a difference in the first few characters by using the `_` wildcard. Here's an example of finding any author with a first name that has *u* as the third character, with the results shown in figure 7.6:

FirstName	LastName
Doug	Li
Paul	Tripp

Figure 7.6 The results of authors who have a first name that has *u* as the third letter

```
SELECT
    FirstName,
```

```
    LastName
FROM author
WHERE FirstName LIKE '__u%'
ORDER BY FirstName ASC;
```

Wildcards other than % and _ are supported by each RDBMS, but because they vary, I won't discuss them in this book. That said, if you're using a particular RDBMS, I encourage you to look into what other wildcards it may support to further enhance your ability to search for patterns of values.

Now let's move on to . . . well, nothing.

7.2   Filtering with null values

Sometimes, database designers create columns that require values for every column, but at other times, a column may allow for the absence of data. If a row does not have any data for such a column, the value shows NULL for that column.

As I noted at the beginning of this chapter, null values are some of the most misunderstood concepts in databases. Put simply, null values are literally nothing: they represent the absence of data. This concept seems simple, but because null values aren't values like 30 or Arizona or 2012-05-12, we need to consider them differently from other values when querying data.

Let's look at an example by reviewing all the columns in the author table. Executing the following query returns all the columns for all 11 rows in the table. One of the first things you may notice is the MiddleName column, which has quite a few values that say NULL. Not everyone has a middle name, so the absence of a middle name for any author is represented by NULL. MySQL Workbench tries to bring this fact to your attention by making NULL look different from other values we've seen so far, in that it is shown with white text in a smaller font and a dark background (figure 7.7).

```
SELECT *
FROM author;
```

AuthorID	FirstName	MiddleName	LastName	PaymentMethod
1	Paul	K	Tripp	Cash
2	Doug	NULL	Li	Check
3	Jen	NULL	Strong	Check
4	Jorge	Armando	Guerra	Check
5	Robert	Grant	Davidson	Check
6	Gail	Anne	Shawn	Check
7	Rebecca	NULL	Miller	Check
8	Andy	NULL	Melkin	Direct Deposit
9	Buck	NULL	Fernandez	Cash
10	Chris	NULL	Walenski	Direct Deposit
11	Deepthi	NULL	Mahadevan	Direct Deposit

Figure 7.7   The results of all columns in the author table, including null values in the MiddleName column

7.2.1 *How not to search for null values*

As I stated in the preceding section, a null value represents the absence of a value, which makes any column containing a null value tricky to query. To avoid some common pitfalls, let's first talk about how *not* to query for null values. If we want to find the rows in the author table that contain null values for MiddleName, none of the next three examples will work:

```
/* This doesn't work because null values are not blank strings. */
SELECT *
FROM author
WHERE MiddleName = '';
```

This query won't return null values because the query is searching for a character string with a length of 0, also known as an *empty* string. I know that's confusing: when I mention "absence of a value" and "empty string," it seems that I'm saying the same thing in different ways. But an empty string is different from a null value because an empty string is still a string. By that, I mean that underneath the covers, your RDBMS is still using bytes to indicate a value for the empty string, so it can be considered for queries that are filtering with many comparison operators, including a wildcard search. Null values use no bytes and are not considered for filtering with comparison operators or wildcards. Here's another common but incorrect way to search for null values:

```
/* This doesn't work because null values are not the word null. */
SELECT *
FROM author
WHERE MiddleName = 'NULL';
```

This query doesn't work because the search condition is for the word "NULL," not a null value. Also, it won't return any rows unless your data is populated with a string of the four characters that make the word "NULL." That may seem unlikely, but sometimes database developers don't understand how to work with null values, so they use the word "NULL" to represent null values. Because the word "NULL" is a string of characters, this can create all sorts of headaches for your queries. Please don't ever do this.

Here's one last incorrect way to search for null values:

```
/* This doesn't work because no value ever equals null. */
SELECT *
FROM author
WHERE MiddleName = NULL;
```

It seems like this query should work, but = is looking for equality, and you can't have equality matches of nothing. At the most basic level, all the comparison operators, including =, are evaluating for search conditions that are either true or not true. Because a null value is nothing, it never equals anything in a search condition, so it never evaluates as being true.

> **Try it now**
>
> Execute any or all of the three preceding queries, and see that they don't return any matching rows.

7.2.2   *How to search for null values correctly*

To search for null values correctly, let's state another verbal example for what we're trying to do. If we want the full name of any author who has a null value for a middle name, we could say the following: "I would like the first, middle, and last name of authors where the middle name is null."

FirstName	MiddleName	LastName
Doug	NULL	Li
Jen	NULL	Strong
Rebecca	NULL	Miller
Andy	NULL	Melkin
Buck	NULL	Fernandez
Chris	NULL	Walenski
Deepthi	NULL	Mahadevan

Figure 7.8   The results of first, middle, and last names in the author table for authors with no middle name

To turn previous verbal declarations like this one into SQL queries, we replaced *is* with the = operator. But because we're dealing with a filter condition involving null values, which don't work with comparison operators, we can instead use a new operator that is literally the last two words of the verbal declaration: IS NULL. Here's what our query will look like, with the results shown in figure 7.8:

```
SELECT
    FirstName,
    MiddleName,
    LastName
FROM author
WHERE MiddleName IS NULL;
```

Pay close attention to null values and the IS NULL operator because null values can be even more problematic. Notice that in figure 7.7, the first of the 11 rows in the author table has a MiddleName value of K. Suppose that you want to query all rows except that one, with an exclusion query (chapter 6). You could do this with the following query, with the results shown in figure 7.9:

FirstName	MiddleName	LastName
Jorge	Armando	Guerra
Robert	Grant	Davidson
Gail	Anne	Shawn

Figure 7.9   The rows returned for any author that does not have a middle name of K, which excludes any author without a middle name

```
SELECT
    FirstName,
    MiddleName,
    LastName
FROM author
WHERE MiddleName <> 'K';
```

You may think this query would return the 10 rows that don't have K as a middle name, but you'd be incorrect. Because the filter is looking for any value that does not equal

K, it discards any results that have null values. Nothing cannot equal (or even not equal) something, so the filter considers only rows that have a non-null value for MiddleName.

It's possible, of course, that you intend this query to return only rows with a value for MiddleName, but if you want all 10 rows to be returned, you need to include the IS NULL operator in your filtering. You'd use an additional OR operator, with the results shown in figure 7.10:

FirstName	MiddleName	LastName
Doug	NULL	Li
Jen	NULL	Strong
Jorge	Armando	Guerra
Robert	Grant	Davidson
Gail	Anne	Shawn
Rebecca	NULL	Miller
Andy	NULL	Melkin
Buck	NULL	Fernandez
Chris	NULL	Walenski
Deepthi	NULL	Mahadevan

Figure 7.10 All rows that don't have a middle name of K are returned, including those with null values

```
SELECT
    FirstName,
    MiddleName,
    LastName
FROM author
WHERE MiddleName <> 'K'
    OR MiddleName IS NULL;
```

7.2.3 *How to search for values that are not null*

Now that we've learned how to include rows with null values, let's look at how to return all rows that do not have a null value. We can start once again by declaring verbally what we want: "I would like the first, middle, and last names of authors where the middle name isn't null."

The word *isn't* is a contraction for *is not*, of course, which is exactly how our next operator will work, shown in the following query and figure 7.11:

FirstName	MiddleName	LastName
Paul	K	Tripp
Jorge	Armando	Guerra
Robert	Grant	Davidson
Gail	Anne	Shawn

Figure 7.11 The results for all rows from the author table with no middle name

```
SELECT
    FirstName,
    MiddleName,
    LastName
FROM author
WHERE MiddleName IS NOT NULL;
```

The IS NOT NULL operator allows us to return all rows with some value other than NULL for a given column. Interestingly enough, we can get the same results using a wildcard we learned about earlier in this chapter:

```
SELECT
FirstName,
    MiddleName,
    LastName
FROM author
WHERE MiddleName LIKE '%';
```

Why does this query work the same way as when we use the IS NOT NULL operator? The % wildcard matches any string of data so long as there is data in the column. Because null values have no data, wildcards never match them or return them in a result set, which is essentially what the IS NOT NULL operator also does.

> **Try it now**
>
> Execute the preceding two queries using IS NOT NULL and the % wildcard, and see that the results are the same as in figure 7.11.

All right—we've spent three chapters examining a multitude of ways to filter results when querying a table. In chapter 8, we'll level up your SQL knowledge even more by learning how to query multiple tables at the same time.

7.3   *Lab*

Let's take a moment to review the ways you've learned to filter rows. Write some SQL queries to find the following:

1 The full names of all authors who have a middle name of Anne or no middle name at all
2 The full names of all authors who have no middle name and have a first name that starts with *D*
3 The title name and price of all titles that start with the word *The* and have a price less than $10.00
4 The title name and publication date of any title that ends with *S* and was published after January 1, 2020
5 The title name of any title containing the word *of* or the word *in*

7.4   *Lab answers*

1 The answer is

```
SELECT
    FirstName,
    MiddleName,
    LastName
FROM author
WHERE MiddleName = 'Anne'
    OR MiddleName IS NULL;
```

2 The answer is

```
SELECT
    FirstName,
    MiddleName,
```

```
        LastName
FROM author
WHERE FirstName LIKE 'D%'
    AND MiddleName IS NULL;
```

3 The answer is

```
SELECT
    TitleName,
    Price
FROM title
WHERE TitleName LIKE 'The%'
    AND Price < 10;
```

4 The answer is

```
SELECT
    TitleName,
    PublicationDate
FROM title
WHERE TitleName LIKE '%s'
    AND PublicationDate > '2020-01-01';
```

5 This question is a bit of a trick question designed to challenge you. You have to consider that depending on how you write the query, you might get more or less data than you want. You might write something as simple as this:

```
SELECT
    TitleName
FROM title
WHERE TitleName LIKE '%of%'
    OR TitleName LIKE '%in%';
```

If you execute that query, you get not only The Call of the While, Anne of Fact Tables, and Catcher in the Try—all of which meet the requirement—but also The Join Luck Club and The DateTime Machine, which don't. The latter two are included in the results because they have a string value matching the value of the letters *in* within their title names.

So how can we exclude those undesired results? One way is to add leading and trailing spaces to the strings we're searching for, like this:

```
SELECT
    TitleName
FROM title
WHERE TitleName LIKE '% of %'
    OR TitleName LIKE '% in %';
```

This query returns the desired results but may not work in a different scenario. Because now we're looking at strings involving leading or trailing spaces, we won't have any results if the title names start or end with the word *in* or *of*. To include any hypothetical results that started or ended with the words we were searching for, we need to include additional conditions:

```
SELECT
    TitleName
FROM title
WHERE TitleName LIKE '% of %'
    OR TitleName LIKE '% in %'
    OR TitleName LIKE 'of %'
    OR TitleName LIKE 'in %'
    OR TitleName LIKE '% of'
    OR TitleName LIKE '% in';
```

Again, this question is admittedly difficult, but it's designed to get you thinking about the possible values of data and how to use what you've learned so far creatively to write an accurate query.

Querying multiple tables

Back in chapter 2, we discussed how relational database management systems (RDBMSes) store data in objects known as *tables*, and since then, we've been examining ways to query these tables. I don't know whether you've been wondering what makes an RDBMS "relational," but I'm going to answer that very question.

One of the primary features of an RDBMS is that it allows a set of data to be stored so that it can relate to other sets of data—hence, the use of the word *relational*. This way of storing data is incredibly powerful because we can not only put the data we have in logical groupings of tables but can also easily retrieve related data from multiple tables with a single query.

Retrieving data this way is done by *joining tables*, which means combining the data in two tables using the values that form the relationship between the tables. Although joining tables is common and relatively easy, you must follow some specific rules to get the desired results. You'll soon learn those rules and see how to write join tables in SQL correctly. First, though, you need to consider a few vital concepts of relational databases and the way they are designed.

8.1 The rules of data relationships

We haven't focused on the words *relational* or *relationship*, but we looked at one aspect of relationships in an RDBMS when we started looking at rows in tables in chapter 2. Think about a single row from any table: it's a collection of values that all relate to one another. The first row in the title table, for example, contains values such as

TitleID, TitleName, and others that relate to the title "Pride and Predicates," so those values all relate to one another. It's the same for every row in the table, except that each row represents related values for a different title.

Although we haven't looked at any examples, values can also relate to other rows in other tables. We've taken all the information specifically related to a single title into the title table, but in the sqlnovel database, we have information that relates to titles elsewhere. One of the tables used to track information about orders of different titles is orderitem. Try the following query, and take a look at the results in figure 8.1:

OrderID	OrderItem	TitleID	Quantity	ItemPrice
1001	1	101	1	9.95
1002	1	101	1	9.95
1003	1	101	1	9.95
1004	1	101	1	9.95
1005	1	101	1	9.95
1006	1	101	1	7.95
1007	1	101	2	7.95
1008	1	101	1	7.95
1009	1	101	1	9.95
1010	1	102	1	9.95

Figure 8.1   The first 10 rows in the orderitem table, including the column TitleID

```
SELECT *
FROM orderitem;
```

The third column is named TitleID, which is the same as the first column in the title table. This name indicates that values in the orderitem table relate to the values in the title table, which makes sense because the titles are what customers are ordering.

But why would we store these values in different tables instead of putting the title-related values we need in the orderitem table? Well, there are several good reasons for storing the data in separate tables. But rather than simply describe these reasons, it might be more helpful to give you an example that shows the reasons using some of the data you've already worked with.

8.1.1 Data without relationships

Suppose that we design a version of the sqlnovel database to track orders, and all the necessary data is stored in this single hypothetical orders table. This table will have columns for order date, title name, price, and customer's first and last names. The table might look something like figure 8.2.

OrderDate	TitleName	Price	FirstName	LastName
2015-06-01 00:00:00	Pride and Predicates	9.95	Chris	Dixon
2015-06-15 00:00:00	Pride and Predicates	9.95	David	Power
2016-09-02 00:00:00	Pride and Predicates	9.95	Chris	Dixon
2016-09-02 00:00:00	The Join Luck Club	9.95	Chris	Dixon
2017-11-14 00:00:00	The Join Luck Club	9.95	David	Power

Figure 8.2   Our hypothetical table, used to track orders, that contains order date, title name, price, and customer name

On the surface, this table appears to be a logical way to track orders, and perhaps you've used a spreadsheet similarly. The table may be fine for tracking a small number of orders, but a closer look at the data reveals quite a few redundant values. In this table, we see what appear to be orders for the same two titles placed by two different customers on different dates. The main problem isn't so much that we're using five rows of data to represent these orders, but that we have to repeat the data values so often.

Imagine that this table has millions of rows. You can see that over time, it could become a problematic waste of query time and storage. This is especially true for the string values of TitleName and customer FirstName and LastName because string values generally take much more storage space than numeric values do.

That problem isn't the only one, though. What would happen if any values of data changed, such as a customer's last name? If a customer changed their last name and placed a new order under their new name, how would we connect the orders placed under the previous name to those placed under the new name? We couldn't do that with this table; with different last names, the orders would appear to be placed by different customers.

The same problem could exist if the data was entered incorrectly. How could we track sales if the last TitleName was inadvertently entered as "The Join Luck Clubs" (with an extra s added to Club)? We couldn't; that value would be a different one. Even though you and I can see that this title is a data-entry mistake, in the data, that entry would be a different title, and it wouldn't show up in results if we wrote a SQL query that used WHERE TitleName = 'The Join Luck Club' as a filter.

As you can see, storing all this data in a single table can lead to lots of problems. Let's look at ways to use some basic relational database concepts to organize this data better.

8.1.2 Data with relationships

In a relational database, we want to eliminate as many redundant occurrences of the same values as possible. We can accomplish this by doing a few things:

- *Organize the data in logical groups of values.* We put these values in separate tables, and we want each row in each table to relate to something unique, such as the title of a book. Think again about how any given row in the title table contains data this way.
- *Determine what column or columns will contain a unique value in each of our new tables.* This column or set of columns will be known as the *primary key*, which allows us to relate data in other tables to this table. In the title table, the primary key is the TitleID column.
- *Replace the data in other tables with these primary-key values to represent the values we want to reference.* Because these key values in our orders table relate to values in other tables, they will be known as *foreign keys*. In the table in figure 8.2, we'll start by replacing the TitleName column with the corresponding TitleID values from the title table because TitleID is the key value.

Let's do this with our orders table. Start by looking again at figure 8.2 to see how to organize the data this way.

First, we have repeating values for TitleName, so it makes sense to create a separate table that stores these title values. The good news, as you've no doubt noticed, is that we already have a title table in our sqlnovel database that stores the data this way. Let's look at the title-table values for TitleID and TitleName for the two titles in our orders table, shown in figure 8.3:

TitleID	TitleName
101	Pride and Predicates
102	The Join Luck Club

Figure 8.3　The results for TitleID and TitleName for the titles Pride and Predicates and The Join Luck Club

```
SELECT
    TitleID,
    TitleName
FROM title
WHERE TitleName IN ('Pride and Predicates', 'The Join Luck Club')
ORDER BY TitleID;
```

NOTE The values for TitleID in the title table must be unique so that we know exactly which row in the title table to reference. If the TitleID values are duplicated, the data becomes inconsistent and confusing; we don't know which values are being referenced.

The TitleID column serves as the primary key, so we can replace the TitleName column in our orders table with TitleID, which corresponds to values in the title table. Figure 8.4 shows what our hypothetical table looks like now.

OrderDate	TitleID	Price	CustomerFirstName	CustomerLastName
2015-06-01 00:00:00	101	9.95	Chris	Dixon
2015-06-15 00:00:00	101	9.95	David	Power
2016-09-02 00:00:00	101	9.95	Chris	Dixon
2016-09-02 00:00:00	102	9.95	Chris	Dixon
2017-11-14 00:00:00	102	9.95	David	Power

Figure 8.4　What it would look like if we replaced TitleName with TitleID in our hypothetical orders table

Now we have a relationship between these tables, which allows us to avoid the problems we discussed earlier—at least as they relate to titles and their names. We're saving space by storing a smaller numeric value instead of a string each time we want to refer to the title. We also have less of a problem with data inconsistency because a single source stores the title name. If any other tables want to reference a particular title name, they too can use the TitleID values.

NOTE This is what makes RDBMSes popular for storing many kinds of data. Storing values in a relational way allows us to store data efficiently, change values easily, and (most important) keep the data consistent throughout the database.

If we look at our orders table, we can consider other ways to store data more efficiently. Customers are unique individuals, so any customer data should be in a separate table, with the data in our orders table being replaced by a key value. Again, we already have a customer table structured with these values and a primary key of CustomerID. Figure 8.5 shows the results of our query of the customer table for the FirstName and LastName values in the orders table:

CustomerID	FirstName	LastName
1	Chris	Dixon
2	David	Power

Figure 8.5 The results from the CustomerID, FirstName, and LastName columns for customers with the name Chris Dixon or David Power

```
SELECT
    CustomerID,
    FirstName,
    LastName
FROM customer
WHERE (FirstName = 'Chris' AND LastName = 'Dixon')
    OR (FirstName = 'David' AND LastName = 'Power')
ORDER BY CustomerID;
```

Now we have three related tables, so let's replace the two customer-name columns in our orders table with a single column referencing the corresponding CustomerID values from the customer table. Figure 8.6 shows the updated orders table.

OrderDate	TitleID	Price	CustomerID
2015-06-01 00:00:00	101	9.95	1
2015-06-15 00:00:00	101	9.95	2
2016-09-02 00:00:00	101	9.95	1
2016-09-02 00:00:00	102	9.95	1
2017-11-14 00:00:00	102	9.95	2

Figure 8.6 Our hypothetical orders table with a CustomerID column to reference names in the customer table

We have a *one-to-many* relationship between the customer table and our orders table. That means that for each order, we have one customer, but any given customer can have more than one order. This type of relationship is common in relational databases.

Our data is organized even more efficiently, but we can make one last change. Consider the third and fourth rows in figure 8.6. It looks like Customer 1 purchased two different items on the same day, which for the purposes of our exercise are considered the same order. This makes sense, and we should expect that many times, customers will order more than one item in a given order.

This poses a problem for creating a unique primary key for our orders table, however, because we can't place a unique key for orders on the rows if there are duplicate rows for any given order. One common way to resolve this problem is to place the items ordered in a separate table, thus dividing the data related to an order into two tables. Because any order can include one or more items, this relationship is also considered a one-to-many relationship.

> **NOTE** Relational databases also have *one-to-one* and *many-to-many* relationships between tables. Generally, these relationships are less common, so we won't look at any examples now. Just know that other kinds of relationships can exist between tables in any database.

If we're going to divide the data in our orders table, we need to consider the following question for all the columns: Do the values relate to a specific item in the order or generally to the order itself? Let's examine the columns:

- *OrderDate*—These values are the same for the entire order because all items are ordered at the same time in a given order.
- *TitleID*—The values are specific to an item because an order can contain more than one title.
- *Price*—This value relates to individual titles, so it is also an item-level value.
- *CustomerID*—This value relates to the entire order because the customer is the same for all items in an order.

Now that we've identified what values go into which tables, we can divide the values in our orders table into two separate tables:

- *orderheader*—Contains the values unique to the entire order. We'll create a primary-key column called OrderID in the orderheader table. This table will also include columns for OrderDate and CustomerID.
- *orderitem*—Contains the values unique to the items in a given order. We'll create a primary-key column called OrderItemID in the orderitem table and a foreign-key column called OrderID to create a relationship between orderitem and orderheader. This table will also include columns for TitleID and Price.

We have organized the data in our hypothetical orders table into the actual tables in the sqlnovel database, and we understand how these tables relate to one another. Let's start writing SQL statements that join the data in these tables using their relationships.

8.2 The way to join data

Now that you have a basic understanding of how tables and keys are used, let's see how they're used in queries. To do this, we'll focus on the FROM clause in queries, which is where we identify the data set to be used.

8.2.1 Joining two tables

If we want to find out which customer placed the first order, which is OrderID 1001, we might start with a query like this:

```
SELECT CustomerID
FROM orderheader
WHERE OrderID = 1001;
```

Try it now

You've waited long enough to write some SQL in this chapter, so execute that query.

There's probably not a lot of value in showing a picture of a single column with a single value in the result set, so if you want to keep reading instead of executing the query, know that the value returned for CustomerID is 1.

Knowing that the CustomerID for the first order is 1 may be useful for a lot of queries, but suppose that we want to know that customer's name. For this task, we need to use the relationship between the orderheader and customer tables by *joining* them in our query. We do this by explicitly stating the second table name (customer) and the column names common to both tables (CustomerID), which we'll use to join the data. We state all this in the FROM clause, using the keywords JOIN and ON.

CustomerID	FirstName	LastName
1	Chris	Dixon

Figure 8.7 The results of joining the orderheader and customer tables to show CustomerID and customer-name values for the first order

The following query uses JOIN and ON to join the orderheader and customer tables to return not only the CustomerID but also the customer's first and last names, as shown in figure 8.7:

```
SELECT
    orderheader.CustomerID,
    customer.FirstName,
    customer.LastName
FROM orderheader
JOIN customer
    ON orderheader.CustomerID = customer.CustomerID
WHERE orderheader.OrderID = 1001;
```

Let's take a closer look at this query. The first thing you may notice is that the JOIN comes after FROM, and ON comes after that. The JOIN keyword is considered part of the FROM clause; it tells our RDBMS that we want to use more data in another table.

Think of using FROM and JOIN a bit like using WHERE and AND for filtering. If we have multiple filtering conditions for the WHERE clause, we start with the keyword WHERE to state the first condition, but every subsequent condition starts with AND. Similarly, in the FROM clause, we start with FROM and then declare the first table from which we want data, which in this query is orderheader. Then, because we also want data from a second table, we connect the data between the two tables by using the JOIN keyword followed by the name of the second table, which in this query is customer. Any subsequent filtering conditions in the WHERE clause will use the AND keyword, and any subsequent table joins in the FROM clause will use the JOIN keyword.

Merely stating that we want to JOIN the tables isn't enough, though, so we also need to say *how* we're relating these tables by explicitly stating the columns we're using to establish the relationship. We do this by using the ON keyword in a predicate. A *predicate* is any part of our SQL statement that evaluates whether something is true, false, or unknown, which is what the ON section of the join does: finds all rows that match CustomerID in each table. If the match is true, the rows are considered for inclusion in our result set.

Although I haven't mentioned it yet, the filtering condition in the WHERE clause of our query is also considered a predicate because we're also asking the RDBMS to evaluate WHERE orderheader.OrderID = 1001. Like that condition, our JOIN is considered an *exclusive condition*, so after evaluating the predicates in our join and our filtering conditions, only those that are considered true matches are returned. We have only one row in our results because only that row's values meet all our conditions.

Also notice that in the ON part of our query, we're using *two-part names* for our columns. This name refers to the syntax of [table name].[column name], and it's crucial because the CustomerID column is included in both tables. We can't simply say ON CustomerID = CustomerID because the RDBMS won't know which CustomerID column we mean. If you think this fact is obvious in the example, rest assured that many databases have tables with columns that relate to one another but that have different column names. For this reason, we need to use two-part names including both the table and column.

> **TIP** Although it doesn't matter which table and column is mentioned first in the ON portion of this JOIN, it's a good idea to start with the table mentioned first. This approach helps with readability and data organization, of course, but as you'll see in chapter 9, it's also crucial for working with other kinds of joins.

These two-part names for columns end up being used throughout the query, mostly for readability. I say *mostly* because we could change almost all the two-part names to use only the column name and not the table name except for any time we use CustomerID. This is because the CustomerID column exists in both tables, so if our query said CustomerID anywhere without a reference to the table, we'd get an error saying that the CustomerID reference is ambiguous.

> **Try it now**
>
> Execute the query used to get the result in figure 8.7. Also change orderheader .CustomerID in the SELECT clause to just CustomerID, and see the error that results in the Output panel.

8.2.2   *Joining more tables*

The great thing about joining tables is we aren't limited to two tables. We can continue to use JOIN to connect more data provided that we know the correct columns used for the relationships between tables.

Recall that we organized our order-specific data into two tables: orderheader and orderitem. If we want to find even more information about the first order, such as the price of the item purchased, we could easily add another join to our query. Because we established previously that the orderheader and orderitem tables will be joined on OrderID, which is the primary key for the orderheader table, we can modify our query with a few more lines of SQL related to the orderitem table. Figure 8.8 shows the results of this query:

```
SELECT
    orderheader.CustomerID,
    customer.FirstName,
    customer.LastName,
    orderitem.ItemPrice
FROM orderheader
JOIN customer
```

```
    ON orderheader.CustomerID = customer.CustomerID
JOIN orderitem
    ON orderheader.OrderID = orderitem.OrderID
WHERE orderheader.OrderID = 1001;
```

In this query, the `JOIN` for the orderitem table comes after the `JOIN` for customer, but in this particular query, the order of these joined tables doesn't matter. We could just as easily have written the query with the `JOIN` for orderitem occurring before the `JOIN` for customer. The arrangement of the order of tables joined comes down to personal preference and readability, so long as both tables used in any `JOIN` have been declared in the `FROM` clause by the time we get to the `ON` portion of the join.

CustomerID	FirstName	LastName	ItemPrice
1	Chris	Dixon	9.95

Figure 8.8   Customer information from the customer table and the price of the item ordered in the first order from the orderitem table

We can add one more table to get the name of the item that was ordered because we have the value for TitleName in a fourth table: title. If you recall, the TitleName is referenced in the orderitem table by the TitleID foreign key, which means that we must include our `JOIN` to the title table after orderitem. Here's the query we'll use to get the results shown in figure 8.9:

```
SELECT
    orderheader.CustomerID,
    customer.FirstName,
    customer.LastName,
    orderitem.ItemPrice,
    title.TitleName
FROM orderheader
JOIN customer
    ON orderheader.CustomerID = customer.CustomerID
JOIN orderitem
    ON orderheader.OrderID = orderitem.OrderID
JOIN title
    ON orderitem.TitleID = title.TitleID
WHERE orderheader.OrderID = 1001;
```

CustomerID	FirstName	LastName	ItemPrice	TitleName
1	Chris	Dixon	9.95	Pride and Predicates

Figure 8.9   Customer information from the customer table, the price of the item ordered in the first order from the orderitem table, and the TitleName from the title table

We can keep joining more tables to get related data, and in later chapters, as we discuss more of the tables in our database, we'll do just that. But as you can see, our queries with all these two-part names make for a lot of words in our SQL query. Even for seasoned query writers, this approach is a wordy way to write a query with a few joins. A much more readable way to write these two-part names involves a familiar concept.

8.3   *Table aliases*

Recall that in chapter 3, we talked about renaming columns in our result set by using *aliases*. We effectively declared that a column would be referenced, at least in the output, but with a different name. Fortunately, the SQL language allows us to use aliases for table names as well.

Our goal in using table aliases is different from our usual goal with column aliases. With columns, we often want to change the column name in the results to be more descriptive, but with table aliases, we want to be less descriptive. Generally, we use an alias of one or two characters to reduce the overall number of characters in our query—which, if done correctly, makes our query easier to read.

One common way to alias the table names is to use one- or two-letter abbreviations for the tables being aliased. We can use an alias of c for the customer table or t for the title table, for example. We could use o as an alias for the orderheader table, but because another table in our query starts with o (orderitem), we can use two-letter aliases for those tables instead. One logical way to use an alias for these tables is to use the first letter of each word in the table names, such as oh for orderheader and oi for orderitem. Here's an example of these types of aliases using the preceding query:

```
SELECT
    oh.CustomerID,
    c.FirstName,
    c.LastName,
    oi.ItemPrice,
    t.TitleName
FROM orderheader oh
JOIN customer c
    ON oh.CustomerID = c.CustomerID
JOIN orderitem oi
    ON oh.OrderID = oi.OrderID
JOIN title t
    ON oi.TitleID = t.TitleID
WHERE oh.OrderID = 1001;
```

Fewer characters fill the screen in that query, which means that we have less information to review if we want to understand this query. We could alias these table names the same way we aliased columns if we wanted to, of course. We could alias orderheader, for example, by saying FROM orderheader AS oh. But this type of aliasing isn't done often because our goal in aliasing table names is to reduce the overall number of characters in a query. For this reason, I highly encourage you to use table aliases as shown here when you join tables in any query because aliases make your queries much easier to read. We have to follow a couple of rules for table names, however:

- Aliases must start with an alphabetical character, not a number or a special character.

- Except for the first character, an alias can contain numbers but not special characters.

The only other consideration for aliases is making them sensible. Don't alias the first table as a, the second table as b, and so on. If your aliases at least remotely represent the actual table names, your SQL queries will be much easier to read and understand.

> **Try it now**
>
> Rewrite any of the queries in section 8.2 to use your own aliases.

8.4 The other way to join data

Earlier in the chapter, I discussed predicates and showed how they evaluate conditions in the joins we use in our FROM clause and the conditions we state in the WHERE clause. Although this method is rarely used, there's a way to combine all the predicates in the WHERE clause.

I mention this technique only because at some point, you'll likely encounter a SQL query written by someone else who uses it for joins. As you'll soon see, this technique is generally discouraged for several reasons. Here's what the preceding query would look like if we used this other way of joining:

```
SELECT
    oh.CustomerID,
    c.FirstName,
    c.LastName,
    oi.ItemPrice,
    t.TitleName
FROM
    orderheader oh,
    customer c,
    orderitem oi,
    title t
WHERE oh.OrderID = 1001
    AND oh.CustomerID = c.CustomerID
    AND oh.OrderID = oi.OrderID
    AND oi.TitleID = t.TitleID;
```

The first thing you might notice is that with this method of joining data, we have an easily readable, comma-separated list of tables in the FROM clause. This format is a bit closer to the verbal English we've been considering throughout the book because we might verbally declare the intentions for this query something like this: "I would like the customer ID, first name, last name, item price, and title name from the orderheader table, customer table, orderitem table, and title table where the order ID is 1001."

But even this method is difficult to convert from a verbal declaration to SQL because we have to tell the RDBMS exactly how all those tables need to be joined. Although this method is a perfectly valid way to join data in SQL, it has some disadvantages:

- When it comes to finding how all these tables are joined, we have to read every row in the WHERE clause to determine how any single join is evaluated. This query may use fewer characters because it doesn't say JOIN for each join, but for this query and more complex queries, we have to scan the entire WHERE clause to find out how any two tables are joined. Combining all these evaluations in the WHERE clause makes troubleshooting much more difficult—like trying to find a particular noodle in a bowl of spaghetti.

- This method allows only a particular type of join. In chapter 9, we'll discuss more-inclusive ways to use JOIN to connect data. We won't be able to connect data in these inclusive ways using this method. For these reasons, you should avoid writing SQL that contains joins in the WHERE clause.

Joins will be critical components of nearly every query you'll write from now on, so if you're unsure how they work, please take time to review this chapter and practice the query examples starting in section 8.2, as well as the following lab exercises. When you're feeling confident about joining tables, I'll see you in chapter 9!

8.5   Lab

1   What is the difference in the output of the following two queries, which use different tables for filtering in the WHERE clause?

```
SELECT
    t.TitleName
FROM orderheader oh
JOIN customer c
    ON oh.CustomerID = c.CustomerID
JOIN orderitem oi
    ON oh.OrderID = oi.OrderID
JOIN title t
    ON oi.TitleID = t.TitleID
WHERE oh.OrderID = 1001;

SELECT
    t.TitleName
FROM orderheader oh
JOIN customer c
    ON oh.CustomerID = c.CustomerID
JOIN orderitem oi
    ON oh.OrderID = oi.OrderID
JOIN title t
    ON oi.TitleID = t.TitleID
WHERE oi.OrderID = 1001;
```

2   How many orders did the customer named Chris Dixon place? Write a query to determine the answer.

3   What are the names of the customers who ordered a title in 2015? Write a query to determine the answer.

4 How could you rewrite the following query, which finds the names of all customers who ordered "The Sum Also Rises," using JOINs and aliases?

```
SELECT
    customer.FirstName,
    customer.LastName
FROM title, orderheader, customer, orderitem
WHERE title.TitleName = 'The Sum Also Rises'
    AND orderheader.OrderID = orderitem.OrderID
    AND orderitem.TitleID = title.TitleID
    AND orderheader.CustomerID = customer.CustomerID;
```

5 We saw in section 8.4 that we can move all the predicates to the WHERE clause. What happens if we move all the predicates to the FROM clause, as in the following query?

```
SELECT
    t.TitleName
FROM orderheader oh
JOIN customer c
    ON oh.CustomerID = c.CustomerID
JOIN orderitem oi
    ON oh.OrderID = oi.OrderID
    AND oh.OrderID = 1001
JOIN title t
    ON oi.TitleID = t.TitleID;
```

8.6   Lab answers

1 The results are the same. Because our query is matching all OrderID values from the orderheader to the orderitem table, the OrderID column from either table can be used in the filtering condition to return the same results.

2 Chris Dixon placed three orders. You could use a query like this one to get the results:

```
SELECT
    oh.OrderID
FROM orderheader oh
JOIN customer c ON oh.CustomerID = c.CustomerID
WHERE c.FirstName = 'Chris'
    AND c.LastName = 'Dixon';
```

3 Eight customers placed an order in 2015:

- Chris Dixon
- David Power
- Arnold Hinchcliffe
- Keanu O'Ward

- Lisa Rosenqvist
- Maggie Ilott
- Cora Daly
- Dan Wilson

You could find them with a query like this:

```
SELECT
    c.FirstName,
    c.LastName,
    oh.OrderDate
FROM orderheader oh
JOIN customer c ON oh.CustomerID = c.CustomerID
WHERE oh.OrderDate >= '2015-01-01 00:00:00'
AND oh.OrderDate < '2016-01-01 00:00:00';
```

4   You could write a query like this using JOINs and aliases:

```
SELECT
    c.FirstName,
    c.LastName
FROM orderheader oh
JOIN customer c
    ON oh.CustomerID = c.CustomerID
JOIN orderitem oi
    ON oh.OrderID = oi.OrderID
JOIN title t
    ON oi.TitleID = t.TitleID
WHERE t.TitleName = 'The Sum Also Rises';
```

5   The query executes successfully with the same result set, but as noted in this chapter, we generally try to avoid combining filtering predicates with join predicates for the sake of readability.

Using different kinds of joins

9

Joining tables is an essential skill for writing SQL queries, but so far, we've tried only one kind of join. To be fair, that type of join is the most common, but as you'll see in this chapter, in plenty of scenarios, that kind of join won't help you produce the results you need.

You might be asked to produce a list of all orders for a given year, for example, and show whether they used a particular discount code. Or you might be asked to find the names of all customers who didn't place an order in a year. Or you might be asked to find a list of all customers in a particular city or state and show which ones placed orders and which did not. You can't accomplish these queries using the join type from chapter 8, so you're going to learn how to use different joins in SQL to fulfill all the preceding requests.

9.1   *Inner joins*

First, let's talk a little bit more about the JOIN keyword we used in chapter 8. This join is a shorthand version of the keyword INNER JOIN, which is a particular type of join. Because it joins only values in both tables that meet the conditions of the join, the results set excludes any rows that don't meet the conditions.

For much of this chapter, we'll use two tables: the orderheader table and a new table named promotion. This new table contains promotion codes that can be used for discounted prices on titles that are ordered. The primary key for the promotion table is PromotionID, and it's referenced by a similarly named PromotionID column in the orderheader table.

The reason we'll use these tables is that there are rows in each table that don't relate to the other table. That is, some rows in the promotion table represent promotions that were never used in any order, and some rows in the orderheader table represent orders that were placed without a promotion code. Also, the relationship between these tables is one-to-many: any promotion code can be used for more than one order, but every order can use only one promotion code.

Also, I should note that there are 12 rows in the promotion table and 50 rows in the orderheader table. I'll refer to the number of rows in these tables throughout the chapter.

Try it now

Use SELECT * FROM promotion and SELECT * FROM orderheader to see how many rows are returned. Check the message in the Output panel to confirm the number of rows in each table. If you prefer, you could count the rows returned yourself, but that's more time-consuming, as well as open to the possibility of human error.

Let's start with the following query, which finds the order ID and promotion code of any order that used a promotion code. Figure 9.1 shows a portion of the results of this query:

```
SELECT
    oh.OrderID,
    p.PromotionCode
FROM orderheader oh
JOIN promotion p
    ON oh.PromotionID = p.PromotionID;
```

OrderID	PromotionCode
1006	2OFF2015
1007	2OFF2015
1008	2OFF2015
1013	2OFF2016
1014	2OFF2016
1015	2OFF2016
1016	2OFF2016
1022	2OFF2017

Figure 9.1 A portion (8 of the 20 rows) of the results showing the OrderID and PromotionCode of all orders that used a promotion code

Looking at the Output window, we see the message 20 row(s) returned. You might notice that the values for Promotion-Code are not 20 unique promotion codes, but the values for OrderID are 20 unique values. Again, this is because of the one-to-many relationship between the tables; each promotion code may be used for multiple orders.

If we want to be more verbose, we could write the same query by describing our join explicitly as an INNER JOIN, returning the same 20 rows:

```
SELECT
    oh.OrderID,
    p.PromotionCode
FROM orderheader oh
INNER JOIN promotion p
    ON oh.PromotionID = p.PromotionID;
```

TIP If you're using only inner joins in a particular query, it's acceptable to write JOIN instead of INNER JOIN. But if a query will include other joins, such as those you're about to learn, you should specify INNER JOIN for clarity and readability.

A common way to show how the values in these tables relate to one another logically is a Venn diagram. Consider two intersecting circles, with each circle including the data of a single table. The intersecting parts of the circles represent the common values between the two tables, and the nonintersecting parts represent the values that are unique to each table.

Figure 9.2 is a Venn diagram of the inner join between the promotion and orderheader tables. We'll look at several Venn diagrams throughout this chapter to help visualize the data included in the different types of joins. The colored part of figure 9.2 represents the data that is returned in our result set, and the noncolored parts represent the data that is omitted from our results.

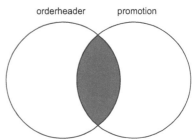

orderheader   promotion

Figure 9.2   A Venn diagram of the inner join used in the preceding query

The data returned by our inner join includes only the common values that meet the condition of our join, where the PromotionID values in each table match. As I mentioned, this option isn't our only one for joining tables. We can also join the tables to include all the values of one table, even if the rows have no related values in the other table. We do this by using OUTER JOIN keywords.

9.2   Outer joins

The syntax used for outer joins is similar to that used for inner joins, in that you use the JOIN keyword to specify the tables you're joining and the ON keyword to identify the condition of the columns used in the relationship between the tables. If additional conditions for the join are necessary, they use the AND keyword.

One big difference between inner and outer joins is that there are different types of outer joins, so you need to state in your SQL which type of outer join you're using. Let's start with the LEFT OUTER JOIN.

9.2.1   Left outer joins

The use of the word *left* in LEFT OUTER JOIN indicates that we want all rows returned from the left table in our join, regardless of whether the rows match. If this keyword seems confusing, think of it as also meaning that we want all the rows from the *first* table noted in our join.

Suppose that we want to see a list of all order IDs, and if they used a promotion code, we want to see which promotion code was used. We'd use the same query as before but change our INNER JOIN to a LEFT OUTER JOIN:

```
SELECT
    oh.OrderID,
```

```
    p.PromotionCode
FROM orderheader oh
LEFT OUTER JOIN promotion p
    ON oh.PromotionID = p.PromotionID;
```

In this query, the left table is orderheader because it's the first table mentioned. In our formatted query, orderheader appears above promotion, not to the left. But if this query was contained on one unformatted line with no carriage returns, orderheader would be to the left of promotion in the query. We represent this kind of left outer join with a diagram like the one in figure 9.3.

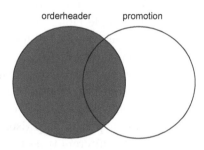

orderheader   promotion

Figure 9.3   A Venn diagram of the left outer join

The message in the Output panel lets us know that this query returns 50 rows, which is to be expected because we learned earlier that the orderheader table contains 50 rows. These 50 rows are a lot to take in, so let's add a filter to limit the results to the first 8 orders placed, as shown in figure 9.4:

```
SELECT
    oh.OrderID,
    p.PromotionCode
FROM orderheader oh
LEFT OUTER JOIN promotion p
    ON oh.PromotionID = p.PromotionID
WHERE oh.OrderID <= 1008;
```

OrderID	PromotionCode
1001	NULL
1002	NULL
1003	NULL
1004	NULL
1005	NULL
1006	2OFF2015
1007	2OFF2015
1008	2OFF2015

Figure 9.4   The results show the OrderID and any PromotionCode used for the first eight orders. A PromotionCode was used only for OrderIDs 1006, 1007, and 1008.

The result set includes a row for every row in the orderheader table that meets our condition of being less than or equal to OrderID 1008, regardless of whether we have a PromotionID value to join to the promotions table. For those orders that don't have a promotion code, the results show a null value in the PromotionCode column.

Although we've done a lot of work with filtering so far, we need to be careful when adding filtering conditions to outer joins. If we add a filtering condition for a specific value in the right table in the WHERE clause of our query with a LEFT OUTER JOIN, we effectively turn our LEFT OUTER JOIN into an INNER JOIN. Filtering on specific values in the right table would eliminate any rows from our result set that might have null values in the right table. We can demonstrate this situation with a similar query that filters on a particular value for the PromotionCode, with the results shown in figure 9.5:

```
SELECT
    oh.OrderID,
    p.PromotionCode
```

```
FROM orderheader oh
LEFT OUTER JOIN promotion p
    ON oh.PromotionID = p.PromotionID
WHERE p.PromotionCode = '2OFF2015';
```

OrderID	PromotionCode
1006	2OFF2015
1007	2OFF2015
1008	2OFF2015

Now the results include only three rows for orders that used PromotionCode 2OFF2015, not a row for every OrderID in orderheader, as we'd expect from a left outer join. Because the condition in the WHERE clause was required of the values in the right table, which in this query is promotion, that condition is applied to the results from both tables. Because of this filtering condition on the right table in the WHERE clause, we could change the LEFT OUTER JOIN in our query to INNER JOIN and get the same results.

Figure 9.5 The results of the left outer join with a filter on the right table (promotion), which reduces our result set to one that would be the same if the join were an inner join

> **Try it now**
>
> Execute the preceding query for a different PromotionCode, such as 2OFF2016. Execute it once with a LEFT OUTER JOIN and again with an INNER JOIN to see that the results are the same.

If we truly wanted to view a list of all orders and see whether they used a specific PromotionCode (such as 2OFF2015) instead of any PromotionCode, we could still do this. We just need to move the filtering from the WHERE clause to the join condition, like this:

```
SELECT
    oh.OrderID,
    p.PromotionCode
FROM orderheader oh
LEFT OUTER JOIN promotion p
    ON oh.PromotionID = p.PromotionID
    AND p.PromotionCode = '2OFF2015';
```

This query returns 50 rows—one for each OrderID—because we're not filtering on the left table. The value of the PromotionCode column in the result set is either 2OFF2015 or NULL.

Please make a note of how this filtering in the join condition works. On many occasions, you'll need to use an outer join while filtering on specific values in two or more tables. If you filter in the WHERE clause for a table joined with an outer join, you may inadvertently create an inner join.

9.2.2 *Right outer joins*

Just as the LEFT OUTER JOIN returns all rows in the left/first table regardless of whether they match the right/second table, the RIGHT OUTER JOIN does the opposite. It returns all rows in the *right* table whether or not they match rows in the left table with the join condition.

Let's use a right join to show all promotional codes regardless of their use, with a portion of the results shown in figure 9.6:

```
SELECT
    p.PromotionCode,
    oh.OrderID
FROM orderheader oh
RIGHT OUTER JOIN promotion p
    ON oh.PromotionID = p.PromotionID;
```

PromotionCode	OrderID
2OFF2015	1008
2OFF2015	1007
2OFF2015	1006
2OFF2016	1016
2OFF2016	1015
2OFF2016	1014
2OFF2016	1013
2OFF2017	1024

Figure 9.6   A portion (8 of the 23 rows) of the results showing all PromotionCodes and OrderIDs if they were used in a promotion

We can visually depict the results of our right join with the diagram shown in figure 9.7.

The preceding query returns 23 rows, which is more than the 12 rows in the promotion table. Look closely, and you'll see that many of the rows include duplicate values for PromotionCode because a code can be used for more than one order. Because of the duplicate use of certain PromotionCodes, we've matched many orders to some of the PromotionCodes.

Scroll through the results, and you'll also see that a few of the PromotionCode values have NULL for OrderID. Those PromotionCodes weren't used in a corresponding order, so they didn't match any order. We have them in our result set anyway because all rows in the promotion table, which is the right table in our query, will have at least one row in our result set from the right outer join.

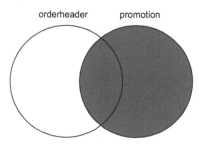

Figure 9.7   A Venn diagram of the right outer join

9.2.3   *Using outer joins to find rows without matching values*

Just as we can use a left or right join to return all rows in a table regardless of whether they match, we can use either kind of outer join to find all the rows that don't match. We do this by saying explicitly that we want to find rows in the matching table with the filter condition IS NULL.

As an example, we can write a query to show only the PromotionCodes that were not used for any order, as shown in figure 9.8, by adding the filter WHERE oh.PromotionID IS NULL to the preceding query:

```
SELECT
    p.PromotionCode,
    oh.OrderID
FROM orderheader oh
RIGHT OUTER JOIN promotion p
    ON oh.PromotionID = p.PromotionID
WHERE oh.PromotionID IS NULL;
```

PromotionCode	OrderID
1OFF2020	NULL
1OFF2021	NULL
2OFF2021	NULL

Figure 9.8   The results for all PromotionCodes that don't have a corresponding OrderID, meaning that the PromotionCode was never used

Although previously, I noted that placing a filtering condition on the joined query will effectively turn an outer join into an inner join, checking for null values is the exception. Remember that checking for a null value isn't checking for equality between two values, but querying for the presence of null values. This kind of query is common; you'll often have to find some value that exists in one table but not in another one. We can represent this concept with a diagram like the one in figure 9.9.

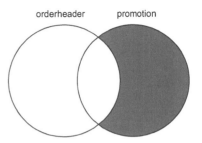

Figure 9.9 A Venn diagram of the right outer join that excludes rows from the left table

9.2.4 *Interchanging left and right joins*

If you try to execute the preceding query in SQLite, it won't work because that relational database management system (RDBMS) doesn't support the `RIGHT OUTER JOIN` command. This won't be a problem for most queries, however. You could simply rewrite the join as a `LEFT OUTER JOIN`:

```
SELECT
    p.PromotionCode,
    oh.OrderID
FROM promotion p
LEFT OUTER JOIN orderheader oh
    ON p.PromotionID = oh.PromotionID
WHERE oh.PromotionID IS NULL;
```

This query produces the same results as those shown in figure 9.8 because all we've done is swap the order of two tables in the `FROM` clause and change the join from `RIGHT OUTER JOIN` to `LEFT OUTER JOIN`. The diagram in figure 9.10 shows what we did.

> **TIP** As much as possible, try to use only left or only right outer joins in any query, not both. You'll need to include both types of outer joins in very few cases, and using only one type of outer join makes your query easier for other people to understand. Also, some

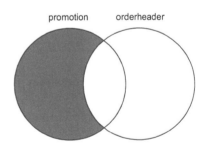

Figure 9.10 A Venn diagram of the left outer join that excludes rows from the right table

RDBMSes don't support right outer joins. For this reason, we'll prefer left outer joins throughout the remainder of this book.

One last note about left and right joins: they don't need to be quite so verbose. Just as `INNER JOIN` can be shortened to `JOIN`, `LEFT OUTER JOIN` and `RIGHT OUTER JOIN` can be shortened to `LEFT JOIN` and `RIGHT JOIN`, respectively. The preceding query can be written without the `OUTER` keyword, which may improve readability:

```
SELECT
    p.PromotionCode,
  oh.OrderID
FROM promotion p
LEFT JOIN orderheader oh
    ON p.PromotionID = oh.PromotionID
WHERE oh.PromotionID IS NULL;
```

> **NOTE** Depending on your RDBMS, you may be able to use a FULL OUTER JOIN or FULL JOIN. This rarely used type of join returns the combined results of a LEFT JOIN and RIGHT JOIN of two tables. We won't be writing any queries with FULL OUTER JOIN because MySQL, Maria DB, and SQLite don't support this type of join, but we'll learn another way to produce this kind of result set in chapter 10.

9.2.5   *The USING keyword*

There are two other ways to write inner, left, right, and outer joins, but they're less common. The first way is to use the USING keyword, which replaces the ON keyword in the join and doesn't require us to specify the table names or aliases. We *can't* specify the table names or aliases because the USING keyword requires the names of the columns used in the relationship to be the same in both tables. We could rewrite the preceding query with USING to get the results shown in figure 9.8 like this:

```
SELECT
    p.PromotionCode,
    oh.OrderID
FROM promotion p
LEFT JOIN orderheader oh
    USING (PromotionID)
WHERE oh.PromotionID IS NULL;
```

The requirement that the column names be identical for a join is usually the biggest deterrent to using . . . well, USING because you'll encounter many databases with related tables that don't share column names. The USING command isn't used frequently, and many other SQL programmers aren't aware of it or its correct use. We're looking at it here only in case you notice it in someone else's SQL queries.

9.2.6   *Natural joins*

The second rare way to write inner, left, right, and outer joins is to use a natural join. With a *natural join,* you don't mention the column names involved in the relationship; seemingly by magic, they join columns of the same name from two tables. We do this by adding the NATURAL keyword while omitting ON or USING. Let's rewrite the preceding query one more time, this time with a natural join:

```
SELECT
    p.PromotionCode,
    oh.OrderID
```

```
FROM promotion p
NATURAL LEFT JOIN orderheader oh
WHERE oh.PromotionID IS NULL;
```

Although they further reduce the amount of SQL you have to write, I highly recommend that you avoid using natural joins. For starters, they don't identify the columns used in the relationship between the tables, so whoever reads your SQL will have no idea how the promotion and orderheader tables are related.

A bigger problem involves similarly named columns. Although our promotion and orderheader tables share only a single easily identifiable column with the same name, in real-world scenarios, many tables contain columns like CreateDate or ModifiedDate to track changes in the values of any rows. Although these columns are often similarly named in a given database, they aren't created to relate data. Using a natural join with tables that contain these commonly named columns would automatically join the data in those columns, which wouldn't produce the expected results.

WARNING Natural joins are not supported in SQL Server.

9.3 *Cross joins*

The last kind of join we'll look at is another unusual one: the cross join. What makes this type of join unusual is that unlike all the other joins we've discussed, it isn't used to find rows with specific values. Rather, a *cross join* finds all possible combinations of rows by matching every row from one table to every row in another.

The cross join is also known as a *Cartesian join* because the results of the cross join reflect the mathematical operation known as a Cartesian product, which describes this result set of all possible paired values from two sets of data. If we want to use a cross join to show all possible combinations of PromotionCodes from the promotion table and OrderIDs from the orderheader table, we could write a query like this:

```
SELECT
    p.PromotionCode,
    oh.OrderID
FROM promotion p
CROSS JOIN orderheader oh;
```

The results of this query reflect all possible combinations of matching values from the two tables, so it should be no surprise that the result set for this query is 600 rows. We have 12 rows in the promotion table and 50 rows in the orderheader table, so a little multiplication (12×50) confirms that 600 rows are to be expected in the results.

Although a cross join isn't helpful for finding particular rows, it's useful when you need to generate a full list of all possible outcomes. You might need to produce a grid for all sizes and colors of a particular product, for example. It can also be beneficial for quickly generating a lot of test data, such as a list of customers or orders that are much larger than what your current data contains.

WARNING   Although I previously noted that you don't need to specify an inner join with the word INNER in MySQL, if you join tables using only the word JOIN and omit a join condition, the results will reflect a cross join, not an inner join as you intended. Other RDBMSes may require ON when using INNER joins.

The cross join is the last of many types of joins we've examined in this chapter. It may seem discouraging that several of the shorter ways to write SQL joins are not recommended, but in chapter 10, we'll look at other ways to join data—more efficient methods that are highly accepted and sometimes more efficient for the RDBMS. For now, let's practice what you've learned.

9.4   Lab

At the beginning of this chapter, I discussed some scenarios that you might encounter. Let's start by using what you've learned to write queries to produce those results. Try to use a left join in each of the first three exercises:

1   Write a query that shows the OrderID and OrderDate of all orders from 2019, as well as the PromotionCode, if one was used.

2   Write a query to show the first and last names of all customers who didn't place an order in 2020.

3   Write a query to show the first and last names of customers as well as the OrderID and OrderDate for any orders placed in 2021 by customers in California (where the value for State in the customer table is CA).

4   This exercise wasn't mentioned at the beginning of the chapter, but write a query using a cross join to generate a list of all possible customer first names from the customer table and last names from the author table.

9.5   Lab answers

1   The answer is

```
SELECT
    oh.OrderID,
    p.PromotionCode
FROM orderheader oh
LEFT JOIN promotion p
    ON oh.PromotionID = p.PromotionID
WHERE oh.OrderDate >= '2019-01-01'
    AND oh.OrderDate < '2020-01-01';
```

2   The answer is

```
SELECT
    c.FirstName,
    c.LastName
FROM customer c
LEFT JOIN orderheader oh
```

```
    ON c.CustomerID = oh.CustomerID
    AND oh.OrderDate >= '2021-01-01'
    AND oh.OrderDate < '2022-01-01'
WHERE oh.CustomerID IS  NULL;
```

3 The answer is

```
SELECT
    c.FirstName,
    c.LastName,
    oh.OrderID,
    oh.OrderDate
FROM customer c
LEFT JOIN orderheader oh
    ON c.CustomerID = oh.CustomerID
    AND oh.OrderDate >= '2021-01-01'
    AND oh.OrderDate < '2022-01-01'
WHERE c.State = 'CA';
```

4 The answer is

```
SELECT
    c.FirstName,
    a.LastName
FROM customer c
CROSS JOIN author a;
```

Combining queries with set operators

10

In the past few chapters, we examined ways to join tables based on the way they relate to one another. Every query we've written has had a single SELECT statement. But this chapter will show how to write a query with multiple SELECT statements and combine the results into a single set of data.

This technique can be useful when we need to evaluate results that require different conditions, such as querying values in different tables with no key to join them. Although we've seen that null values are excluded from results when we use joins, we'll see how to use SQL to include null values if those values exist in two data sets and we want to include them in our results.

10.1 *Using set operators*

We've written a lot of queries that start with SELECT, and each resulted in a single result set. That's what SELECT queries do: produce a set of results. More specifically, they produce a set of rows that meet the various conditions of our queries.

At times, though, we want to combine or evaluate two or more result sets, and to do this, we need to use special keywords known as *set operators*. Though SQL doesn't have many set operators, all of them use the same syntax to evaluate two result sets:

```
SELECT <some column>, <another column>
FROM <some table>
WHERE <some condition>
<set operator>
SELECT <some column>, <another column>
```

```
FROM <some table>
WHERE <another condition>;
```

Even though we're using two different `SELECT` statements in our query, the set operator allows us to evaluate the results into a single result set. The most common evaluation is to combine them, but as we'll see later in this chapter, we can do more. First, though, we must adhere to a few rules for using set operators:

- *The number of columns needs to match.* This rule is the most obvious one because we know from our introduction to tables that every row in a table must have the same number of columns. Our result set using a set operator is no different. Attempting to evaluate queries with a different number of columns will result in an error.
- *The data type of each column needs to match.* We haven't talked much about data types yet, but we've seen that there are different data types for numbers, characters, and dates. If we attempt to combine different data types in a result set, we'll receive an error message.
- *The names of columns in the first query are used in the result set.* This rule means that we can evaluate columns with different names, but their ordinal positions must be the same in each `SELECT` statement. If we're using column aliases, only those used in the first `SELECT` statement apply to the results. We can add column aliases to any `SELECT` statement other than the first one in our queries without causing an error, but remember that the relational database management system (RDBMS) will ignore those aliases, which won't affect the result set. Understanding this rule is also important because of the last rule.
- *An `ORDER BY` clause can appear only in the final `SELECT` statement.* An `ORDER BY` is the last evaluation in any query, and as such, it's allowed only after the last `SELECT` statement. If we try to sort the results in any other `SELECT` statement, we'll receive an error message.

10.2   UNION

The most common set operator is `UNION`, which allows us to combine the results of two or more `SELECT` statements into a single result set, removing any duplicates.

> **TIP**   One of the most important things to remember about `UNION` is that it removes duplicate rows from your result set. Don't forget!

As an example, we can combine the names of all the people in our sqlnovel database into a single set of names. That is, we can select the first and last names from the customer and author tables into a single result set. Let's select the names from tables and order by last name and first name (results shown in figure 10.1):

```
SELECT FirstName, LastName
FROM customer
UNION
SELECT FirstName, LastName
```

```
FROM author
ORDER BY LastName, FirstName;
```

FirstName	LastName
Sandra	Calderon
Cora	Daly
Kevin	Daly
Robert	Davidson
Tara	Di Silvestro
Chris	Dixon
Jordan	Ericsson
Buck	Fernandez

The results of our two SELECT statements have been combined into a single result set and ordered as we directed in figure 10.1. But why do we use the word UNION? Well, if we wanted to verbally declare what we're requesting with our SQL, we'd say something like this: "I would like the first and last names from the customer table, and I would like to combine the results with the first and last names from the author table."

Figure 10.1   A portion (8 of the 31 rows) of the results of first and last names from the customer and author tables

Although the word *combine* accurately describes what we're doing, as we'll see throughout this book, there are all sorts of ways to combine things in SQL. We can combine rows, columns, values, and entire result sets in different ways, so the word *combine* isn't specific enough to describe what we're requesting. Instead, we use the word *union* to describe combining two or more data sets into a single result.

In English, the noun *union* often describes the uniting in marriage of people from two different families into one new family, so it may be helpful to think of the UNION operator as marrying two different data sets into a single result set. Our verbal declaration becomes a bit more descriptive with the word *union:* "I would like the first and last names from the customer table, and I would like to union the results with the first and last names from the author table."

FirstName	LastName	TableName
Sandra	Calderon	customer
Cora	Daly	customer
Kevin	Daly	customer
Robert	Davidson	author
Tara	Di Silvestro	customer
Chris	Dixon	customer
Jordan	Ericsson	customer
Buck	Fernandez	author

Although we don't inherently know whether any given row was selected from the customer table or the author table, we can verify the table of origin by adding a third column with literal values to indicate the table from which the row came. We'll add these literal values to both SELECT statements, but we need to add the column name only to the first SELECT statement, as shown in figure 10.2. As I noted earlier, the column names in the result set are chosen from the first SELECT statement:

Figure 10.2   A portion (8 of the 31 rows) of the results of first and last names from the customer and author tables, as well as a third column indicating the table that the rows came from

```
SELECT FirstName, LastName, 'customer'
      TableName
FROM customer
UNION
SELECT FirstName, LastName, 'author'
FROM author
ORDER BY LastName, FirstName;
```

The most common way to use a union is to combine various filtering conditions, especially ones that might be contradictory, in a single SELECT statement, such as values from different tables. Let's add some filtering conditions for LastName from the customer table and FirstName from the author table (results shown in figure 10.3):

```
SELECT FirstName, LastName, 'customer' TableName
FROM customer
WHERE LastName LIKE 'D%'
UNION
SELECT FirstName, LastName, 'author'
FROM author
WHERE FirstName LIKE 'C%'
ORDER BY LastName, FirstName;
```

In figure 10.3, only five rows meet the filtering criteria, and we have at least one row from each table. Notice that there are duplicate values for first name (Chris) and last name (Daly). Recall from earlier in this chapter that duplicate rows in which all values match are removed from our results when we use UNION.

FirstName	LastName	TableName
Cora	Daly	customer
Kevin	Daly	customer
Tara	Di Silvestro	customer
Chris	Dixon	customer
Chris	Walenski	author

Figure 10.3 The results for the full names of customers whose last name starts with *D* and authors whose first name starts with *C*, ordered by last name and first name

We can verify this fact by making a few changes in our query. Two rows in figure 10.3 have the first name Chris, which appears once in each table we're querying. Let's omit the LastName and TableName columns from our results because those extra columns create unique rows for the rows that have Chris as a value for FirstName. With these columns omitted, we should expect Chris to appear in only one row because duplicates will be removed when we use UNION.

In addition to omitting those columns, we'll change the ORDER BY from LastName to FirstName. When we're using a set operator like UNION, we can sort the results only by columns included in the SELECT statement. We've removed LastName from the SELECT statement, so if we left the SQL for ordering by LastName in our next query, we'd get an error on execution, indicating that LastName is an "unknown column." Here's our new query (results shown in figure 10.4):

```
SELECT FirstName
FROM customer
WHERE LastName LIKE 'D%'
UNION
SELECT FirstName
FROM author
WHERE FirstName LIKE 'C%'
ORDER BY FirstName;
```

FirstName
Chris
Cora
Kevin
Tara

Figure 10.4 The results of first names from the customer table whose last names start with *D*, combined with a UNION with the results of first names from the author table whose first names start with *C*. The two rows for Chris are represented by a single row because UNION removed the duplicate row from the result set.

But what if we don't want the duplicate rows to be removed? What if instead, we want any duplicate rows to be *included* in a result set? For that scenario, let's look at the next set operator: UNION ALL.

10.3   *UNION ALL*

The UNION ALL set operator is very much like the UNION operator, with the main difference being that it doesn't remove duplicate rows. Instead, UNION ALL instructs the RDBMS to read all the data as requested by each SELECT statement and return the results as they were read. We can modify the set operator from the preceding query from UNION to UNION ALL to see this difference (results shown in figure 10.5):

```
SELECT FirstName
FROM customer
WHERE LastName LIKE 'D%'
UNION ALL
SELECT FirstName
FROM author
WHERE FirstName LIKE 'C%'
ORDER BY FirstName;
```

Both rows for Chris are included in the results in figure 10.5 because UNION ALL doesn't remove duplicate rows from the result set. Because UNION ALL doesn't remove duplicates, the filtering conditions it uses can

FirstName
Chris
Chris
Cora
Kevin
Tara

Figure 10.5   The results of first names from the customer table whose last names start with *D*, combined with a UNION ALL with the results of first names from the author table whose first names start with *C*

function similarly to the filtering in a WHERE clause. There are no differences between the results of these two queries, for example:

```
SELECT LastName
FROM customer
WHERE LastName = 'Daly'
UNION ALL
SELECT LastName
FROM customer
WHERE LastName = 'Dixon'
ORDER BY LastName;

SELECT LastName
FROM customer
WHERE LastName = 'Daly'
    OR LastName = 'Dixon'
ORDER BY LastName;
```

Try it now

Execute the two preceding queries to verify that both return the same results.

Both queries return a result set with three rows—two for Daly and one for Dixon—although they do so in different ways. The first query executes two SELECT statements against the customer table and then combines the results, with each query searching for rows that meet a single condition. The second query instead executes a single SELECT, which searches for rows that meet multiple conditions.

> **TIP** As you progress in your knowledge of SQL, it's always good to know different ways to produce the same results because you may encounter situations in which one technique performs better than others. Depending on factors that are covered in later chapters, a query with a UNION ALL may produce results much faster than a similar one with an OR, even though the UNION ALL is executing two SQL statements to find the same results. For now, remember to always consider different ways to find results if your query performs worse than expected.

One other difference between UNION and UNION ALL is that queries with UNION are generally slower than those with UNION ALL because the RDBMS has to do more work to remove the duplicate rows. If the result set from a UNION ALL is very large and full of duplicates, however, UNION queries could be faster because there would be less data in the result set to send over the network. Keep these facts in mind when you write SQL statements that query hundreds of gigabytes of data or more when using either UNION or UNION ALL.

Last, we can use UNION ALL to achieve the same results as a FULL OUTER JOIN, which (as noted in chapter 9) is not a supported type of join in MySQL, MariaDB, and SQLite.

10.4 *Emulating FULL OUTER JOIN in MySQL*

As noted at the end of chapter 9, a FULL OUTER JOIN returns not only the rows that match between two tables but also the unmatched rows from both tables. Figure 10.6 shows how we would represent these results in a Venn diagram if we could write such a query by searching for promotion codes shared by the promotion and orderheader tables.

Here's what the SQL would look like. This type of query won't execute in MySQL, but it will execute in another RDBMS that allows FULL OUTER JOIN:

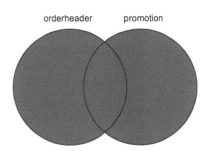

```
SELECT
    p.PromotionCode,
    oh.OrderID
FROM orderheader oh
FULL OUTER JOIN promotion p
    ON oh.PromotionID = p.PromotionID
```

Figure 10.6 A Venn diagram of the values included in a query of the orderheader table with a FULL OUTER JOIN of the promotion table

The results of a FULL OUTER JOIN are very similar to the results of executing a LEFT JOIN and

RIGHT JOIN at the same time, but because we can't do this in MySQL, we can emulate it with the left and right joins combined with a UNION ALL. UNION ALL is preferred in this case because it doesn't remove duplicate rows, which may exist between the tables and would be returned with a FULL OUTER JOIN.

The one tricky thing to remember is that when we're emulating a FULL OUTER JOIN in this way, we need to modify one of the joins to exclude common values. If we don't, we will end up with duplicate rows because both left and right joins include the common values that an INNER JOIN would return.

The following query demonstrates how to emulate a FULL OUTER JOIN in MySQL using UNION ALL. We'll prevent the duplicate representation of matching rows by excluding them from our second SELECT by filtering on WHERE oh.PromotionID IS NULL, which we learned about in chapter 9:

```
SELECT
    p.PromotionCode,
    oh.OrderID
FROM orderheader oh
LEFT JOIN promotion p
    ON oh.PromotionID = p.PromotionID
UNION ALL
SELECT
    p.PromotionCode,
    oh.OrderID
FROM orderheader oh
RIGHT JOIN promotion p
    ON oh.PromotionID = p.PromotionID
WHERE oh.PromotionID IS NULL;
```

This query returns 53 rows, which include

- Rows that match PromotionID values in both tables
- Rows in orderheader that don't contain PromotionID values
- Rows in promotion that contain PromotionID values that weren't used in the orderheader table

It may be helpful to use Venn diagrams to show specifically what each of the two SELECT statements in our query is doing. The first query finds the first two of our three sets of rows noted earlier, which are rows that match PromotionID values in both tables and rows in orderheader that don't contain PromotionID values. The diagram in figure 10.7 represents these values.

The second query finds the last item, which are rows in promotion that contain Pro-motionID values that weren't used in the orderheader table. The diagram in figure 10.8 represents these values.

By using a UNION ALL, we effectively combined all these results into a single result, as shown in figure 10.6 earlier in this section.

UNION and UNION ALL are useful set operators. But nearly every RDBMS has two other set operators that you should know about: INTERSECT and EXCEPT.

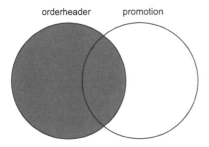 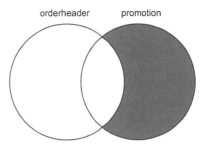

Figure 10.7   A Venn diagram of the values included in a query of the orderheader table with a left outer join of the promotion table

Figure 10.8   A Venn diagram of the values included only in a query of the promotion table, with a right outer join of the orderheader table

> **WARNING**   MySQL didn't support INTERSECT and EXCEPT until version 8.0.31. If you're using an earlier version, you'll encounter errors when attempting to use these operators.

10.5   *INTERSECT*

Another set operator that may prove useful is INTERSECT, which can return results similar to those of a query with an INNER JOIN. There are two important differences between their results, however:

- Where INNER JOIN will return duplicate values, INTERSECT will not. This fact is similar to the differences in the results of UNION ALL and UNION.
- An INNER JOIN will never return null values because nothing can't equal nothing. Because INTERSECT is looking for common values between two data sets and not evaluating equality, the results of INTERSECT will also include any null values that match in the results of the two queries.

Let's review an inner join to demonstrate the differences. Here's how we can use an INNER JOIN to find PromotionID values in both the orderheader and promotion tables:

```
SELECT
    oh.PromotionID
FROM orderheader oh
INNER JOIN promotion p
    ON oh.PromotionID = p.PromotionID;
```

If we wrote this query for an RDBMS that supports INTERSECT, our query would look like this:

```
SELECT
    PromotionID
FROM orderheader
```

```
INTERSECT
SELECT
    PromotionID
FROM promotion;
```

Although we used only one column in this example, INTERSECT supports the use of multiple columns in your SELECT statements. Although the column names don't need to be the same, all queries must have the same number of columns, and the columns must be selected in the same order for INTERSECT to evaluate them.

10.6   *EXCEPT*

Another set operator frequently supported by other RDBMSes can return data in one set that is not included in a second set. That set operator is EXCEPT, which excludes results similar to a method we learned about in discussing left joins in chapter 9.

> **NOTE**   Oracle doesn't support the EXCEPT operator, but it has a MINUS operator that is identical in function and use.

Suppose that we want to find all the PromotionID values in the promotion table that weren't used in any orders in the orderheader table, as represented by the diagram in figure 10.9. We already know that we can find them with a statement like this:

```
SELECT
    p.PromotionID
FROM promotion p
LEFT JOIN orderheader oh
    ON p.PromotionID = oh.PromotionID
WHERE oh.PromotionID IS NULL;
```

We can achieve a result set very similar to this use of a LEFT JOIN that filters on null matches in the joined table by using EXCEPT:

```
SELECT
    PromotionID
FROM promotion
EXCEPT
SELECT
    PromotionID
FROM orderheader;
```

As with INTERSECT, the results of EXCEPT have two significant differences from those of LEFT JOIN:

- A LEFT JOIN will return duplicate values, but EXCEPT won't.
- A LEFT JOIN will never return null values because nothing can't equal nothing.

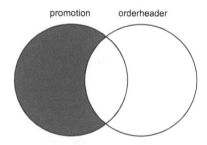

Figure 10.9   A Venn diagram of the values included only in a query of the promotion table, with a left outer join of the orderheader table

Because EXCEPT is looking for common values between two data sets, not evaluating equality, the results of EXCEPT will also include any null values that exist in the results of the first query and not the second.

Although INTERSECT and EXCEPT are used far less frequently than INNER JOIN and LEFT JOIN, keep them in mind if you're using an RDBMS that supports these keywords and you need to have null values returned in your result set.

That's plenty of information on how to use set operators. In chapter 11, we'll examine other ways to join tables and other data sets by using logical operators.

10.7 Lab

1 In this chapter, we learned that the column names in queries with UNION and UNION ALL come from the first SELECT statement. What do you think will happen with a query like this one that has no column name for the last column in the first query? Try it to find out:

```
SELECT FirstName, LastName, 'customer'
FROM customer
UNION
SELECT FirstName, LastName, 'author' TableName
FROM author
ORDER BY LastName, FirstName;
```

2 Considering that there are rows in the customer table for customers Cora Daly and Kevin Daly, will the results of these two queries be the same? If not, what will the differences be?

```
SELECT LastName
FROM customer
WHERE FirstName = 'Cora'
OR FirstName = 'Kevin';

SELECT LastName
FROM customer
WHERE FirstName = 'Cora'
UNION
SELECT LastName
FROM customer
WHERE FirstName = 'Kevin';
```

3 We've looked at the different behaviors of UNION and UNION ALL, but we haven't used them in the same query. It's inadvisable to use them in the same query, though, and depending on the RDBMS you're using, you may get an error message if you attempt to do so. Even if you don't, the results can be unpredictable. To demonstrate this situation, try executing the following two queries. Notice that they have different results. Why do you think the results are different?

```
SELECT LastName
FROM customer
WHERE FirstName = 'Cora'
UNION
SELECT LastName
FROM customer
WHERE FirstName = 'Kevin'
UNION ALL
SELECT LastName
FROM customer
WHERE LastName = 'Daly';

SELECT LastName
FROM customer
WHERE LastName = 'Daly'
UNION ALL
SELECT LastName
FROM customer
WHERE FirstName = 'Kevin'
UNION
SELECT LastName
FROM customer
WHERE FirstName = 'Cora';
```

10.8   Lab answers

1   Because no column name is supplied for the last column in the first SELECT statement, the literal value `'customer'` is used for the final column name in the result set.

2   The results won't be the same. The first query, which uses OR for filtering, returns two rows—one for each match. The second query, which uses UNION, returns only one row because UNION removes duplicates from the results.

3   The first query returns three rows, and the second query returns one. At first glance, these results may be confusing because the second query simply reverses the order of the SELECT statements.

The answer lies in precedence, which indicates the order in which the SELECT statements are presented. The first UNION or UNION ALL is applied first, and the second one is applied next. Remember that UNION eliminates duplicates, and UNION ALL doesn't.

In the first query, each of the first two SELECT statements returns one row with the value `'Daly'`, and because the UNION eliminates duplicates, the result is one row—so far. But the third SELECT statement returns two rows, which, when evaluated with a UNION ALL, create a result set of three rows—one row from the first two SELECT statements and two rows from the last SELECT statement.

In the second query, we combine the first SELECT statement, which returns two rows, with the second SELECT statement, which returns one row, and we do this with a UNION ALL. If we executed only this part of the query, we'd get three rows returned. But then we combine another SELECT statement that returns one row with a UNION, which removes all the duplicates from our result set. That's why the second query returns only one row.

If this explanation is more than a little confusing, don't worry. As long as you avoid combining UNION and UNION ALL in the same query, you'll never have to worry about this headache.

Using subqueries and logical operators

In chapter 10, we expanded the scope of our thinking a bit. We saw how to use SQL not only to query tables but also, with the help of set operators such as UNION or INTERSECT, to combine the results of two or more SELECT statements to form a single result set. In this chapter, we'll build on that knowledge by examining an important method of evaluating the results of multiple SELECT statements in the same query: the subquery.

Subqueries are simply queries nested into another query. We use subqueries when we can't achieve the desired results from a single SELECT statement, so instead of writing two or more queries, we combine them into a single query. Don't worry—this process isn't as complicated as it sounds.

By the end of this chapter, you'll see how subqueries allow you to evaluate the results of SELECT statements in ways beyond the capabilities of the set operators you learned about in preceding chapters. We have a lot of ways to use subqueries to discover, so let's get started.

11.1 A simple subquery

As I've noted throughout the book, a SELECT statement is a type of SQL query that returns a set of data known as a *result set*. So far, you've executed dozens of queries that produce result sets. You've queried one or more tables, producing result sets that look a lot like tables. By that, I mean the results have rows and columns, and the columns have names.

Let's take that scenario a step further. Because query results produce a result set similar to a table, we can evaluate the results of SELECT statements in many of the same ways that we evaluate the data in a table. This means we can join and filter these results as though they were tables, and the way to do this is to use subqueries. Rather than continue to speak theoretically, I'll give you an example.

Suppose that we want to find the order ID and order date for any orders placed after a particular order by a customer named Margaret Montoya. We're using this customer because they placed only one order. If we want to verbally declare this request, we might say the following: "I would like the order ID, customer ID, and order date from the customer table, but I want only the orders placed after the one order placed by the customer named Margaret Montoya."

This statement is the first time we've declared something in a compound sentence, with two separate clauses. With what we've learned so far, we could write two separate queries to get the desired results. The first query, to find the order placed by Margaret Montoya, might look like this:

```
SELECT
    oh.OrderID,
    oh.OrderDate
FROM orderheader oh
INNER JOIN customer c
    ON oh.CustomerID = c.CustomerID
WHERE c.FirstName = 'Margaret'
    AND c.LastName = 'Montoya';
```

The result of this query shows that Margaret Montoya placed only one order, on April 23, 2021. Now that we have that date, we could include it in a second query to find the results shown in figure 11.1. The query might look something like this:

```
SELECT
    OrderID,
    CustomerID,
    OrderDate
FROM orderheader
WHERE OrderDate > '2021-04-23';
```

Writing two queries to find this result is cumbersome, which is why we'd replace the hardcoded date with a subquery. All we need to do is replace the hardcoded order date of '2021-04-23' with the first query, which is now a subquery, and surround the subquery with parentheses.

OrderID	CustomerID	OrderDate
1044	19	2021-06-06 00:00:00
1045	11	2021-10-01 00:00:00
1046	4	2021-11-13 00:00:00
1047	19	2021-11-28 00:00:00
1050	1	2022-03-10 00:00:00

Figure 11.1 The OrderID, CustomerID, and OrderDate of all orders placed after Margaret Montoya placed her only order on April 23, 2021

WARNING When filtering with a subquery, we can have only one column returned because SQL allows us to evaluate only one value or set of values at a time in the WHERE clause. If we select more than one column in the subquery used next, our query will result in an error.

Here's what a SELECT statement with a subquery that produces the same results as the two preceding queries might look like:

```
SELECT
    OrderID,
    CustomerID,
    OrderDate
FROM orderheader
WHERE OrderDate > (
    SELECT
        oh.OrderDate
    FROM orderheader oh
    INNER JOIN customer c
        ON oh.CustomerID = c.CustomerID
    WHERE c.FirstName = 'Margaret'
        AND c.LastName = 'Montoya'
    );
```

The results of this query are the same as the results shown in figure 11.1 because we've combined the logic of two queries into one.

The subquery has the containing parentheses on different lines above and below the subquery. Although you don't need to format your subqueries this way, this method of formatting has benefits. For one thing, the code is a bit easier to read than it would be if you placed the parentheses at the beginning and end of the subquery. Perhaps more important, it's easier to drag the cursor over the subquery, highlight only the subquery, and execute it alone. When you're writing your own SQL, this technique is helpful for verifying that the subquery produces the desired results.

> **Try it now**
>
> Execute the preceding subquery. Then highlight and execute only the lines of the sub-query inside the parentheses to validate that the value returned is 2021-04-23.

In this query, we used a comparative operator, >, with our subquery, but other comparison operators such as = and <> have the limitation of being able to compare only one value. To unlock the full potential of subqueries, we need to use an entirely different set of keywords, known as *logical operators*.

11.2 Logical operators and subqueries

Logical operators are a bit like comparison operators in that they test whether some condition is true, false, or unknown. You've already used a few of these operators: IN, NOT IN, BETWEEN, and LIKE. Some comparison operators are unable to evaluate a result set with more than one row, so let's look at an example of a subquery that returns more than one row.

OrderID 1034 includes more than one title, as we see in figure 11.2. If we need to write SQL to find what titles are included, we can write something like this:

```
SELECT
    t.TitleName
FROM title t
INNER JOIN orderitem oi
    ON oi.TitleID = t.TitleID
WHERE OrderID = 1034;
```

TitleName
The Join Luck Club
Catcher in the Try
Anne of Fact Tables
The DateTime Machine

Figure 11.2 The four titles included in order 1034

Let's rewrite this query using a subquery by moving the part of the query that filters on OrderID into its own query, place that part in the WHERE clause as a subquery, and filter on where the TitleID from the title table is equal, using = to match the value of the results of our subquery:

```
SELECT
    t.TitleName
FROM title t
WHERE TitleID = (
    SELECT TitleID
    FROM orderitem
    WHERE OrderID = 1034
    );
```

This query doesn't work, though. If you try executing it, the Output panel displays the error message "Subquery returns more than 1 row." This is true. We know from the preceding query that this order includes four titles, which means that the subquery returns four rows. Our subquery can't be evaluated by = because that comparison operator is trying to determine whether every TitleID in the title table equals a single value. This query would work if there were only one title in the order, but there are four, and unfortunately, the = operator can't evaluate more than one value. For this scenario, our first logical operator, ANY, can help.

> **Try it now**
>
> Execute the preceding query, and notice the error in the Output panel.

11.2.1 *The ANY and IN operators*

The ANY logical operator evaluates a set of values to see whether any of them have equality to the values you're attempting to match—hence, the name ANY. You can think of ANY as being a helper for = (or any other comparison operator), allowing any value to be included in the subquery. To get the preceding query to work, simply add the ANY operator after = in the WHERE clause:

```
SELECT
    t.TitleName
FROM title t
WHERE TitleID = ANY (
    SELECT TitleID
    FROM orderitem
    WHERE OrderID = 1034
    );
```

The results of this query are the same as the results shown in figure 11.2. We can verbally declare what we're doing like this: "I would like the title name from the title table, and I would like the titles to match any of the titles from order 1034."

> **NOTE** Most relational database management systems (RDBMS), including MySQL, also support the SOME logical operator, which is identical to ANY in use and function. It's used much less frequently than ANY, however.

We can also get the same results by replacing ANY with a different logical operator: the IN keyword. We can make a similar verbal declaration of our intention: "I would like the title name from the title table, and I would like the titles to be in titles from order 1034." Our query would look like this:

```
SELECT
    t.TitleName
FROM title t
WHERE TitleID IN (
    SELECT TitleID
    FROM orderitem
    WHERE OrderID = 1034
    );
```

So now that you can use either of two logical operators with a subquery to get the same results, which should you choose? Well, the answer depends on whether you need to use a comparison operator too. If you have to use >, >=, <, or <=, you have to use ANY because IN doesn't allow those kinds of comparisons. If you don't need to use one of those comparison operators, however, you can use IN, which is used for these kinds of subqueries far more often than = ANY. Next, let's look at the opposite way to filter: excluding the results of our subquery.

11.2.2 *The ALL and NOT IN operators*

Suppose what we need is to find the names of titles that are *not* in order 1034, as shown in figure 11.3. We might say, "I would like the title name from the title table, and I would like the titles to not be in titles from order 1034." Just as we added the word *not* to our verbal declaration, we can do the same thing with our SQL:

```
SELECT
    t.TitleName
FROM title t
WHERE TitleID NOT IN (
```

```
    SELECT TitleID
    FROM orderitem
    WHERE OrderID = 1034);
```

TitleName
Pride and Predicates
The Great GroupBy
The Call of the While
The Sum Also Rises

Our sqlnovel database contains eight titles, and order 1034 includes four of them, as shown in figure 11.2. Now we know the other four titles that were not in that order. Our SQL statement is evaluating all the titles in order 1034 and then finding the titles in the title table that aren't any of those included in the order.

Figure 11.3 The four titles not included in order 1034

This brings us to another way we may be tempted to verbally declare the desired results of this query: "I would like the title name from the title table, and I would like the titles to not match any of the titles from order 1034." At first glance, we might think we can use the ANY operator to get these results by using it with the not-equal operator, <>:

```
SELECT
    t.TitleName
FROM title t
WHERE TitleID <> ANY (
    SELECT TitleID
    FROM orderitem
    WHERE OrderID = 1034
    );
```

Although this query will execute without error, it won't provide the desired results. This query is evaluating all the titles in the title table to see which ones don't match any of the titles in our subquery. Because our subquery contains more than one title, every title in the title table will be a match because at least one title in the subquery isn't the same.

Try it now

Execute this query, and notice that it returns every title in the title table.

To get the results we want, we need to use the ALL operator instead of ANY because we want titles that don't match *all* the titles in the subquery:

```
SELECT
    t.TitleName
FROM title t
WHERE TitleID <> ALL (
    SELECT TitleID
    FROM orderitem
    WHERE OrderID = 1034
    );
```

Executing this query produces the results shown in figure 11.3, which is what we intended. As with IN and ANY, the decision to use NOT IN or ALL comes down to whether a comparative operator is required.

NOTE I haven't mentioned this topic yet, but be aware that by using subqueries, you're asking the RDBMS to execute two queries at the same time and evaluate the results of one against the other. Generally speaking, using subqueries requires more processing and memory, so when writing SQL, you should consider carefully whether using a subquery is necessary.

11.2.3 *The EXISTS and NOT EXISTS operators*

Two other operators can make subqueries more efficient than the ones we've seen so far: EXISTS and NOT EXISTS. These operators are appealing because they don't evaluate the values of every row in the subquery; rather, they check only for *any* matching rows. When a match for a value is found, other matches are not evaluated for equality or inequality.

First, we'll look at EXISTS, which is used similarly to the way we used = ANY and IN earlier to find the titles included in order 1034. The difference is that when we use EXISTS, we must include a kind of join in the WHERE clause of the subquery. Here's what this query would look like:

```
SELECT
    t.TitleName
FROM title t
WHERE EXISTS (
    SELECT TitleID
    FROM orderitem oi
    WHERE OrderID = 1034
        AND t.TitleID = oi.TitleID
    );
```

Executing this query provides the results shown in figure 11.2, returning the names of all the titles in order 1034. Notice that we used EXISTS in the WHERE clause, and now we have an additional line in the WHERE clause of the subquery: AND t.TitleID = oi .TitleID. This is where the evaluation for matching values in the subquery takes place. Because the evaluation occurs there, what we put in the SELECT clause of our subquery doesn't matter.

For this reason, you'll often see subqueries used with EXISTS in other people's SQL that has something that seems nonsensical in the SELECT clause, like this subquery, which has SELECT 1 in the SELECT clause:

```
SELECT
    t.TitleName
FROM title t
WHERE EXISTS (
    SELECT 1
    FROM orderitem oi
    WHERE OrderID = 1034
        AND t.TitleID = oi.TitleID
    );
```

Try it now

Execute the preceding query to see for yourself that it returns the results shown in figure 11.2. Try replacing the 1 in the SELECT clause of the subquery with any other value to see that the value there becomes irrelevant.

Also, we can use NOT EXISTS to find the titles that are *not* included in order 1034. Executing the following query returns the results shown in figure 11.3:

```
SELECT
    t.TitleName
FROM title t
WHERE NOT EXISTS (
    SELECT 1
    FROM orderitem oi
    WHERE OrderID = 1034
        AND t.TitleID = oi.TitleID
    );
```

Again, the main reason to use EXISTS or NOT EXISTS with subqueries is to query larger data sets because these operators provide better performance than IN/NOT IN, ANY, and ALL.

11.3 Subqueries in other parts of a query

So far in this chapter, we've looked only at subqueries used for filtering in the WHERE clause. But we can use subqueries in other clauses as well.

11.3.1 Subqueries in the FROM clause

We can write a query to return the results shown in figure 11.2 with a join in the FROM clause, for example. To do this, we move our subquery into a join in the FROM clause—in this case, using an inner join. We don't need any operators because we aren't evaluating the subquery for filtering. We're simply joining the results of the subquery, and any evaluation occurs with the ON part of the join.

Also, because our subquery doesn't have a name for the resulting data set, we'll need to use an alias so that we can join it to another table:

```
SELECT
    t.TitleName
FROM title t
INNER JOIN (
    SELECT TitleID
    FROM orderitem
    WHERE OrderID = 1034
    ) oisq
    ON t.TitleID = oisq.TitleID;
```

By moving the subquery to the FROM clause, we're treating our subquery results as though they were a table, with those results being joined to the title table by TitleID. The results of the subquery aren't a table, but they have to be computed by the RDBMS before we can determine if any rows from the results of our subquery can be joined to the title table.

What's interesting is that because the subquery is in the FROM clause, it can be used in our query like a table. As a result, we're no longer limited to having one column in our subquery, so we can add more columns to the subquery if necessary for joining or filtering purposes.

> **Try it now**
>
> Execute the preceding query, change SELECT TitleID to SELECT TitleId, OrderID, and execute that query as well.

We can also use a join in the FROM clause to find values that aren't in the subquery by using the LEFT OUTER JOIN method from chapter 9. We can use this kind of join with a filter on the null values in the second data set, which in this case is the subquery, to find values existing in the first table but not in the joined table:

```
SELECT
    t.TitleName
FROM title t
LEFT JOIN (
    SELECT TitleID
    FROM orderitem
 WHERE OrderID = 1034
    ) oisq
    ON t.TitleID = oisq.TitleID
WHERE oisq.TitleID IS NULL;
```

The results of this query are the same as those shown in figure 11.3.

11.3.2 Subqueries in the SELECT clause

A final way to use subqueries is the SELECT clause. We can get the same TitleNames shown in figure 11.2 by using a subquery in the SELECT clause, although we have to rearrange the query by switching the subquery from the filtering query on orderitem to the selection of the TitleName from the title table:

```
SELECT
    (
    SELECT TitleName
    FROM title t
    WHERE t.TitleID = oi.TitleID
    ) AS TitleName
FROM orderitem oi
WHERE oi.OrderID = 1034;
```

WARNING This approach is a highly unusual way to find this result set. I'm presenting this example only to show you what a subquery in the SELECT clause looks like. Writing subqueries in the SELECT clause is rarely the best way to write SQL.

We've seen several ways to use subqueries and the options they afford us in writing SQL. Note, however, that subqueries should be used thoughtfully because they often have a negative effect on query performance. The fact that each subquery executes an additional SELECT statement means our SQL statements with subqueries typically create more work for the RDBMS.

Chapter 12 looks at ways to group data sets to find calculations like the minimum and maximum values of those sets. First, though, you get to put your new subquery skills to use.

11.4 Lab

1 Write a query using a subquery with IN to get the names of the title(s) in the only order placed by Joe Pagenaud.

2 Look again at the queries in section 11.1, where we tried to find the orders placed after Margaret Montoya's order. Write a similar query to find the order ID, customer ID, and order date for any orders placed after all of Cora Daly's orders.

3 Selecting 1 divided by 0 returns a null value. Could you use SELECT 1/0 instead of SELECT TitleID in the SELECT clause of the subquery of the first query in section 11.2.3 and still get the correct results?

11.5 Lab answers

1 You have many ways to do this, depending on which queries you join in the subquery. Here's one way:

```
SELECT
    t.TitleName
FROM title t
INNER JOIN orderitem oi
    ON t.TitleID = oi.TitleID
WHERE oi.OrderID IN (
    SELECT
    oh.OrderID
    FROM orderheader oh
    INNER JOIN customer c
        ON oh.CustomerID = c.CustomerID
    WHERE c.FirstName = 'Joe'
        AND c.LastName = 'Pagenaud'
    );
```

2 Your query may vary, but here's a way to find the intended order information:

```
SELECT
    OrderID,
```

```
        CustomerID,
        OrderDate
FROM orderheader
WHERE OrderDate > ALL (
    SELECT
        oh.OrderDate
    FROM orderheader oh
    INNER JOIN customer c
        ON oh.CustomerID = c.CustomerID
WHERE c.FirstName = 'Cora'
    AND c.LastName = 'Daly'
    );
```

3 Yes, because the value or column used in the SELECT clause of a subquery is not evaluated by EXISTS or NOT EXISTS.

Grouping data

If you're accustomed to working with spreadsheets, rather than relational data in a database, the past three chapters may have been a bit challenging for you. After all, in spreadsheets you often work with a single set of data instead of multiple sets. If the concepts in those chapters are new to you, take heart; this chapter covers concepts that should be very familiar to most spreadsheet users.

One useful aspect of spreadsheets is that they allow us to do mathematical calculations on a range of data quickly. If we want to find the total of all values in a column, for example, we can click the AutoSum button, which places the desired sum amount in a particular cell. If we highlight that cell, we see that the spreadsheet used the word SUM with the defined range of cells. SUM represents a *function*, which is a command that performs a predefined calculation.

Although we have no button in the SQL language to calculate totals automatically, we do have functions like SUM to help us perform mathematical calculations. Moreover, in a relational database, we have much more flexibility in the way we perform these calculations than we have in spreadsheets.

12.1 Aggregate functions

Throughout the rest of this book, we'll be discussing different kinds of functions in SQL. A *function* is a keyword that makes it easy to perform calculations or other actions. SQL has many functions for calculating all sorts of values for converting dates, formatting data, and doing much more.

This chapter focuses on the main *aggregate functions*, which are functions that perform a calculation over a range of data in a column. When you need to perform basic calculations, these aggregate functions are indispensable.

12.1.1 The SUM function

The most basic function we can use is SUM, which returns the sum total of all values in a column of data. If we want to know the total number of titles ordered, for example, we could sum the Quantity column in the orderitem table. We could declare this intention verbally by using the word *sum* to describe what we want: "I would like the sum of the quantity of titles in the orderitem table." This declaration isn't far off from our SQL, which looks like this (results shown in figure 12.1):

```
SELECT SUM(Quantity)
FROM orderitem;
```

Note a few things before we go any further. First, we need to use parentheses to identify what column we're choosing for the SUM. If we don't use the parentheses, the query will result in a syntax error.

SUM(Quantity)
70

Figure 12.1
The quantity of all orders is shown in a column with no alias. The default column name is the calculation.

Also, if you execute this query, you'll notice that the column uses your calculation as the name of the column, which may not be helpful. When you use aggregate functions, you usually want to specify a name for the column by using an alias, which helps you identify the meaning of the returned values. If you want to execute this query again, you should modify it to use an alias that reflects the aggregate calculation:

```
SELECT SUM(Quantity) AS TotalQuantity
FROM orderitem;
```

> **WARNING** Keep in mind that the SUM function is intended to be used only with numeric data values. If you try to use this function with date or character values, the result may not be meaningful.

> **TIP** When you use an alias for an output column, avoid using the name of the table column as the alias. In addition to possibly confusing anyone who might read your output, some relational database management systems (RDBMSes) don't allow this action.

12.1.2 The COUNT function

Although SUM calculates the sum total of all values, if we want to know the quantity of values that exist in a column, we need to use a different function. The COUNT function counts the number of rows in a column. This statement seems relatively obvious, but note one important feature of aggregate functions: by default, they exclude null values.

Let's look at the orderheader table to see how many rows it contains. We can do this easily by selecting the COUNT of all the OrderIDs, for which every row has a value. Figure 12.2 shows the result of this query:

```
SELECT COUNT(OrderID) AS TotalOrders
FROM orderheader;
```

TotalOrders
50

Figure 12.2
A total of 50 rows in the orderheader table have a value for OrderID, which is all the rows in the table.

The results indicate that we have 50 rows in the orderheader table, which is correct. But if we try to count the number of Promotion-Codes used by selecting the COUNT of the PromotionID column, we'll get a different result (shown in figure 12.3):

```
SELECT COUNT(PromotionID) AS TotalOrdersWithPromotionCode
FROM orderheader;
```

The results now show only 20 rows, which means that only 20 of the 50 rows in the orderheader table have a value for PromotionID. The other 30 rows have a null value for PromotionID.

The COUNT function also has a unique, widely used feature: you can use it to return the number

TotalOrdersWithPromotionCode
20

Figure 12.3   Only 20 rows in the orderheader table have a value for PromotionID.

of rows in a table without specifying a column. If you don't know the names of any columns in the orderheader table, you could easily find them by using the asterisk (*), as you learned when selecting all columns in chapter 3:

```
SELECT COUNT(*) AS TotalOrders
FROM orderheader;
```

The results of this query will be the same as those shown in figure 12.2, which is noteworthy because even if there are null values in any of the columns, selecting COUNT(*) always returns the total number of rows in a table.

> **WARNING**   SELECT COUNT(*) is a useful method for quickly determining the number of rows in most tables, but be careful when using it with tables that have millions or billions (or more) rows. This kind of query can use excessive computer resources and create delays for other queries.

12.1.3   *The MIN function*

The MIN function returns the minimum, or lowest, non-null value for a column. If we want to find the least expensive item from all orders, as shown in figure 12.4, we can use a query like this:

```
SELECT MIN(ItemPrice) AS MinimumItemPrice
FROM orderitem;
```

MinimumItemPrice
4.95

Figure 12.4
The minimum price of any item in the orderitem table is $4.95.

12.1.4   *The MAX function*

MIN has a commonly used partner function: the MAX function. Whereas the MIN function returns the lowest value for a row, the MAX function returns the maximum, or highest, value. Let's change the function used in the preceding query to find the highest price for any item, as shown in figure 12.5:

MaximumItemPrice
12.95

Figure 12.5
The maximum price of any item in the orderitem table is $12.95.

```
SELECT MAX(ItemPrice) AS MaximumItemPrice
FROM orderitem;
```

Although the SUM function can be used only with numeric data, in MySQL and many other RDBMSes, you can use the MIN and MAX functions with non-numeric data. When these functions are used with non-numeric data, they return the first or last value, respectively, as though the data were sorted on that column in ascending order. Although using MIN and MAX with date values is rarely problematic, the warnings for string values about collation in earlier chapters apply here as well: sometimes lower- and uppercase letters, as well as nonalphabetic characters, are ranked differently by different collations.

> **Try it now**
>
> Write a short query to select the MIN value for the FirstName column of the author table.

12.1.5   *The AVG function*

The last aggregate function we'll use in this chapter is AVG, will computes the average of all non-null values in a column. If we want to find the average price of the titles in the title table, as shown in figure 12.6, we could use the AVG function like this:

```
SELECT AVG(Price) AS AveragePrice
FROM title;
```

It looks as though the average price of the titles in our database is about $9.70. You surely noticed a lot of extra zeros in the result; those zeros appear because the AVG function is attempting to calculate the average value to a higher level of precision. This situation isn't a problem because the value is accurate; chapter 14 discusses how to modify the precision of the result if necessary.

AveragePrice
9.700000

Figure 12.6
The average price of all titles in the title table

> **WARNING**   Like the SUM function, the AVG function should be used only with numeric values.

12.1.6   *Filtering and aggregating combined values*

We can also use a filter with our aggregate functions. Suppose that we want to determine the average price of all titles published after January 1, 2019. Let's try our verbal declaration: "I would like the average price of all titles with a publication date greater than January 1, 2019." This declaration converts easily to the following SQL query:

```
SELECT AVG(Price) AS AveragePrice
FROM title
WHERE PublicationDate > '2019-01-01';
```

We can even combine our functions in the same query. If we want to know the dates of the first and last orders in the orderheader table, for example, we can use the MIN and MAX values because they work with date values:

```
SELECT
    MIN(OrderDate) AS FirstOrder,
    MAX(OrderDate) AS LastOrder
FROM orderheader;
```

Something else we can do with aggregate queries is use a mathematical calculation inside the parentheses. We need to do this in queries that require the values from more than one column, such as determining the total dollar value of all items sold. If we conclude that we can determine the total dollar value for any row of items by multiplying Quantity by ItemPrice, we can use that calculation with a SUM function to determine the total sales value for all the rows in our orderitem table, with the result shown in figure 12.7:

TotalOrderValue
573.50

**Figure 12.7
The total value of
all orders in the
orderitem table is
$573.50.**

```
SELECT SUM(Quantity * ItemPrice) AS TotalOrderValue
FROM orderitem;
```

As easy as it is to determine total overall sales, until now we've been limited to evaluating values at table level or basing evaluations on filtered data from a table. What if we want to know the SUM of each order, the quantity of items sold for each Promotion-Code, or the number of titles sold by each author?

12.2 Aggregating data with GROUP BY

If we want to analyze data at a deeper level, we need a new set of keywords: GROUP BY. GROUP BY isn't just a couple of keywords but also a new clause that allows us to divide one set of data into groups on which we can perform our aggregations. That explanation may seem theoretical, so the following section provides a practical example.

12.2.1 GROUP BY requirements

In the preceding query, we selected the total dollar value for all orders. If we want to find the total dollar value for each individual order, we would divide our data into groups of values for each order and then perform the same calculation as previously. We divide our values by grouping them, in this case by OrderID. Given the formula we used before, a verbal declaration might look something like this: "I would like the sum of the quantity multiplied by the item price of all the ordered items, and I want to group the sum by order ID."

Here is how this declaration looks as a query. We'll add an ORDER BY to sort the data by OrderID for readability (result shown in figure 12.8):

```
SELECT OrderID, SUM(Quantity * ItemPrice) AS OrderTotal
FROM orderitem
GROUP BY OrderID
ORDER BY OrderID;
```

This query is similar to the last one except that now we're grouping our data into logical sets of values for each OrderID and then calculating SUM(Quantity * ItempPrice) for each set. We do this by adding first GROUP BY OrderID and then ORDERID to our SELECT clause.

> **NOTE** When you use GROUP BY, every column in SELECT must be included in the GROUP BY clause or must have an aggregate calculation. If a column in SELECT doesn't meet either requirement, you'll get a syntax error.

You may have noticed that the GROUP BY clause is used after the FROM clause and before the ORDER BY clause. GROUP BY needs to be after the WHERE clause as well, if we have one. Knowing this, if we want to limit our orders to those placed after January 1, 2019, we must join to our orderheader table to add this filter, and we probably should alias the column names as well:

OrderID	OrderTotal
1001	9.95
1002	9.95
1003	9.95
1004	9.95
1005	9.95
1006	7.95
1007	15.90
1008	7.95

Figure 12.8
Eight of the 50 rows returned show the calculated OrderTotal for all orders.

```
SELECT
    oi.OrderID,
    SUM(oi.Quantity * oi.ItemPrice) AS OrderTotal
FROM orderitem oi
INNER JOIN orderheader oh
    ON oi.OrderID = oh.OrderID
WHERE oh.OrderDate > '2019-01-01'
GROUP BY oi.OrderID
ORDER BY oi.OrderID;
```

Adding this filter on OrderDate reduces the result set from 50 rows to 21, but keep in mind that we are still performing the calculation on each data set based on OrderID for those 21 rows.

12.2.2 *GROUP BY and null values*

The GROUP BY clause has another useful feature: it allows us to perform aggregations on columns with null values. You may remember from section 12.1.2 that we used the COUNT function to find promotions used in orders, and the null values were excluded. When we use the GROUP BY clause, we can account for null values too.

Suppose that we want to account for those 30 orders that were placed without a promotion code, as shown in figure 12.9. Without a promotion code, these orders are represented by a null value in the PromotionID column of the orderheader table. Because these PromotionID values are null, they were excluded from our query with COUNT in section 12.1.2. But we can use GROUP BY to group the orders logically by PromotionID because GROUP BY includes null values:

PromotionID	RowCount
NULL	30
1	3
2	4
3	3
4	1
5	2
6	1
7	2
9	2
12	2

```
SELECT PromotionID, COUNT(*) AS RowCount
FROM orderheader
GROUP BY PromotionID
ORDER BY PromotionID;
```

Figure 12.9 The PromotionID values in the orderheader table. This result includes null values because GROUP BY doesn't exclude nulls.

In this query, we're not filtering the results. Filtering can be a bit tricky when we use GROUP BY because the aggregations can't be filtered in the WHERE clause. If we want to filter the results of our aggregations, we have to introduce another clause.

12.3 Filtering with HAVING

The HAVING clause is the partner clause to GROUP BY, in that it's where we filter on the aggregations we're calculating. It's used similarly to the WHERE clause. The main difference is that the WHERE clause filters rows, whereas the HAVING clause filters groups of aggregated values. The good news is that we can apply any of the filtering methods we've learned in the HAVING clause if necessary.

Let's work through an example. Suppose that we want to find the PromotionCodes used in orders and to see which ones were used at least three times. We could start by writing a query to find all PromotionCodes used, joining the orderheader table to promotion on PromotionID, grouping the values by PromotionCode, and then counting the times a PromotionID was used in the orderheader table. We'll alias the tables and order the results for readability:

```
SELECT
    p.PromotionCode,
    COUNT(oh.PromotionID) AS OrdersWithPromotionCode
FROM orderheader oh
INNER JOIN promotion p
    ON oh.PromotionID = p.PromotionID
GROUP BY p.PromotionCode
ORDER BY p.PromotionCode;
```

NOTE If you've executed all the queries in this chapter so far, you may wonder what happened to the null values in the results of the preceding query. Well, those null values for PromotionID exist in the orderheader table, but they don't exist in the promotion table, And even if they did, an INNER JOIN would exclude them, so the results include only matching values from both tables.

Now that we have our basic query to view which PromotionCodes were used and how often they were included in an order, we can add the HAVING clause to filter on codes used three or more times, with the results shown in figure 12.10:

PromotionCode	OrdersWithPromotionCode
2OFF2015	3
2OFF2016	4
2OFF2017	3

Figure 12.10   The only PromotionCodes that were used at least three times

```
SELECT
    p.PromotionCode,
    COUNT(oh.PromotionID) AS OrdersWithPromotionCode
FROM orderheader oh
INNER JOIN promotion p
    ON oh.PromotionID = p.PromotionID
GROUP BY p.PromotionCode
HAVING COUNT(oh.PromotionID) >= 3
ORDER BY p.PromotionCode;
```

Now that we've added our HAVING clause, we've filtered our results down to three rows. If we want to, we can use the alias of our aggregation (OrdersWithPromotionCode) in the HAVING clause like this:

```
SELECT
    p.PromotionCode AS PromoCode,
    COUNT(oh.PromotionID) AS OrdersWithPromotionCode
FROM orderheader oh
INNER JOIN promotion p
    ON oh.PromotionID = p.PromotionID
GROUP BY p.PromotionCode
HAVING OrdersWithPromotionCode >= 3
ORDER BY p.PromotionCode;
```

The query should return the results shown in figure 12.10. This outcome may seem contradictory because in earlier chapters, I noted that you can't use a column alias in the WHERE clause. The next section is probably a good time to talk about something that's important in SQL and the queries we write: the logical order in which the RDBMS reads our queries.

12.4   *Logical query processing*

Up to this point, you've learned about several clauses in SQL statements and the order in which you must write them. At a simplified level, SQL clauses are ordered like this:

1   SELECT

2   FROM (including JOINs)

3   WHERE (including ANDs and ORs)

4   GROUP BY

5 HAVING

6 ORDER BY

This order, however, isn't the one in which the MySQL RDBMS reads your queries. It reads them in this order:

1 FROM (including JOINs)

2 WHERE (including ANDs and ORs)

3 SELECT

4 GROUP BY

5 HAVING

6 ORDER BY

This order in which the RDBMS reads your queries is known as *logical query processing*, which defines the logical order in which the RDBMS processes your query. This concept is important to understand because it will not only help you troubleshoot your queries when they return unexpected or incorrect results but also help you determine when you can use table and column aliases.

The order of logical query processing may seem strange, but it's optimal for the RDBMS to follow in processing your query:

1 Evaluate the data in the tables your query will use in the FROM clause.

2 Filter the data to reduce the result set in the WHERE clause.

3 Gather the columns to be returned in the SELECT clause.

4 Group those columns in the GROUP BY clause for aggregation.

5 Filter the aggregations in the HAVING clause.

6 Sort the results in the ORDER BY clause.

Now you see why table aliases can be used throughout the query: they're logically established in the earliest processing of our query in the FROM clause. You also see why you can use column aliases established in the SELECT clause in the HAVING and ORDER BY clauses but not in the WHERE clause.

> **WARNING** Although MySQL performs logical query processing as described in this section, other RDBMSes may follow a different order by logically processing the SELECT clause after GROUP BY and HAVING. For this reason, you shouldn't get into the habit of using column aliases in your HAVING clause.

12.5 *The DISTINCT keyword*

We have one more keyword to cover in this chapter: DISTINCT. This helpful keyword is used frequently, but it's a bit misunderstood.

We can use the DISTINCT keyword in a SELECT clause to avoid having repeating values. If we want to see the names of all titles ever ordered, as shown in figure 12.11, we could write a query like this using DISTINCT:

```
SELECT DISTINCT t.TitleName
FROM title t
INNER JOIN orderitem oi
    ON t.TitleID = oi.TitleID
ORDER BY t.TitleName;
```

TitleName
Anne of Fact Tables
Catcher in the Try
Pride and Predicates
The Call of the While
The DateTime Machine
The Great GroupBy
The Join Luck Club
The Sum Also Rises

Figure 12.11 The distinct title names included in orders in the orderitem table

Although the table contains 50 orders, some of which were placed for more than one title, the query returns only one row for each title. DISTINCT can be very useful for determining the range of values in any table quickly, and I'm sure you'll see it used often in other people's queries. So why is it covered in a chapter about aggregation? When you use SELECT DISTINCT, your RDBMS is doing an aggregation to return your distinct values, and that aggregation is extra work. By using DISTINCT in the preceding query, we're essentially asking the RDBMS to process this query:

```
SELECT t.TitleName
FROM title t
INNER JOIN orderitem oi
    ON t.TitleID = oi.TitleID
GROUP BY t.TitleName
ORDER BY t.TitleName;
```

> **Try it now**
>
> Run the two preceding queries with DISTINCT and GROUP BY, respectively, and notice that they both produce the results shown in figure 12.11.

Now that you're aware of what DISTINCT does, try to limit its use in your SQL, especially with large data sets. Aggregating data isn't problematic when you're querying the small tables in this book's example database, but it can be difficult when you're querying larger tables elsewhere.

TIP   One of the most common misuses of DISTINCT is to eliminate duplicates from query results when multiple data sets are joined. If you're tempted to use DISTINCT to remove duplicates from the results of a query with multiple joins, take a second look at the join conditions to make sure you're joining on the correct columns. Incorrect joins often cause unwanted duplicate rows in a result set.

12.6   *Lab*

1   In this chapter, I noted that you can't use certain functions with certain data types. To better understand this limitation, select the SUM of the OrderDate in the orderheader, and see what the result is.

2   Why won't this query work?

```
SELECT
    p.PromotionCode AS PromoCode,
    COUNT(oh.PromotionID) AS OrdersWithPromotionCode
FROM orderheader oh
INNER JOIN promotion p
    ON oh.PromotionID = p.PromotionID
WHERE PromoCode = '2OFF2015'
GROUP BY p.PromotionCode
HAVING OrdersWithPromotionCode >= 3
ORDER BY p.PromotionCode;
```

3 Write a query to count the number of rows in the author table.

4 Write a query to select the minimum and maximum values of the publication dates from the titles table.

5 In this chapter, you determined the total dollar value of all orders by using the equation `Quantity * ItemPrice` on the orderitem table. Write a query using GROUP BY to determine the average total dollar value for each individual order. (Hint: you may need to use a subquery.)

12.7 Lab answers

1 You may have missed it, but in chapter 5, I noted that date and time values are stored as numeric values that your RDBMS can interpret as dates and times. Although it's practically useless, the value you see here is the RDBMS trying to make sense of using a SUM of date values.

2 The query fails because a column alias is used in the WHERE clause, and the logical query processing order is to evaluate the WHERE clause before the SELECT clause. For this reason, the RDBMS doesn't know what PromoCode is when it evaluates the WHERE clause because the alias is determined in the SELECT clause that is processed later in the query.

3 To count the number of rows in a table, you can use COUNT(*):

```
SELECT COUNT(*)
FROM author;
```

4 To select the minimum and maximum publication dates, you can use the MIN and MAX functions:

```
SELECT
    MIN(PublicationDate) AS FirstPublication,
    MAX(PublicationDate) AS LastPublication
FROM title;
```

5 You have a few ways to do this. The first way is to group the total value of all orders as we did in section 12.2.1 and then select an average value of those order totals, like this:

```
SELECT AVG(OrderTotals.OrderTotal)
FROM (
    SELECT OrderID, SUM(Quantity * ItemPrice) AS OrderTotal
    FROM orderitem
    GROUP BY OrderID
    ) OrderTotals;
```

Using variables

We've written and executed a lot of SQL queries so far, and a good number of those queries involved filtering the results on specific values. Through many examples, we've seen how to filter on a particular order or title ID, customer name, or date range, and every time, we've specified the literal value for filtering in our SQL. A *literal* value is specific, such as the number 4 or the date 2020-10-06. Using literal values is helpful for learning and practice, but when you use SQL outside this book, you'll need to write more flexible queries.

If you want to look at the total sales of a title for a given month, such as March 2021, you can write a query to do that now. But what if you want to run a similar query for April or need total sales for a different title or a different range of dates? Do you have to write a different query for each title and date range?

I assure you that you don't. All you have to do is learn how to use variables. A *variable* is a memory-based object that stores a value that, once defined, can be used repeatedly throughout a query or in subsequent queries. More important, the stored value can vary from one execution to another, which means that the value is *variable*—hence, the name.

Considering the flexibility that variables provide, you'll use them with great frequency throughout your SQL. Let's get started!

13.1 *User-defined variables*

Although there are different kinds of variables, the ones we'll use in this chapter are known as *user-defined variables*. The name is self-explanatory because the user (you or

I) will *define* these variables, which means assigning them a name and a value. All these variables start with the at sign (@), so when you see @ in SQL, you're likely to be looking at a variable.

Before we use any variable, we must declare it. Since chapter 2, we've verbally declared our intentions in English to help us understand the syntax of queries, but sometimes, we also need to declare things in our SQL. Let's look at how to do that in MySQL.

13.1.1 Declaring your first user-defined variable

Declaring a variable typically requires two pieces of information to start: the *name* of the variable and the *value* of the variable. Suppose that we want to write a query to filter on title name. We could start with a sensible variable name like @TitleName and the value 'The Sum Also Rises'. We could make a straightforward verbal declaration: "I would like to declare a variable named @TitleName, and I would like to assign it the value of The Sum Also Rises." The SQL used for this declaration is similar in logic, using the new keyword SET:

```
SET @TitleName = 'The Sum Also Rises';
```

As with many things in SQL, the syntax is similar to the order of our verbal declaration. We declare a variable by setting its name with SET and then assign a value using = and a literal value.

> **NOTE** When you use SET, you can use either = or := as the assignment operator. Which one you use is a matter of personal preference, although as you'll see later in the chapter, in at least one instance, you must use := for your variable declaration.

You may have noticed that we didn't specify what data type to use. That's because MySQL determines the data type based on the value we used. In our example, we used a character string ('The Sum Also Rises') as the value of the variable, so our variable is a string data type.

Other permissible data types for variables include integer, decimal, and float, which are numeric data types. If the data for the variable doesn't fit one of the permissible types, the relational database management system (RDBMS) will convert the values to a permissible data type. Date and time values, which we've used throughout this book, are treated as strings.

> **WARNING** This method of declaring variables in MySQL isn't universal. When you use a different RDBMS, such as SQL Server or PostgreSQL, you have to declare a user-defined variable using the DECLARE keyword and also assign it a specified data type.

If necessary, we can confirm the value of our variable at any time with a simple SELECT statement, as shown in figure 13.1:

```
SELECT @TitleName;
```

Although selecting a variable to confirm its value may seem trivial, you'll use this method quite a bit when you use variables. When you write a SQL query, this method is useful for checking the values of a variable periodically; it's also helpful for troubleshooting complex SQL scripts that aren't returning the desired values.

@TitleName
The Sum Also Rises

Figure 13.1
The results of selecting
`@TitleName`, **which shows**
the value of the variable.
It also shows the variable
name in the header.

13.1.2 Understanding rules for user-defined variables

I should note a few rules about using variables before we go any further. There aren't many rules, and they aren't difficult to remember, but they're crucial to using variables correctly:

- *The first character of a variable name must be* @. Using @ in the variable name tells the RDBMS you're working with a variable.
- *The remaining characters in a variable name must be alphabetic or numeric.* As you can see with the use of @, nonalphanumeric characters can have special meanings in SQL. Use only letters and numbers in your variable names.
- *Variable names can be no more than 64 characters.* You want to use descriptive variable names so that others who read your SQL can easily understand their purposes. But if the name of any of your variables is anywhere near 64 characters, you're probably being a bit too descriptive.
- *Variable names are not case-sensitive.* If you declare a variable named `@Variable`, any use of `@VARIABLE`, `@variable`, or `@VaRiAbLe` will refer to the same one.
- *A user-defined variable can hold only a single value.* You can't include multiple values, although you can change the value of a variable throughout your SQL if you so desire.
- *A user-defined variable exists only for the duration of the connection.* Databases and tables *persist*, which means that they exist until they're explicitly removed. Unlike those objects, variables don't persist, so when you close MySQL Workbench or any other application you use to connect to a database, any variables you've declared no longer exist.

13.1.3 Using your first user-defined variable

With all those rules out of the way, we're ready to put variables to use. Let's write some SQL to use a variable that helps us select the TitleID, TitleName, and PublicationDate from the title table, with the results shown in figure 13.2:

```
SET @TitleName = 'The Sum Also Rises';
SELECT
    TitleID,
    TitleName,
```

```
    PublicationDate
FROM title
WHERE TitleName = @TitleName;
```

Now we have this bit of SQL, which admittedly is rather short. Suppose that we had much more SQL to execute for a given title—perhaps to find the number of titles sold or the states of residence of customers who purchased the title. Whatever the case, if we set and filtered on a variable throughout the query as we did earlier, to query a different title, we'd have to make the change in only one part of our SQL.

TitleID	TitleName	PublicationDate
108	The Sum Also Rises	2021-11-12 00:00:00

Figure 13.2   The TitleID, TitleName, and PublicationDate from the title table for 'The Sum Also Rises', as filtered using a user-defined variable

Here's how that task looks in practice. Let's change the variable to 'Pride and Predicates' and execute our query again. The following query produces the results shown in figure 13.3:

```
SET @TitleName = 'Pride and Predicates';
SELECT
    TitleID,
    TitleName,
    PublicationDate
FROM title
WHERE TitleName = @TitleName;
```

Again, this bit of SQL is simple, but I hope it helps you see the power of using variables to make your script more flexible and reusable. Variables are used in nearly every programming language, and plenty of examples in this chapter and subsequent chapters show how to use them effectively.

TitleID	TitleName	PublicationDate
101	Pride and Predicates	2015-04-30 00:00:00

Figure 13.3   The TitleID, TitleName, and PublicationDate from the title table for 'Pride and Predicates', as filtered using a user-defined variable

Try it now

Declare a variable with a name of your choosing, and use it to select the TitleID, TitleName, and PublicationDate from the title table for any particular title.

13.2   *Filtering with variables in FROM and HAVING clauses*

Let's look at some practical ways to use variables in SQL. Suppose that we want the date of every order of any particular title. We can use a variable for this task, and in this case, we'll start with 'The Sum Also Rises'. With the table-joining logic we've used before, we could write something like this (results shown in figure 13.4):

```
SET @TitleName = 'The Sum Also Rises';

SELECT
    oh.OrderDate
FROM orderheader oh
INNER JOIN orderitem oi
    ON oh.OrderID = oi.OrderID
INNER JOIN title t
    ON oi.TitleID = t.TitleID
WHERE t.TitleName = @TitleName;
```

You can change that title name to any other valid title and return the corresponding set of order dates. As you might imagine, if your variable is set to a value that's not included in the title table, your result set would be zero rows.

OrderDate
2021-11-13 00:00:00
2021-11-28 00:00:00
2022-03-10 00:00:00

Figure 13.4
The OrderDate for any order that included the title 'The Sum Also Rises'

Another common way to use variables is to find information about orders on a particular day, week, month, or year. Let's find the names of all customers who placed orders for any titles in November 2021, as shown in figure 13.5. In this case, we'll use two variables to represent the start and end dates of our range:

```
SET @DateStart = '2021-11-01',
    @DateEnd = '2021-11.30';

SELECT
    c.FirstName,
    c.LastName,
    oh.OrderDate
FROM customer c
INNER JOIN orderheader oh
    ON c.CustomerID = oh.CustomerID
WHERE oh.OrderDate BETWEEN @DateStart and @DateEnd;
```

Interestingly, we can put this filter in a different part of the predicate. Instead of putting the filter in the WHERE clause, we can make it a condition in the JOIN. (This isn't typically how filtering is done in SQL, although you may notice it in other people's code.) Here's what the preceding query would look like if we filtered on our variables in the FROM clause as part of a JOIN condition:

FirstName	LastName	OrderDate
Keanu	O'Ward	2021-11-13 00:00:00
Monica	Newgarden	2021-11-28 00:00:00

Figure 13.5   The FirstName and LastName of any customer who placed an order in November 2021, along with the OrderDate

```
SET
    @DateStart = '2021-11-01',
    @DateEnd = '2021-11-30';

SELECT
    c.FirstName,
    c.LastName,
```

```
    oh.OrderDate
FROM customer c
INNER JOIN orderheader oh
    ON c.CustomerID = oh.CustomerID
    AND oh.OrderDate BETWEEN @DateStart and @DateEnd;
```

We can also use a variable to see how many titles sold above a specific quantity. We can apply the aggregation techniques we learned in chapter 12 here, with a HAVING clause as a filter that uses a variable. Let's get a list of all the TitleNames that sold 10 or more copies, as shown in figure 13.6:

TitleName	TotalQuantitySold
Pride and Predicates	25
The Join Luck Club	13
Catcher in the Try	11
The DateTime Machine	13

Figure 13.6   The TitleName and TotalQuantitySold of all titles that sold at least 10 copies

```
SET @MinimumQuantitySold = 10;

SELECT
    t.TitleName,
    SUM(oi.Quantity) AS TotalQuantitySold
FROM orderitem oi
INNER JOIN title t
    ON oi.TitleID = t.TitleID
GROUP BY t.TitleName
HAVING SUM(oi.Quantity) >= @MinimumQuantitySold;
```

The results show four titles that meet the threshold of at least 10 copies (Quantity) sold. If we want to change the threshold of our filter to another value, all we need to do is change the value of the @MinimumQuantitySold variable.

13.3   Assigning an unknown value to a variable

One useful aspect of variables allows us to create and use a variable even when we don't know the explicit value on which we want to filter. If I asked you the value of TitleID for TitleName The Sum Also Rises, would you know it? Honestly, I wrote everything in this database, and even I can't recall that value.

Although we may not have memorized the TitleID values, we've used them countless times in our queries because these values constitute the relationship between the orderheader and title tables.

13.3.1   Reviewing how a query works

Let's take a moment to consider how TitleID is used in the first query in section 13.2 and how we can use one variable to collect the value for another variable. Here's that query, which looks for the order dates of the title The Sum Also Rises:

```
SET @TitleName = 'The Sum Also Rises';

SELECT
    oh.OrderDate
```

```
FROM orderheader oh
INNER JOIN orderitem oi
    ON oh.OrderID = oi.OrderID
INNER JOIN title t
    ON oi.TitleID = t.TitleID
WHERE t.TitleName = @TitleName;
```

Let's walk through the joins in this table, starting at the bottom and working our way up. Why do it this way? Your RDBMS will probably start finding your results by filtering rows in the title table. Filtering typically means fewer rows to read, and fewer rows to read means fewer rows to join with other tables, which is more efficient than reading all the rows in all the tables, joining them, and then applying filtering.

In this query, we used the variable `@TitleName` to find any rows in the title table that matched our query, which happens to be one row. Then we join that row to any related rows to orderitem via the matching TitleID values, and we join to any related rows in orderheader using the matching OrderID values in both tables. When we have related values through all tables, we can select the values for OrderDate to determine when the titles were ordered.

13.3.2　*Assigning an unknown variable with SELECT*

This query is a relatively simple one with a couple of joins. It's important to note, though, that joins require the RDBMS to do extra work because it has to read and relate the data in different tables. Fortunately, we can reduce the number of joins in our query in section 13.3.1 by creating a variable for the TitleID values because we know that only one value in the title table matches the TitleName value for The Sum Also Rises.

We can find the value for TitleID, which is unknown, by declaring our variable a bit differently. We're going to use a SELECT statement instead of SET because we're selecting a value from an existing table to use in our variable.

First, though, let's take a step back. Suppose that we want to return the value of TitleID instead of using it to assign a value to our `@TitleID` variable. We might write our SQL this way, using a `@TitleName` variable for the name of the title:

```
SET @TitleName = 'The Sum Also Rises';

SELECT TitleID
FROM title
WHERE TitleName = @TitleName;
```

Try it now

I keep talking about this value, so execute this query to find the TitleID value for The Sum Also Rises.

We can use the logic from this query to assign the value of this
TitleID to a new @TitleID variable. Figure 13.7 shows the output
for the assigned value:

```
SET @TitleName = 'The Sum Also Rises';

SELECT @TitleID := TitleID
FROM title
WHERE TitleName = @TitleName;
```

@TitleID := TitleID
108

Figure 13.7
Selecting an
unknown value
for TitleID in @
`TitleID` **will**
result in output
that shows the
value that was
selected—in this
case, 108.

The FROM and WHERE clauses are identical to those in the preceding
query, but the SELECT clause looks unlike anything we've done so
far. With the logic of SELECT @TitleId := TitleID, we can do two
things at the same time with our SELECT clause: select the TitleID
value and assign that value to our @TitleID variable.

Also notice that we used the := operator instead of = in our SQL. Earlier in this chapter, I mentioned that you can use = or := when you assign a value to a variable using SET.
When you assign a value to a variable using SELECT in MySQL, however, you can use only
the := operator.

> **WARNING** As I noted earlier for the SET keyword, this method of assigning an
> unknown value to a variable is different in nearly every RDBMS. Although the
> process is fundamentally similar, it's important to know the correct syntax for
> your RDBMS.

One other interesting side effect of assigning a value to a variable with SELECT is the
fact that the results are output to the Results panel. SELECT statements result in output
in MySQL, and in this case, the result shows the value that was assigned to the variable,
with the SQL used in the SELECT statement as the column header.

13.3.3 *Considering performance with variables*

Now that we've learned how to assign a value to a variable using SELECT, let's see how
this looks with the overall query that was intended to find the order dates for The Sum
Also Rises (results shown in figure 13.8):

```
SET @TitleName = 'The Sum Also Rises';

SELECT @TitleID := TitleID
FROM title
WHERE TitleName = @TitleName;

SELECT
    oh.OrderDate
FROM orderheader oh
INNER JOIN orderitem oi
    ON oh.OrderID = oi.OrderID
WHERE oi.TitleID = @TitleID;
```

This latest query uses two variables but requires only one join in the final statement instead of two. Although this query is still relatively trivial in terms of work required of the RDBMS, in queries against larger sets of data, reducing joins as we've done here can offer significant improvements in performance.

> **NOTE** If you look closely at the Results panel, you'll see two sets of results, with two separate tabs at the bottom of the panel. Those shown in figure 13.8 are the results you wrote your SQL to determine, but as you may have guessed, the results in the "hidden" tab are the output from the first SELECT where the variable value was assigned.

OrderDate
2021-11-13 00:00:00
2021-11-28 00:00:00
2022-03-10 00:00:00

Figure 13.8
The OrderDate for any order that includes the title The Sum Also Rises. This time, we used the SELECT keyword instead of SET keyword to get the results shown in figure 13.4.

13.3.4 Troubleshooting considerations with variables

Consider a request to find the title, quantity, and price of the first order in a particular year, such as 2021. To do this, first we need to find the date of the first order in 2021; then, using that value, we find the information about the order placed on that date. Our database contains so few orders that there are no more than one per day, which makes the task simpler. Let's start by determining the date of the first order in 2021, as shown in figure 13.9.

I haven't covered this topic yet, but we could use the SET method to assign an unknown value to our variables instead of SELECT. To do this, however, we'd have to use a kind of subquery, like this:

FirstOrderDate
2021-01-15 00:00:00

Figure 13.9
The OrderDate of the first order placed in 2021, which is shown only because of the SELECT statement. We'll use this value later to determine more information about the order placed on that day.

```
SET @FirstOrderDate = (
    SELECT MIN(OrderDate)
    FROM orderheader
    WHERE OrderDate BETWEEN '2021-01-01' AND '2021-12-31');

SELECT @FirstOrderDate AS FirstOrderDate;
```

This query produces the correct result, but we can see the value assigned to the variable only if we explicitly use a separate SELECT statement. As we saw earlier, using SELECT instead of SET to assign this value also shows us the value assigned to the variable (figure 13.10):

```
SELECT @FirstOrderDate := MIN(OrderDate)
FROM orderheader
WHERE OrderDate BETWEEN '2021-01-01' AND '2021-12-31';
```

Whichever method you use is a matter of preference. This is largely determined by whether you want the output to show

@FirstOrderDate := MIN(OrderDate)
2021-01-15 00:00:00

Figure 13.10
The OrderDate of the first order placed in 2021, shown without a second SELECT statement. The SQL used in the SELECT statement is the column header.

whether the correct value is being used because SET doesn't show the value of a variable by default, as SELECT does. As you write a query, it may be helpful to use the SELECT method to verify that the values assigned to your variables are correct to prevent incorrect results. Seeing the values in the Results panel may give you more confidence in the effectiveness of your SQL.

For now, let's use the method with SELECT to determine the first order of 2021 and to select the title, quantity, and price of that order. The following query returns the results shown in figure 13.11:

TitleName	Quantity	ItemPrice
The DateTime Machine	1	7.95

Figure 13.11   The TitleName, Quantity, and ItemPrice of the items in the first order placed in 2021

```
SELECT @FirstOrderDate := MIN(OrderDate)
FROM orderheader
WHERE OrderDate BETWEEN '2021-01-01' AND '2021-12-31';

SELECT
    t.TitleName,
    oi.Quantity,
    oi.ItemPrice
FROM orderheader oh
INNER JOIN orderitem oi
    ON oh.OrderID = oi.OrderID
INNER JOIN title t
    ON oi.TitleID = t.TitleID
WHERE oh.OrderDate = @FirstOrderDate;
```

It's good to have options for using variables in your SQL. Now you should have a better understanding of the pros and cons of using SET or SELECT to assign value to your user-defined variables.

13.4   Other notes about variables

Before we get to the lab exercises, we have a few more points about variables to consider.

13.4.1   Assigning a literal value using SELECT

Although I didn't cover this topic, we can use SELECT to assign a literal value instead of SET. The choice is mostly a matter of preference, but we've seen throughout the chapter that SELECT offers more options for working with FROM, WHERE, and other clauses. We'd use this syntax to assign a date value, for example:

```
SELECT @SomeDate := '2021-11-30';
```

13.4.2   Assigning a value of NULL to a variable

Often, we want to start with a variable with a null value assigned to it and see later in our SQL whether it gets another value assigned. The variable type doesn't matter until a value gets assigned, in which case the variable type will change to the data type of the value. We can assign a null value to a variable with SET or SELECT, using either of the following lines of SQL:

```
SET @NullVariableWithSET = NULL;

SELECT @NullVariableWithSELECT;
```

13.4.3 *Changing the type of data used by a variable*

In MySQL, variables can have different values assigned to them throughout your SQL. As I just noted, the variable data type can change if you start with NULL but later assign a string, integer, or other kind of value. There aren't many use cases for changing the data type of a variable, but if you want to, you can even assign different data types to a variable throughout your SQL. In the following example, the first assigned value is a number, and a string data type is assigned later:

```
SET @SomeVariable = 1;

SELECT @SomeVariable AS FirstValue;

SET @SomeVariable = 'The Sum Also Rises';

SELECT @SomeVariable AS SecondValue;
```

Although it's possible to change a variable type throughout your SQL, doing so falls in the category "Things You Can Do but Shouldn't." I note this option only in case you make a mistake and accidentally reuse a variable more than once; you won't get an error message or warning that you've done so.

13.5 *Lab*

1 In this chapter, I noted that in MySQL you must use := when assigning a value using SELECT. What happens if you use = instead?

2 I also noted that you can assign only a single value to a variable. What happens if you execute the following query? Is a value assigned to the variable, and if so, what is the value?

```
SELECT @TitleID := TitleID
FROM title;
```

3 Review the final query in section 13.3.4, and update it, using variables for the start date and end date.

4 Write a query to find total sales dollars (in terms of Quantity times Price) for any customer, with the customer's FirstName and LastName as variables.

13.6   *Lab answers*

1   If you use = instead of := to assign values to a variable in a SELECT statement, the value of the variable will be null. The MySQL RDBMS uses = to test for equality, as we've seen numerous times when using filters and joins. In the SELECT statement, it determines that the two values are not equal because the variable has no value. Remember: null is the absence of data.

2   The value is 108, although if you execute the query, you see all the values for TitleID in the results. Because only one value can be assigned to the variable, the final value is assigned. For this reason, be careful to select only a single value when using this method to assign values to a variable.

3   You could use SQL this way to add more flexibility to this query, allowing for easy changes at the top to examine different ranges of data:

```
SET
    @DateStart = '2021-01-01',
    @DateEnd = '2021-12-31';

SELECT @FirstOrderDate := MIN(OrderDate)
FROM orderheader
WHERE OrderDate BETWEEN @DateStart and @DateEnd;

SELECT
    t.TitleName,
    oi.Quantity,
    oi.ItemPrice
FROM orderheader oh
INNER JOIN orderitem oi
    ON oh.OrderID = oi.OrderID
INNER JOIN title t
    ON oi.TitleID = t.TitleID
WHERE oh.OrderDate = @FirstOrderDate;
```

4   You have a few ways to do this. Here's one way:

```
SET @FirstName = 'Chris';
SET @LastName = 'Dixon';

SELECT @CustomerID := CustomerID
FROM Customer
WHERE FirstName = @FirstName
    AND LastName = @LastName;

SELECT
    @FirstName AS FirstName,
    @LastName AS LastName,
    SUM(oi.Quantity * oi.ItemPrice) AS TotalSalesDollars
FROM orderheader oh
INNER JOIN orderitem oi
    ON oh.OrderID = oi.OrderID
WHERE oh.CustomerID = @CustomerID;
```

Querying with functions

Chapter 12 looked at a handful of functions—commands that perform some sort of predefined calculation. We looked specifically at basic aggregate functions that allow us to quickly calculate things like the sum of a range of values, as well as the minimum, maximum, and average values for a given range.

This chapter examines even more functions that open more possibilities in SQL, including those that allow us to select and filter specific string, date and time, and other informational values. First, though, we'll take a broader look at when we should and shouldn't use functions.

14.1 The problems with functions

Functions are incredibly useful for selecting specific parts of values, calculating values, and manipulating values in SQL. They're like magic spells we can perform by adding an extra word in our SQL. Functions, however, have two big problems that we need to discuss before we use them throughout our queries.

14.1.1 Function commands vary for each RDBMS

The core keywords and clauses we've used up to now are universal for the most part. When we write SQL using SELECT, FROM, WHERE, and GROUP BY, we know that the code will work not only in MySQL but also in any relational database management system (RDBMS) we use. Functions, however, are not universal, and many of the functions we examine in this chapter have some variation for one or more RDBMSes.

Now, that doesn't mean the functions you'll learn and practice are only for MySQL; many of them work in another RDBMS. But it does mean that if you try to use them in another RDBMS and encounter a syntax error, you'll likely need to do a little research to find out the correct keyword for that particular RDBMS. That said, I'll do my best to note these variations throughout this chapter because they can be obstacles to taking your new SQL skills to another RDBMS.

14.1.2 Function commands can be inefficient

I noted at the end of chapter 12 that the DISTINCT keyword has to do extra work by reading all the values in a range and returning the requested values without duplicates. I noted that it should be used very carefully with large sets of data because you don't want to use server resources unnecessarily.

Depending on their use, nearly all the functions discussed in this chapter also need to read all the values in a range. Although functions are incredibly useful and appear to be shortcuts to achieving a desired output, we need to be mindful of their use with large sets of data. Although using functions with a large data set can get us the correct answers, functions may use more resources and therefore may not be the most efficient way to use SQL.

Again, these warnings aren't meant to discourage you from using functions. You just need to be aware of their limitations and effects.

14.2   String functions

String functions allow us to select parts of string data, which we often have to do when we need to present data in a way that differs from how it's stored in the database. Examples of these situations are returning customer names in uppercase for a mailing list and eliminating unnecessary leading or trailing spaces from a value.

14.2.1 Case functions

The first string function we'll try is the UPPER function, which converts a string of characters to uppercase characters. We'll use it here to view only the customers in California, which are identified by the State value of CA and shown in figure 14.1. We'll also include the actual values stored for FirstName and LastName for comparison:

```
SELECT
    FirstName,
    LastName,
    UPPER(FirstName),
    UPPER(LastName)
FROM customer
WHERE State = 'CA';
```

The syntax for UPPER, as for most functions, is to call the function and then contain the column name, variable, or other value where the function is applied inside parentheses. For this reason, you'll often see functions with parentheses in their names, such as UPPER().

Although you may have observed that the third and fourth columns in figure 14.1 are uppercase characters, as expected, also notice the names of the columns returned. Those names are the columns as they appear in our SELECT clause, which will be the default name if one is not assigned. Let's run the query again, this time using column aliases of the prefix Upper with assigned column names (results shown in figure 14.2):

FirstName	LastName	UPPER(FirstName)	UPPER(LastName)
Cora	Daly	CORA	DALY
Tara	Di Silvestro	TARA	DI SILVESTRO
Margaret	Montoya	MARGARET	MONTOYA

Figure 14.1 **The first and last names of all customers in California, first as they exist in the customer table and then in uppercase when we use the UPPER function**

```
SELECT
    FirstName,
    LastName,
    UPPER(FirstName) AS UpperFirstName,
    UPPER(LastName) AS UpperLastName
FROM customer
WHERE State = 'CA';
```

That result is more readable, and we could use similar logic with another function to make all the characters in the columns lowercase. There are few reasons to present values in lowercase, but if lowercase is required, this function is available. For this task, we can use LOWER instead of UPPER (results shown in figure 14.3) with corresponding column aliases:

```
SELECT
    FirstName,
    LastName,
    LOWER(FirstName) AS LowerFirstName,
    LOWER(LastName) AS LowerLastName
FROM customer
WHERE State = 'CA';
```

FirstName	LastName	UpperFirstName	UpperLastName
Cora	Daly	CORA	DALY
Tara	Di Silvestro	TARA	DI SILVESTRO
Margaret	Montoya	MARGARET	MONTOYA

Figure 14.2 **The first and last names of all customers in California, first as they exist in the customer table and then as all uppercase when we use the UPPER function with defined column names**

FirstName	LastName	LowerFirstName	LowerLastName
Cora	Daly	cora	daly
Tara	Di Silvestro	tara	di silvestro
Margaret	Montoya	margaret	montoya

Figure 14.3 **The first and last names of all customers in California, first as they exist in the customer table and then as all lowercase when we use the LOWER function with defined column names.**

14.2.2 Trim functions

The other thing we want to try is removing leading or trailing spaces. We have a few options for this task, with three separate functions: RTRIM, LTRIM, and TRIM. The RTRIM function removes all *trailing spaces* from a value—all spaces to the right of the last non-space character. LTRIM removes all *leading spaces* from a value—all spaces to the left of the first nonspace character. TRIM is the same as applying both LTRIM and RTRIM to a value; it removes all leading and trailing spaces.

> **NOTE** You could use two functions on the same value, such as SELECT (RTRIM(LTRIM(SomeValue)). Make sure that your logical order is correct because the innermost function will be executed first. You may encounter SQL like this written by folks who lacked either the knowledge or ability to use the TRIM function to remove both leading and trailing spaces.

Let's try these functions using a variable with leading and trailing spaces. This example may seem nonsensical, but I assure you that if you ever need to program an interface for manual data entry, you'll have to deal with leading and trailing spaces in the data.

Our variable will have three leading spaces and two trailing spaces. We'll also assign column names in our query (trimmed results shown in figure 14.4):

```
SET @Word = '   word   ';
SELECT
    @Word AS WordAsEntered,
    LTRIM(@Word) AS WordLTRIM,
    RTRIM(@Word) AS WordRTRIM,
    TRIM(@Word) AS WordTRIM;
```

Admittedly, we can't see the spaces in the results too well just by looking at them. But we can use another function to verify that leading and trailing spaces have been removed: LENGTH. This function returns the length in terms of the number of characters, including spaces, for each value.

WordAsEntered	WordLTRIM	WordRTRIM	WordTRIM
word	word	word	word

Figure 14.4   The results of selecting the character string '   word   ', which has three leading spaces and two trailing spaces, with the three trim-related functions. LTRIM removes the left leading spaces, RTRIM removes the right trailing spaces, and TRIM removes both leading and trailing spaces.

We'll have to do a little math for the next example, but only basic addition and subtraction. The word *word* has four characters, and if we add three leading spaces and two trailing spaces, the length of our word as entered should be nine characters.

If we trim the three left (leading) spaces, our LTRIM value should be 6 (9 minus 3). If we trim the two right (trailing) spaces, our RTRIM value should be 7 (9 minus 2). Finally, if we trim all leading and trailing spaces, we should have a length of four characters for the word *word*.

Test this with SQL and the LENGTH function by wrapping it around the functions you used for trimming spaces. That's right—you can execute a function from inside another function. When you do this, though, remember that the innermost function always gets executed first. Figure 14.5 shows the results of this code:

```
SET @Word = '   word   ';
SELECT
```

```
LENGTH(@Word) AS WordAsEnteredLength,
LENGTH(LTRIM(@Word)) AS WordLTRIMLength,
LENGTH(RTRIM(@Word)) AS WordRTRIMLength,
LENGTH(TRIM(@Word)) AS WordTRIMLength;
```

WordAsEnteredLength	WordLTRIMLength	WordRTRIMLength	WordTRIMLength
9	6	7	4

Figure 14.5   The results of selecting the length of the strings with the LENGTH function after applying different trim functions to the string 'word'. Because the removal of leading and trailing spaces can be difficult to see, we can use LENGTH to validate the results.

Again, trimming data this way is important because you generally don't want to store or display data with leading spaces. Those spaces not only take up unnecessary space in your database but also can cause problems with common tasks such as filtering and sorting.

> **NOTE**   SQL Server has no LENGTH function. Instead, use LEN to find the length of a string.

14.2.3 Other string functions

Although each RDBMS has its own set of string functions, some functions are so commonly used that they're available in nearly every RDBMS. Table 14.1 lists a few of those functions.

Table 14.1   Common string functions and definitions available in most RDBMSes

Function name	Description
LEFT	Gets a specified number of leftmost characters from a string
REPLACE	Searches and replaces a substring of values in a string
RIGHT	Gets a specified number of rightmost characters from a string
SUBSTRING	Gets a substring starting from a specified position with a specific length

14.3   Date and time functions

We can not only parse string values with functions but also do the same with date and time values. Most RDBMSes have appropriately named functions for determining the YEAR, MONTH, DAY, HOUR, MINUTE, and SECOND, which can be useful when we want to find information based on one or more parts of the date.

14.3.1 Date functions that return numeric values

Suppose that we want to find a list of all order IDs from 2015 like the one shown in figure 14.6. We could use the YEAR function in a query that checks the year of all orders in the orderheader table and returns the requested data. Let's include OrderID and OrderDate in our query:

```
SELECT
    OrderID,
    OrderDate
FROM orderheader
WHERE YEAR(OrderDate) = 2015;
```

You could do the same thing with one of the other six functions related to date and time. I'm sure you're already thinking about how to use variables in this kind of search to add even more flexibility for filtering. Or maybe you're starting to consider that you could also use the functions to select parts of a date and time value.

Let's use all these functions on the OrderDate of the first order. That order has an OrderID of 1001 (results shown in figure 14.7):

```
SELECT
    OrderDate,
    YEAR(OrderDate),
    MONTH(OrderDate),
    DAY(OrderDate),
    HOUR(OrderDate),
    MINUTE(OrderDate),
    SECOND(OrderDate)
FROM orderheader
WHERE OrderID = 1001;
```

OrderID	OrderDate
1001	2015-06-01 00:00:00
1002	2015-06-15 00:00:00
1003	2015-07-03 00:00:00
1004	2015-08-12 00:00:00
1005	2015-09-05 00:00:00
1006	2015-11-02 00:00:00
1007	2015-11-15 00:00:00
1008	2015-11-22 00:00:00

Figure 14.6   **The results of all OrderIDs and OrderDates from orders placed in 2015. We got these results by using the** YEAR **function.**

OrderDate	YEAR(OrderDate)	MONTH(OrderDate)	DAY(OrderDate)	HOUR(OrderDate)	MINUTE(OrderDate)	SECOND(OrderDate)
2015-06-01 00:00:00	2015	6	1	0	0	0

Figure 14.7   **The results of all the date and time parts of the OrderDate of the first order in the orderheader table**

These functions may not seem helpful now, but chapter 15 suggests some practical ways to use date and time parts to determine the results of various calculations. Also, these functions aren't the only date and time functions. Section 14.3.2 discusses two others that may interest you.

14.3.2   *Date functions that return string values*

The DAYNAME and MONTHNAME functions give you a little more information about date values by returning string values for the names of the month and day of a given date. Although the month may seem obvious if you know the numeric value, it's highly unlikely that you'll remember the name of the day of the week on which the order was placed. Modify the preceding query to use these functions so you can find out (results shown in figure 14.8):

```
SELECT
    OrderDate,
    YEAR(OrderDate),
    MONTHNAME(OrderDate),
    DAY(OrderDate),
    DAYNAME(OrderDate)
FROM orderheader
WHERE OrderID = 1001;
```

OrderDate	YEAR(OrderDate)	MONTHNAME(OrderDate)	DAY(OrderDate)	DAYNAME(OrderDate)
2015-06-01 00:00:00	2015	June	1	Monday

Figure 14.8 The results of using the `MONTHNAME` **and** `DAYNAME` **to determine the names of the month and day of the first order in the orderheader table**

TIP Remember these functions when you have to compile reports that need a date time value formatted a certain way or the name of the month or day specified.

14.3.3 *Other date and time functions*

Table 14.2 lists some common date and time functions that are available in nearly every RDBMS.

Table 14.2 Common date and time functions available in most RDBMSes

Function name	What It Gets
DATE	Only the date from a date and time value
DAYOFWEEK	The numeric day of the week for a date value
DAYOFYEAR	The numeric day of the year for a date value
LAST_DAY	The last date of the month for a date value
QUARTER	The quarter of the year for a date value
TIME	Only the time from a date and time value
WEEKOFYEAR	The numeric week of the year for a date value

As you can imagine, these functions have many potential uses for finding information about date and time values stored in a database. But what if you need to find information about right now, such as the who, where, and when of a query? Fortunately, functions are available to answer these questions.

14.4 *Informational functions*

Each RDBMS has its own set of ways to answer the who, where, and when of a query, although some common functions are typically used. Let's start with the when, as in "When does a query occur?"

14.4.1 *Date and time information*

To determine when "right now" is, you commonly use the function CURRENT_
TIMESTAMP. This function grabs the current time on the server where your database
is located, which in this case is most likely the computer you're using for your local
installation of the sqlnovel database. The format of the date and time will be similar to
what you've seen for the date and time values so far, in the format [year-month-day
hour:minute:second].

Note that when you use CURRENT_TIMESTAMP, you still need to use parentheses as you
would with any function, even though you don't pass a value:

```
SELECT CURRENT_TIMESTAMP() AS RightNow;
```

I'm not going to show you the results because my results will be different from yours,
and your results will be different every time you execute this function.

> **Try it now**
>
> Determine the current time on your database server, using the CURRENT_TIMESTAMP
> function.

This function isn't the only one related to the current time. If you need only the day or
the time, most RDBMSes have the CURRENT_DATE and CURRENT_TIME functions as well.
You can try these functions with a query like this one:

```
SELECT
    CURRENT_DATE() AS CurrentDate,
    CURRENT_TIME() AS CurrentTime;
```

Because CURRENT_TIMESTAMP is a bit longer than most function names, many RDBMSes
have another function that does the same thing with fewer letters. In MySQL, this
function is NOW. You can use the following SQL to confirm this fact and see that both
functions return the same value:

```
SELECT
    CURRENT_TIMESTAMP() AS RightNow,
    NOW() AS AlsoRightNow;
```

One last thing to note about these functions is that you can use them with other functions covered in this book. If you need to return the name of today's day of the week,
for example, you could determine it with a query like this:

```
SELECT DAYNAME(NOW()) AS CurrentDayOfWeek;
```

14.4.2 Connection information

Now let's move on to a final set of functions that tell you who and where you are. Although you're working with only one database throughout this book, in professional experience, you're likely to connect to multiple databases at various times to query different data. If you're ever uncertain about which database you're connected to, you can identify it with the DATABASE function (result shown in figure 14.9):

```
SELECT DATABASE();
```

DATABASE()

sqlnovel

**Figure 14.9
The results of
selecting the
current database
used by the
connection,
which is the
sqlnovel
database**

Also, you may use more than one login to connect to a database. This can happen when you change between your personal login to another used by a specific application or report system, often for testing. You can determine the username being used by your connection with the CURRENT_USER function:

```
SELECT CURRENT_USER();
```

> **NOTE** MySQL has both the USER and CURRENT_USER functions, both of which return information about the username. Most RDBMSes include CURRENT_USER but not USER.

Finally, as I noted in the installation directions in chapter 1, the MySQL database engine gets periodic updates that are represented in the version number. When you're connecting to a database, the version number is rarely obvious. If you want to see the current version number, use the VERSION function:

```
SELECT VERSION();
```

The version is returned as a string of three numbers separated by periods; the first number is the main version. For the exercises in this book, you should be using version 8 or later.

That should be enough new functions for now. In chapter 15, you'll discover even more functions that allow you to manipulate values and perform calculations in many practical ways.

14.5 Lab

1 I noted that most functions take a parameter of some kind, but I didn't use any parameters with CURRENT_TIMESTAMP. What happens if you pass a value to CURRENT_TIMESTAMP, such as the number 2?

2 Using the date functions discussed in this chapter, how can you determine a count of orders that were placed on a Monday?

3 What two variables can you use to determine the longest title name in the title table? How can you write a query to determine this name?

14.6   *Lab answers*

1 The CURRENT_TIMESTAMP function accepts integers as parameters; they determine the precision used in the date and time value returned. Adding 2 also return milliseconds of the date and time:

```
SELECT CURRENT_TIMESTAMP(2);
```

2 You can use the DAYNAME function, which allows you to filter rows in the orderheader table with an order date on a Monday:

```
SELECT COUNT(OrderID) AS MondayOrders
FROM orderheader
WHERE DAYNAME(OrderDate) = 'Monday';
```

3 You can use the MAX and LENGTH functions to determine the longest title name in the title table:

```
SELECT MAX(LENGTH(titlename))
FROM title;
```

The next part may be a bit more challenging because it involves a subquery. You can filter on titles with the length determined by the preceding query by using a subquery in the predicate to determine the name of the longest title with a length matching the MAX length:

```
SELECT TitleName
FROM title
WHERE LENGTH(TitleName) =
    (SELECT MAX(LENGTH(TitleName))
    FROM title);
```

Combining or calculating
values with functions

Chapter 14 looked at several functions that allow us to return parts of data. This chapter looks at a few more functions that let you combine values in different ways and even perform calculations. Depending on the nature of the data you're working with, I'm sure you'll find some functions in this chapter that you'll use frequently. If you work with address data, for example, how can you combine all the columns for street, city, and more into a single column? Or if you work with financial reports, how can you make all your calculations show the desired precision of currency?

This chapter looks at these scenarios and more. We'll start with using functions to combine values.

15.1 Combining string values

I haven't discussed this topic yet, but you can use SQL to perform basic calculations, such as addition. Here's an example of basic addition (result shown in figure 15.1):

1 +
1
2

```
SELECT 1 + 1;
```

**Figure 15.1
The results of
calculating
1+1 using SQL**

Being able to perform addition is useful if you're working exclusively with numeric data, but what if you need to combine string values? Unfortunately, as you can see in figure 15.2, using the plus sign (+) doesn't allow you to combine string values to get a desired result:

```
SELECT 'I' + ' ' + 'love' + ' ' + 'books!';
```

'I' + ' ' + 'love' + ' ' + 'books!'
0

Instead of getting the result "I love books!," we get a result of 0. This result indicates that the calculation couldn't be completed because MySQL doesn't know how to "add" words together mathematically.

Figure 15.2 The results of combining string values with the plus operator, which doesn't combine all the values into a string

> **NOTE** You can use the plus sign to combine strings in SQL Server, but this approach won't work in most relational database management systems (RDBMSes).

A specific verb describes what we're trying to do here by combining two or more string values to form a single value. That verb is *concatenate*, and it's important to know because the function we'll use to concatenate our string values is CONCAT.

15.1.1 CONCAT

If we want to concatenate string values, we can use the CONCAT function to combine multiple values by specifying the list of values separated with commas. For the preceding query, we'd use this function as follows and get the result shown in figure 15.3:

CONCAT('I', ' ', 'love', ' ', 'books!')
I love books!

```
SELECT CONCAT('I', ' ', 'love', ' ', 'books!');
```

Figure 15.3 The results of using the CONCAT function to create a single string value from multiple string values to form the "I love books!" output

This example may seem a bit silly, but as you'll soon see, this function is powerful. String values don't exist only in literal values like the ones we used in that query, of course. They also exist in the columns of tables or in variables. We can combine any of these string values with CONCAT just as easily. Let's create a variable for a title review and concatenate it with all the title names in the title table (results shown in figure 15.4):

```
SET @Review = ' is a great book!';
SELECT CONCAT(TitleName, @Review) AS TitleReview
FROM title;
```

We can even use CONCAT with numeric or date data types. When we do so, however, we need to be aware that all values will be converted to string data types to concatenate values with different data types. This operation sometimes causes unexpected results in the sorting of concatenations that involve numeric or date values.

To demonstrate, let's combine the Price and TitleName values in the title table as shown in

TitleReview
Pride and Predicates is a great book!
The Join Luck Club is a great book!
Catcher in the Try is a great book!
Anne of Fact Tables is a great book!
The DateTime Machine is a great book!
The Great GroupBy is a great book!
The Call of the While is a great book!
The Sum Also Rises is a great book!

Figure 15.4 The results of concatenating the values of the TitleName column in the title table with a string variable to form a single column of output

figure 15.5. We'll separate the values with spaces for readability. We want to sort the output from lowest values to highest, so we'll specify ascending order with ASC for emphasis:

```
SELECT CONCAT(Price, ' ', TitleName) AS PriceAndTitle
FROM title
ORDER BY PriceAndTitle ASC;
```

PriceAndTitle
10.95 The Great GroupBy
12.95 Anne of Fact Tables
7.95 The DateTime Machine
7.95 The Sum Also Rises
8.95 Catcher in the Try
8.95 The Call of the While
9.95 Pride and Predicates
9.95 The Join Luck Club

Figure 15.5 The results of the concatenated values of Price and TitleName with a space to separate them, sorted in ascending order of the concatenated value

What happened here? Numerically, the values 10.95 and 12.95 should be at the end of ascending order, but here, they appear at the beginning. This occurs because these numeric values had to be converted to string values for the concatenation, and they're sorted by the order of the characters. In this case, the first character in these concatenated values is 1, which ordinally comes before the first characters of the other values, which are 7, 8, and 9.

We can get the desired sorting in our output by using ORDER BY with the specific column we want to sort on, which in this case is Price. Even though the Price column by itself isn't in the result set, we can use it when sorting data, as the resulting rows show (figure 15.6):

```
SELECT CONCAT(Price, ' ', TitleName) AS
    PriceAndTitle
FROM title
ORDER BY Price;
```

PriceAndTitle
7.95 The DateTime Machine
7.95 The Sum Also Rises
8.95 Catcher in the Try
8.95 The Call of the While
9.95 Pride and Predicates
9.95 The Join Luck Club
10.95 The Great GroupBy
12.95 Anne of Fact Tables

Figure 15.6 The results of the concatenated values of Price and TitleName with a space to separate them, sorted in ascending order of Price

In case you've forgotten, I talked about this concept in chapter 4. To reiterate, just because a column isn't in the output doesn't mean you can't sort by that column in the ORDER BY clause. You can sort by any value or combination of values in the table that's in the FROM clause, provided that you aren't aggregating with a GROUP BY clause. This means your concatenated values can be ordered not only by price or title but also by title ID or publication date.

Try it now

Use the preceding query to select Price and TitleName as a concatenated value, but add '$' before the Price value to indicate the type of currency. If you're still sorting by Price rather than by the concatenated value, the order should still be in the expected ascending value. You can try sorting by TitleName or another column in the title table to change the order of the results.

You may not need to concatenate values of different data types often, as you just did, but if you work with customer data, you may need to produce output that concatenates first and last names in a single column. This output could be used in mailing lists, form emails, name badges, and so on.

As you might guess, concatenating first and last names is easy to do with CONCAT. Let's concatenate the values for FirstName and LastName in the author table, separated with a space and aliased as AuthorName (results shown in figure 15.7):

```
SELECT CONCAT(FirstName, ' ', LastName) AS AuthorName
FROM author;
```

15.1.2 CONCAT_WS

As useful as the CONCAT function is, if we need to concatenate several values using the same separator, there may be an even better function. Although not every RDMBS supports it, most of them include a CONCAT_WS function to make concatenation with a separator a bit easier. The CONCAT_WS function is similar to CONCAT, with the exception that the first value provided is the separator used between all other values. We could produce the results shown in figure 15.7 with the following query, which uses the CONCAT_WS function with a space as the first value like this:

```
SELECT CONCAT_WS(' ', FirstName, LastName) AS AuthorName
FROM author;
```

AuthorName
Paul Tripp
Doug Li
Jen Strong
Jorge Guerra
Robert Davidson
Gail Shawn
Rebecca Miller
Andy Melkin
Buck Fernandez
Chris Walenski
Deepthi Mahadevan

**Figure 15.7
The results of the FirstName and LastName columns of the author table concatenated into a single value and separated with a space**

Using CONCAT_WS doesn't make this particular SQL query any shorter. But if we had to separate more than two columns with a space or some other separator, the CONCAT_WS function is preferable to CONCAT because we need to specify the separator only once.

Because there happens to be a MiddleName column in the author table, let's try using CONCAT_WS to add it as well and concatenate each author's full name (results shown in figure 15.8):

```
SELECT CONCAT_WS(' ', FirstName, MiddleName, LastName) AS AuthorName
FROM author;
```

The CONCAT_WS function provides easy concatenation of all author names, which is remarkable if you consider that some of the middle names have null values. CONCAT_WS automatically accounts for those nulls and replaces them with empty strings when concatenating values, which CONCAT typically doesn't do.

With CONCAT, the nulls are not converted to empty strings, which can be problematic.

AuthorName
Paul K Tripp
Doug Li
Jen Strong
Jorge Armando Guerra
Robert Grant Davidson
Gail Anne Shawn
Rebecca Miller
Andy Melkin
Buck Fernandez
Chris Walenski
Deepthi Mahadevan

**Figure 15.8
The results of using CONCAT_WS to concatenate the FirstName, MiddleName, and LastName of all rows in the author table**

As discussed in chapter 7, null values represent the absence of data, so any time we concatenate another value that isn't null to a null value, the result is always null.

Let's look at this concept in practice. If we attempt to produce the same results as those shown in figure 15.8 by using CONCAT, we'll be disappointed by the results. As figure 15.9 shows, any row with a null value for MiddleName will return a result of NULL:

```
SELECT CONCAT(FirstName, ' ', MiddleName, ' ', LastName) AS AuthorName
FROM author;
```

15.1.3 COALESCE

If we must account for possible null values when concatenating with the CONCAT function or any other function that doesn't change null values, the SQL language offers an additional function we can use. The COALESCE function is supported by every RDBMS and can be used to handle null values in concatenation functions. COALESCE takes a list of values that are provided to the function (similarly to how we provided a list of values to CONCAT) and returns the first non-null value from the list.

AuthorName
Paul K Tripp
NULL
NULL
Jorge Armando Guerra
Robert Grant Davidson
Gail Anne Shawn
NULL
NULL
NULL
NULL
NULL

Figure 15.9 The results of using CONCAT to concatenate the FirstName, MiddleName, and LastName of all rows in the author table. The rows with NULL results are caused by null values in MiddleName.

For the example shown in figure 15.10, we'll use COALESCE with the value for MiddleName as the first value in the list and then an empty string for the second value. Because we know that the empty string isn't null, we can trust that COALESCE will return non-null values for MiddleName or an empty string for null values.

We'll replace the MiddleName selection in the preceding query with the COALESCE function as described to ensure that there are no null values in the results (figure 15.10):

```
SELECT CONCAT(
    FirstName, ' ', COALESCE(MiddleName, ''), ' ', LastName
    ) AS AuthorName
FROM author;
```

Although COALESCE solved the problems created by the null values for MiddleName, if you look closely, you may see that in those rows, we now have two spaces between first and last names. Nothing is inherently wrong with that result, but in this case, using CONCAT_WS returned better-formatted results.

AuthorName
Paul K Tripp
Doug Li
Jen Strong
Jorge Armando Guerra
Robert Grant Davidson
Gail Anne Shawn
Rebecca Miller
Andy Melkin
Buck Fernandez
Chris Walenski
Deepthi Mahadevan

Figure 15.10 The results of using CONCAT to concatenate the FirstName, MiddleName, and LastName of all rows in the author table. The COALESCE function replaced the null values for MiddleName with empty strings.

If you work with an RDBMS that doesn't offer CONCAT_WS, and you need to concatenate values like these and change the double spaces to single spaces, you can. You just need to use another common function that can convert a string of some values to another value.

15.2 Converting values

Now that we've combined multiple values to create a new value, let's look at a few more functions we can use to change values.

15.2.1 REPLACE

We can use the REPLACE function to change the occurrence of any combination of one or more characters within a string to some other combination. This combination is known as a *substring* because it is part of the overall string being evaluated.

The REPLACE function takes three values as input, in this order: the string you're going to search, the substring you want to replace, and the substring that will be the replacement.

Here's a simple example. If we wanted to change the way that the American word *check* is displayed to the British version, *cheque*, we could replace the letters *ck* in the word *check* with *que*, as shown in figure 15.11. We could write the following query using the REPLACE function:

> REPLACE('check', 'ck', 'que')
> cheque

Figure 15.11   The results of replacing ck **in the string** 'check' **with** que **to convert the word from the American English to British English**

```
SELECT REPLACE('check', 'ck', 'que');
```

Returning to our problem of changing two spaces to one with our concatenated names in section 15.1.3, we can add a REPLACE function to our query to replace any occurrence of a double space with a single space (results shown in figure 15.12):

```
SELECT REPLACE(
    CONCAT(
        FirstName, ' ', COALESCE(MiddleName, ''), ' ', LastName
    )
    , '  ', ' ') AS AuthorName
FROM author;
```

To solve this particular problem, you used three functions. As you grow in your experience using SQL, this strategy won't be uncommon; every function performs a specific task, and you may have to think of ways like this to use more than one function in a query creatively.

AuthorName
Paul K Tripp
Doug Li
Jen Strong
Jorge Armando Guerra
Robert Grant Davidson
Gail Anne Shawn
Rebecca Miller
Andy Melkin
Buck Fernandez
Chris Walenski
Deepthi Mahadevan

**Figure 15.12
The results of the concatenated author names, replacing the null values with an empty string using** COALESCE **and the resulting double spaces with a single space using** REPLACE

15.2.2 CONVERT and CAST

Two functions are commonly used to convert values from one data type to another: CAST and CONVERT. Both functions convert a value from one data type to a different specified data type. We saw in chapter 13 that MySQL has some built-in functionality to convert values to different data types automatically, but not every RDBMS has this functionality. For many RDBMSes, you need to use one of these two functions to handle any type of data conversion. Also, although many RDBMSes offer both of these functions, some offer only one or the other. Fortunately, MySQL supports both, so you can practice some queries for each function.

Here's a simple example. The current date values are stored with both date and time. The time portion of this data isn't helpful in our sqlnovel database because we haven't captured any data for hours, minutes, or seconds. All we have are zeros for all the time values of PublicationDate. If we want to display only the date part of PublicationDate in the title table, we need to use one of these functions.

PublicationDate	PublicationDateNoTime
2015-04-30 00:00:00	2015-04-30
2016-02-06 00:00:00	2016-02-06
2017-04-03 00:00:00	2017-04-03
2018-01-12 00:00:00	2018-01-12
2019-02-04 00:00:00	2019-02-04
2019-12-23 00:00:00	2019-12-23
2020-03-14 00:00:00	2020-03-14
2021-11-12 00:00:00	2021-11-12

Let's look first at CONVERT, which requires two values: the value we're changing and then the desired data type to which we want to convert the data. In this example, we want to convert the data type from DATETIME, as it is stored in the title table, to DATE. Let's select both the original PublicationDate and our converted value to see the difference (results shown in figure 15.13):

Figure 15.13   The results of selecting PublicationDate from the title table and converting it to remove the time portion of the value

```
SELECT
    PublicationDate,
    CONVERT(PublicationDate, DATE) AS PublicationDateNoTime
FROM title;
```

The data types to which we can change our values vary by RDBMS. But be aware that converting string values such as names to a numeric or date value usually won't give you a useful result and may even return an error.

> **Try it now**
>
> Use the SQL in this section to convert the PublicationDate of the title table to DATE value; then try converting the TitleName to a DATE value as well. In MySQL, you should get a null value for the converted TitleName values because a string can't be converted to a valid date.

The CAST function is similar to CONVERT but has slightly different syntax. Instead of passing two separate values to the function, we pass a kind of phrase that uses the word AS instead of a comma. Here's how we'd use CAST for the preceding example:

```
SELECT
    PublicationDate,
    CAST(PublicationDate AS DATE) AS PublicationDateNoTime
FROM title;
```

Executing this query returns the same results as those shown in figure 15.13.

Why would you use one function instead of the other? Aside from personal preferences, you're likely to prefer CAST because it's considered to be a standard function of SQL; CONVERT is not. For this reason, you're much more likely to see CAST included in the list of functions for a given RDBMS, which means that SQL written for one RDBMS that includes CAST is more likely to be usable in another RDBMS.

> **NOTE** Although these two functions effectively do the same thing, the CONVERT function often has additional functionality that allows you to pass a third value for formatting the output. Check the documentation of your RDBMS to see whether CONVERT is supported and has additional options.

15.3 *Numeric calculations with functions*

In chapter 12, we discovered aggregate functions such as MIN, MAX, AVG, and SUM. These aggregate functions are types of numeric functions, which can be applied to numeric values for various calculations.

Many other numeric functions are available, but most of them perform specific mathematical calculations, such as the square root of a value, the logarithm, or the tangent. For now, let's focus on one mathematical function that most users can employ in some practical cases.

The ROUND function provides an easy way to solve common problems in which a value needs to be rounded with fewer decimal places—to convert decimal values of currency to integer values for simplicity, for example. Most businesses wouldn't publicly proclaim, for example, that they sold $1,000,000.32 in merchandise. Instead, they'd round the number to $1,000,000.

Although the sqlnovel database doesn't contain $1 million in sales, we can still use ROUND to produce the total sales in whole dollars for a given year without cents (fractions of a dollar). Let's see how we'd use the ROUND function to calculate the integer value for total sales value for all orders. Chapter 12 made a calculation on this very value by using the SUM function. Here, we'll add a second column that wraps around that calculation, using the ROUND function. Let's select both the sum and the rounded sum to show the difference (results shown in figure 15.14):

TotalOrderValue	TotalOrderValueRounded
573.50	574

Figure 15.14 The results of the total value of all sales in dollars and cents, along with the same value rounded to an integer

```
SELECT
    SUM(Quantity * ItemPrice) AS TotalOrderValue,
    ROUND(SUM(Quantity * ItemPrice)) AS TotalOrderValueRounded
FROM orderitem;
```

Note that the rounding in this case made the value increase because anything equal to or greater than .50 is rounded to a higher value, whereas any value less than .50 is rounded to a lower value. We can easily prove this with a simple SELECT statement that rounds the value 573.49 to a lower value.

Try it now

Execute SELECT ROUND(573.49); to verify that this value will be rounded down to 573.

One other thing to note about the ROUND function: it has two parameters. The first parameter is for the number value, which we've used in this chapter. The second parameter, however, is optional; it specifies the number of places beyond the decimal point to which the number should be rounded. If a value for the second parameter isn't passed, it converts to an integer value (0 spaces beyond the decimal).

If you work with calculations involving currency, you'll likely need to use ROUND with both parameters. Suppose that you need to calculate the added sales tax for a purchase of a title that costs $9.95. If the tax is 5%, you could calculate that amount by multiplying $9.95 by .05. If you do, however, the resulting value for the tax value will be more than two decimal places. Because customers can't be charged fractions of cents, you can pass a value of 2 to the second parameter of ROUND to make the tax value match the currency. Use the following query to validate these results, showing both the calculated tax and the rounded tax (figure 15.15):

CalculatedTax	CalculatedTaxRounded
0.4975	0.50

Figure 15.15 The results of using ROUND to round 573.49 from two decimal places to one, which rounds the value slightly higher

```
SELECT
    9.95 * .05 AS CalculatedTax,
    ROUND(9.95 * .05, 2) AS CalculatedTaxRounded
```

If you're required to work with more complicated calculations, your RDBMS likely has dozens of additional functions for mathematical equations. Table 15.1 lists some common mathematical functions that are available in nearly every RDBMS.

Table 15.1 Common mathematical functions available in most RDBMSes

Function name	What it produces
ABS	The absolute value of a number
CEIL	The smallest integer not less than a number (rounding up)
FLOOR	The largest integer not more than a number (rounding down)
MOD	The remainder (modulo) of a number divided by another
SQRT	The square root of a number

    NOTE   In SQL Server, the CEIL function is replaced by CEILING.

So far, we've spent every chapter looking at ways to use SQL to select data from tables in a database and present the resulting output in different ways. In chapter 16, we'll start to look at ways to change data in tables through data manipulation.

15.4   Lab

1   In the author table, select a single column aliased as AuthorName for all author first and last names, but in the format LastName, FirstName (such as Iannucci, Jeff).

2   Write a query for which the output is a sentence that declares the Publication-Date of the first title. The output can be something like "The first title was published on 2001-01-30" except that you use the PublicationDate formatted with the date, not the time.

3   It's common practice to ignore articles like the word *The* when sorting titles alphabetically. Write a query that returns the TitleName of all titles in the title table sorted alphabetically in this manner.

15.5   Lab answers

1   You can use the CONCAT_WS function to format the names with a query like this:

```
SELECT CONCAT_WS(', ', LastName, FirstName) AS AuthorName
FROM author;
```

2   Depending on which function you prefer to use, you can achieve this output in one of several ways. If you use CAST, your query might look like this:

```
SELECT CONCAT(
    'The first title was published on ', CAST(PublicationDate AS DATE),
    '.'
    ) AS FirstPublicationDate
FROM title
WHERE TitleID = 101;
```

You could get the same output with CONVERT:

```
SELECT CONCAT(
    'The first title was published on ', CONVERT(PublicationDate, DATE),
    '.'
    ) AS FirstPublicationDate
FROM title
WHERE TitleID = 101;
```

You could also use the DATE function, discussed in chapter 14:

```
SELECT CONCAT(
    'The first title was published on ', DATE(PublicationDate), '.'
```

```
    ) AS FirstPublicationDate
FROM title
WHERE TitleID = 101;
```

3 This one may be a bit tricky because it requires using the REPLACE function in the ORDER BY clause, which you haven't done yet. By doing this, you can replace the word *The* in the TitleName with an empty string for sorting. Be sure to include the space after the word *The* to achieve the correct sort order:

```
SELECT TitleName
FROM title
ORDER BY REPLACE(TitleName, 'The ', '');
```

Inserting data

16

For 15 chapters, we've examined ways to read data using the SELECT statement. But all that data we read using the SELECT statement had to get into the tables somehow, so in this chapter, we'll learn how to insert data.

Throughout this book, we've seen that the syntax of SQL is often like the English language. When it comes to inserting rows of data, this similarity holds true because the new keyword we'll be using is INSERT. Let's look at some ways to use INSERT to add data to the tables in our database.

16.1 Inserting specific values

The first way to insert data is to use specific values. The main idea to keep in mind is that when we insert data, we're inserting a new row into an existing table.

Chapter 2 talked about rows, columns, and values. All tables in our relational database management system (RDBMS) have rows of data, and each row has a specific set of properties defined by the columns of the table. Each property in the columns is represented by some value of a particular data type, sometimes using NULL to represent the absence of a value for a particular column.

I hope that by now, the preceding paragraph makes total sense to you, especially given all the SQL queries you've written so far. If anything about it is unclear, I encourage you to review chapter 2 to solidify your understanding of rows, columns, and values. If everything makes sense, you can proceed to inserting some data.

16.1.1 Inserting a new row

As noted, we'll use INSERT as the keyword to insert data, and if we want to insert some specific values, we'll also use the keyword VALUES. For our first query, we'll insert a new row into the title table, but first, let's look at the data in that table.

In chapter 3, I warned you about using SELECT *, but because this table is small, you can use it to save yourself from typing all the column names in this ad hoc query. You'll use this logic a few times in this chapter to glance at the rows of data in tables (figure 16.1):

```
SELECT *
FROM title;
```

TitleID	TitleName	Price	Advance	Royalty	PublicationDate
101	Pride and Predicates	9.95	5000.00	15.00	2015-04-30 00:00:00
102	The Join Luck Club	9.95	6000.00	12.00	2016-02-06 00:00:00
103	Catcher in the Try	8.95	5000.00	10.00	2017-04-03 00:00:00
104	Anne of Fact Tables	12.95	10000.00	15.00	2018-01-12 00:00:00
105	The DateTime Machine	7.95	5500.00	15.00	2019-02-04 00:00:00
106	The Great GroupBy	10.95	0.00	20.00	2019-12-23 00:00:00
107	The Call of the While	8.95	2500.00	15.00	2020-03-14 00:00:00
108	The Sum Also Rises	7.95	5000.00	12.00	2021-11-12 00:00:00

Figure 16.1   The results of all rows and columns in the title table

If we're going to insert a new row into the table shown in figure 16.1, we need to have values for all columns of data, and we need to use the correct data types. For readability, our query will specify the columns in the order in which they appear in the table: TitleID first, TitleName second, and so on.

Here's the query we'll use to insert a new row for the David Emptyfield title. We'll refer to this kind of query as an INSERT statement:

```
INSERT INTO title (
    TitleID,
    TitleName,
    Price,
    Advance,
    Royalty,
    PublicationDate
    )
VALUES (
    109,
    'David Emptyfield',
    9.95,
    0.00,
    10.00,
    '2022-01-16'
    );
```

In the preceding query, we're adding the next sequential TitleID (109), the TitleName, and the values for Price (9.95), Advance (0.00), Royalty (10.00), and PublicationDate (2022-01-16). If we execute this query, we should see a success message in the Output panel: 1 row(s) affected.

Try it now

Write and execute the preceding query. Typing all the column names of the title table may seem like a pain, but remember that you can use the Shift key to select all the column names in the Navigator panel and then drag them to your Query panel. If you don't recall how, see chapter 3 to refresh your memory.

Something else to notice about our query is that both the column names and the value names are surrounded by parentheses. When we use parentheses, we define the order of both the columns and values used by our INSERT statement.

Interestingly, we could just as easily have written the preceding query with a different column order. The only consideration would be that we'd need to rearrange the values in the same order in which the columns are specified in the INSERT statement.

Here's an example with the order of the columns reversed. If you executed the preceding INSERT statement, don't execute this:

```
INSERT INTO title (
    PublicationDate,
    Royalty,
    Advance,
    Price,
    TitleName,
    TitleID
    )
VALUES (
    '2022-01-16',
    10.00,
    0.00,
    9.95,
    'David Emptyfield',
    109
    );
```

Why would you change the column order for an INSERT statement? Well, normally, you wouldn't; that could confuse anyone who might read your SQL statement. If you find yourself inserting data into a table that has dozens or hundreds of columns, however, your SQL might be more readable if you organize column names alphabetically in your INSERT statement instead of in the order of the columns in the table. Apart from that example, you're probably better off ordering the column names in your INSERT statement in the same order as the columns of the table.

16.1.2 *Inserting multiple new rows*

Another interesting thing about enclosing values in parentheses is that the parentheses indicate all the values used for inserting a single row, which means we can also insert multiple rows if necessary. Just as we use a comma to indicate separate columns and values in our INSERT statement, we can use a comma to indicate separate sets of values to be inserted as rows. Here's an example of inserting two more rows into the title table using multiple values in the VALUES portion of our INSERT statement:

```
INSERT INTO title (
    TitleID,
    TitleName,
    Price,
    Advance,
    Royalty,
    PublicationDate
    )
VALUES (
    110,
    'Red Badge of Cursors',
    7.95,
    0.00,
    15.00,
    '2022-03-29'
    ),
    (
    111,
    'Of Mice and Metadata',
    8.95,
    0.00,
    12.00,
    '2022-05-17'
    );
```

This example notes only two additional rows, but there's no defined limit to how many rows you could insert into a table. Realistically, the only limitation is the amount of storage space in your database, which is difficult to determine with any kind of general SQL statement and thus is beyond the scope of this book. That said, unless you're inserting thousands or millions of rows, you probably don't have to worry about storage space.

> **NOTE** Speaking of general SQL statements, as you review SQL in another RDBMS, you may notice that someone else's SQL omits the word INTO from INSERT statements. That is, the SQL reads something like INSERT [table name] VALUES (…). Omitting INTO is not optional in all RDBMSes, so I recommended that you get into the habit of including it in your code so you don't have to worry about syntax errors if you work with multiple RDBMSes.

So far, all the INSERT statements in this chapter involve inserting an entire row or rows of data. As you work with SQL, sometimes you'll need to insert values for every column but may be programmatically prevented from doing so. Let's look at how we can handle inserting a partial row.

16.1.3 *Inserting a partial row*

The term *partial row* may be confusing because I noted in chapter 2 that all rows in a given table must include values for all columns. This statement is still true, but two considerations allow us to insert a partial row of data.

The first consideration is when a table includes columns that allow null values. Let's look at the author table for an example (figure 16.2):

```
SELECT *
FROM author;
```

AuthorID	FirstName	MiddleName	LastName	PaymentMethod
1	Paul	K	Tripp	Cash
2	Doug	NULL	Li	Check
3	Jen	NULL	Strong	Check
4	Jorge	Armando	Guerra	Check
5	Robert	Grant	Davidson	Check
6	Gail	Anne	Shawn	Check
7	Rebecca	NULL	Miller	Check
8	Andy	NULL	Melkin	Direct Deposit
9	Buck	NULL	Fernandez	Cash
10	Chris	NULL	Walenski	Direct Deposit
11	Deepthi	NULL	Mahadevan	Direct Deposit

Figure 16.2   The results of all rows and columns in the author table

As we can see in figure 16.2, the MiddleName column allows null values because not all authors have a middle name. Although this nullable column presented challenges when we worked with functions and concatenation in chapter 15, it affords us the option to ignore it when inserting rows.

If we want to insert a row with a value of NULL for MiddleName, we can ignore the column in our INSERT statement. Doing this will result in a value of NULL by default. Here's an example:

```
INSERT INTO author (
    AuthorID,
    FirstName,
    LastName,
    PaymentMethod
    )
VALUES (
    12,
    'Whitney',
```

```
'Miller',
'Cash'
);
```

We can execute this query without any error because the MiddleName column allows a value of NULL and enters it as a default for our new row. If we execute the preceding query and then select all the rows in the author table, we can verify this result (figure 16.3).

AuthorID	FirstName	MiddleName	LastName	PaymentMethod
1	Paul	K	Tripp	Cash
2	Doug	NULL	Li	Check
3	Jen	NULL	Strong	Check
4	Jorge	Armando	Guerra	Check
5	Robert	Grant	Davidson	Check
6	Gail	Anne	Shawn	Check
7	Rebecca	NULL	Miller	Check
8	Andy	NULL	Melkin	Direct Deposit
9	Buck	NULL	Fernandez	Cash
10	Chris	NULL	Walenski	Direct Deposit
11	Deepthi	NULL	Mahadevan	Direct Deposit
12	Whitney	NULL	Miller	Cash

Figure 16.3   The results of all rows and columns in the author table, including the new row in which AuthorID is 12, which has a value of NULL for MiddleName

Not entering a value in this query may seem lazy, but you'll encounter tables in which you want to insert rows that have null values for certain columns. One common example is a table with columns for modification date and modification user to track when data was changed and who changed it. As we insert new data, we want those columns to be null to show that the data hasn't been modified since it was initially added to the table. Chapter 17 discusses modifying data in greater detail.

Getting back to entering partial rows, the second reason we may need to enter a partial row of data is that there are default constraints on one or more columns on a table. The architect of a table creates a *default constraint* to set a defined value for a column when data is inserted, which means that data for one or more columns is automatically populated instead of entered by our INSERT statement.

Let's look at the author table again. Notice that the first column is AuthorID and that it features an incremental sequence of numbers from 1 to 12. We need these numbers to be unique for each row because they represent the key values used to relate to data in other tables. (Chapter 8 talks about key values.)

Because these values need to be unique, database architects often put a default constraint on the first column. This constraint automatically populates that column with an identity value that uniquely identifies each row. This ensures that you and I don't acci-dentally enter the same identity value for different rows in the author table. If we did that, the relationships with data in any table using AuthorID would become ambiguous because they'd have relationships with one or more author rows.

Our author table currently has no default constraint for automatically populating the AuthorID column with a default value. We know this because we manually entered a value of 12 for the row we inserted. If a default constraint for an identity value were in place, we wouldn't be allowed to enter a value for AuthorID. In that case, which often occurs in database tables with ID values, we'd write our INSERT statement to omit the AuthorID column, like this:

```
INSERT INTO author (
    FirstName,
    MiddleName,
    LastName,
    PaymentMethod
    )
VALUES (
    'Whitney',
    NULL,
    'Miller',
    'Cash'
    );
```

Again, the database isn't set up with a default constraint on the author table, so don't execute this query. Just know that you'll need to account for these kinds of columns with partial inserts in many real-world databases.

16.1.4 *A word of caution about omitting columns*

You may see another kind of omission in the INSERT statement when you work with someone else's real-world SQL: the omission of the table columns in the INSERT INTO portion of the statement. You could write an INSERT statement like this one, for exam-ple, and execute it successfully:

```
INSERT INTO author
VALUES (
    12,
    'Whitney',
    NULL,
    'Miller',
    'Cash'
    );
```

This approach may be tempting, but if you consider what I've discussed in this chapter, you can already see why this option is dangerous:

- *This technique works only if you have values for all the columns in the table and have all the values in the correct order.* If you have one value too many or one value too few, the query will fail with an error. If you have the values in the wrong order, at best you'll have created a row with inaccurate data and at worst will encounter an error. (An execution error may be preferable to inaccurate data because you'd still have data integrity.)

- *This kind of query starts failing if you change the underlying table.* It's not uncommon to add columns to a table, and if you add a new column to the author table, this query will no longer execute successfully because you have more columns than values.

- *The table could have default constraints that prevent you from entering values for certain columns.* If the table had any default constraints, an INSERT statement without columns specified would fail to execute.

For all these reasons, you should always write INSERT statements that specify column names. If you see any SQL that doesn't, see whether you can rewrite it to include column names.

With that topic out of the way, let's move on to more options for inserting data. So far, we've used the VALUES keyword to insert rows of data, but we have other options. The good news is that you already know them.

16.2   *Inserting a row with a query*

When we use VALUES as we've used it in our INSERT statements thus far, we're telling the RDBMS, "Hey, RDBMS, I have these values, and I want to insert them into this table." In both SQL and English, our statement has two parts: the location of the insertion and the declaration of the values to be inserted.

To use a method instead of VALUES for our INSERT statement, we simply replace the latter part with a SQL query that has columns selected in an order and data type that match the columns of the table into which we're inserting, as defined in the first part of our query.

Because we've already inserted a new title (David Emptyfield) and a new author (Whitney Miller), we can relate this title to this author by using the titleauthor table. I haven't talked about this table yet, so let's look at it with an ad hoc SELECT * query (results shown in figure 16.4):

```
SELECT *
FROM titleauthor;
```

This table has three columns: TitleID, AuthorID, and AuthorOrder. As you may guess, TitleID relates to the TitleID column in the title table, and AuthorID relates to the AuthorID column in the author table. Notice that we don't necessarily have unique values for either column in this table. This table represents a many-to-many

TitleID	AuthorID	AuthorOrder
101	2	1
102	3	1
103	4	1
104	5	1
105	6	1
106	7	1
107	11	1
107	1	2
108	8	1
108	9	2
108	10	3

Figure 16.4   The results of all rows and columns in the titleauthor table

relationship because any title could have more than one author and any author could
have contributed to more than one title.

The third column is AuthorOrder, which refers to the order of the authors as displayed on the cover of a title. The value in this column is always 1 for one author, which
is what matters for the new row of data we're going to enter.

Let's start with a SELECT statement that allows us to query the required tables. Because
this data isn't related yet, we can use subqueries as discussed in chapter 11:

```
SELECT
    (
    SELECT TitleID
    FROM title
    WHERE TitleName = 'David Emptyfield'
    ) AS TitleID,
    (
    SELECT AuthorID
    FROM author
    WHERE FirstName = 'Whitney'
        AND LastName = 'Miller'
    ) AS AuthorID;
```

> **NOTE**   In chapter 11, I noted that using subqueries in SELECT statements is
> rarely the best idea, but in this INSERT statement, using a subquery makes sense
> because it's an easy way to add these values to the titleauthor table.

This query serves as the starting point for our insert. Note that although column aliases
are not required, they've been added for readability and to help us match the resulting
values to the columns in the titleauthor table.

Let's add the necessary parts to make this query an INSERT statement, including adding a value of 1 for the AuthorOrder column. Here's what our final query will look like:

```
INSERT INTO titleauthor (
    TitleID,
    AuthorID,
    AuthorOrder
    )
SELECT
    (
    SELECT TitleID
    FROM title
    WHERE TitleName = 'David Emptyfield'
    ) AS TitleID,
    (
    SELECT AuthorID
    FROM author
    WHERE FirstName = 'Whitney'
        AND LastName = 'Miller'
    ) AS AuthorID,
    1 AS AuthorOrder;
```

Again, the columns in the SELECT clause are aliased for readability. But the important part is that we have the columns in both the INSERT and SELECT parts of the query in matching order.

> **Try it now**
>
> If you haven't already done so, execute the SQL that inserts David Emptyfield into the title table (section 16.1.1) and Whitney Miller into the author table (section 16.1.3), followed by the INSERT statement that relates them in the titleauthor table. You'll use this data in chapter 17.

16.3 Inserting a row with variables

Now let's look at another way to insert data: using variables. In chapter 13, we worked with many SELECT queries that used variables, which are highly desirable for any kind of repeatable SQL we need to use. We can declare and use variables in an INSERT statement that uses SELECT to make easily repeatable SQL that needs only the variables changed. Here's an example that we can use to add A Table of Two Cities to the title table:

```
SET
    @TitleID = 112,
    @TitleName = 'A Table of Two Cities',
    @Price = 9.95,
    @Advance = 0.00,
    @Royalty = 15.00,
    @PublicationDate = '2022-08-07';

INSERT INTO title (
    TitleID,
    TitleName,
    Price,
    Advance,
    Royalty,
    PublicationDate
    )
VALUES (
    @TitleID,
    @TitleName,
    @Price,
    @Advance,
    @Royalty,
    @PublicationDate
    );
```

This example is only one way to use variables to insert data. If you've read chapter 13, I'm sure that you're already thinking of other ways to use variables to add data to tables in a database.

By learning how to add data with INSERT statements, you've started executing SQL statements that are categorized as data manipulation. *Data manipulation* refers to the process of changing data, and it applies not only to adding data but also to modifying or even removing data. In chapter 17, you'll expand your data-manipulation skills by learning how to modify and remove data.

16.4 Lab

1 Will this SQL, which has different alias column names from the table column names, execute successfully?

```
INSERT INTO titleauthor (
    TitleID,
    AuthorID,
    AuthorOrder
    )
SELECT
    (
    SELECT TitleID
    FROM title
    WHERE TitleName = 'David Emptyfield'
    ) AS TID,
    (
    SELECT AuthorID
    FROM author
    WHERE FirstName = 'Whitney'
        AND LastName = 'Miller'
    ) AS AID,
    1 AS AO;
```

2 Will this SQL, with no table column names specified, execute successfully?

```
INSERT INTO author
VALUES (
    13,
    'Jeff',
    'Iannucci'
    );
```

3 Insert a new row into the promotions table, using the following values:

- PromotionID—13
- PromotionCode—2OFF2022
- PromotionStartDate—May 1, 2022
- PromotionEndDate—May 15, 2022

4 Insert a new row into the customer table for Gianluca Rossi. The CustomerID should be 21, but all other information will be the same as that of Mia Rossi, whose CustomerID is 20. For this exercise, you should use SELECT instead of VALUES for the insert.

16.5   *Lab answers*

1 Yes. The column names, whether or not they're noted in the aliases in the SELECT clause, don't need to match the column names in the table where the data is being inserted. What matters is that you have the same number of columns with matching data types.

2 No. Execution of this query will result in an error message indicating that the column count doesn't match because the author table has four columns, and this query is attempting to insert values for only three values. This result is one reason why you should always specify the columns in the table into which the data is being inserted.

3 Your code should look something like this:

```
INSERT INTO promotion (
    PromotionID,
    PromotionCode,
    PromotionStartDate,
    PromotionEndDate
    )
VALUES (
    13,
    '2OFF2022',
    '2022-05-01 00:00:00',
    '2022-05-15 00:00:00'
    );
```

4 Although you could specify all the values being inserted for the new row with literal values, you could also copy the existing values where CustomerID=20 except CustomerID and FirstName, like this:

```
INSERT INTO customer (
    CustomerID,
    FirstName,
    LastName,
    Address,
    City,
    State,
    Zip,
    Country
    )
SELECT
    21,
    'Gianluca',
    LastName,
    Address,
    City,
    State,
    Zip,
    Country
FROM customer
WHERE CustomerID = 20;
```

17
Updating and deleting data

Chapter 16 discussed inserting new rows of data into tables and contained our first exercises for doing something with SQL other than reading data. The chapter also briefly mentioned that the INSERT keyword is one of several used for data manipulation.

This chapter examines two other ways of manipulating data: updating and deleting. Because SQL is designed to be intuitive for English speakers, we'll work with the keywords UPDATE and DELETE, respectively.

17.1 Updating values

Updating data is a bit different from inserting data, in that we're manipulating data at the column level instead of the row level. Recall that tables have rows, and rows have properties represented by columns. When we update data in SQL, we're updating the values of those properties, so we're making changes at the column level.

These changes may or may not include all columns in a given row, and they may or may not involve updating the values of one or more columns of every row in the table. The point is that we have many options for updating data in SQL. If this discussion is confusing, some examples may help you understand the options.

17.1.1 Working with data manipulation in real time

Before we begin, I want to draw your attention to a feature of SQL and relational databases that often catches people off guard. You may be accustomed to working with a word processor, a spreadsheet, or another application that contains some kind of data and saves your changes only when you click a particular button or press a certain series of keys. In these applications, if you make a mistake, you can always go back and undo the changes before you save them.

Unlike in those applications, any data manipulation you make in a relational database happens in real time and is permanent. If you have an "oops" moment, you have no way to undo the changes; they are committed instantly. This fact may seem alarming, but it's necessary to enable a relational database management system (RDBMS) to provide up-to-date data quickly and accurately to hundreds or thousands of users who are connected to and continually querying a database.

> **WARNING** It's important to understand that every data change we'll make in this chapter will happen in real time. The RDBMS has no Save button or keystroke.

Because these changes happen instantly and humans have a knack for making mistakes, the MySQL Workbench has a built-in safety feature called Safe Updates. Safe Updates is enabled by default, and it reduces the chance of an accidental data change that can affect every row in a table.

With Safe Updates enabled, for example, we can't make any updates that don't specify the key value of a table. Because our tables currently don't have key values, we need to disable this feature to make updates. If we don't, our SQL statements in this chapter will result in errors.

You have a few ways to disable this feature, but the most complete way is to choose Edit > Preferences in the top-left corner of the MySQL Workbench. This command opens the Workbench Preferences dialog box, shown in figure 17.1. Select SQL Editor in the pane on the left side; then clear the Safe Updates check box in the main pane. After clearing the check box, click OK to close the window, and then close and restart Workbench. Now that Safe Updates is disabled, we can begin (carefully) to update our data.

17.1.2 *Requirements for updates*

For our first example, we want to update the price of a single title, Pride and Predicates, from $9.95 to $8.95. As in so many statements in SQL, let's start with an English verbal declaration: "I would like to update the price of Pride and Predicates to $8.95."

This statement is a good starting point, and it's close to what the SQL will be, but we have to make a few changes to account for table and column names: "I would like to update the price to $8.95 where the title name is Pride and Predicates."

Our verbal statement is closer to the SQL. We have our filter ("where the title name is Pride and Predicates"), but we need to mention the table that contains the data. We do this by saying we want to update the table and then setting one or more column values to some other value: "I would like to update the title table. I would like to set the price to $8.95 where the title name is Pride and Predicates."

This verbal statement is perfect. Let's convert it to a SQL statement:

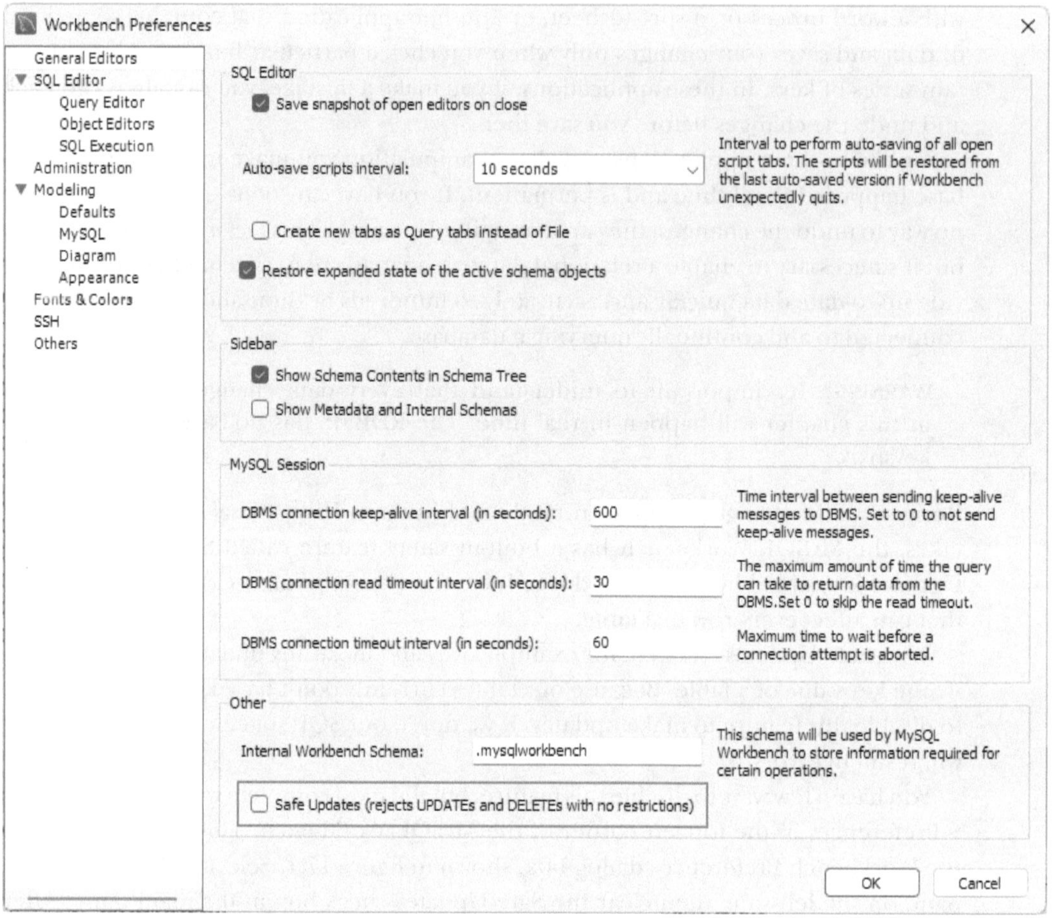

Figure 17.1   Safe Updates disabled in the Workbench Preferences dialog box

```
UPDATE title
SET Price = 8.95
WHERE TitleName = 'Pride and Predicates';
```

We have one new keyword, UPDATE, and one we've used with variables, SET. We use UPDATE to indicate the table in which data is to be updated, and we use SET to assign new values much the same way that we did when assigning values to variables. This UPDATE statement highlights the three requirements for any update and the order they must be in to create a valid SQL statement:

1 The table to be updated, using UPDATE

2 The column name(s) and new values to be assigned, using SET

3 The filter condition to determine which rows are to be updated, using WHERE in this case

WARNING   Although it's technically not required, the WHERE clause is perhaps the most critical. If you don't write *and execute* the filtering condition, you'll update *every* row in the table. Because these changes are made in real time, always take the utmost care to write and execute the filter to change only the values in the intended rows.

17.1.3 Updating values in one or more columns

As you may have noticed in the second requirement for update statements, you can update values in one or more columns. Much as you use commas to indicate multiple columns in a SELECT statement, you can use commas to indicate two or more desired updates in an UPDATE statement.

NOTE   All values to be changed in an UPDATE statement must be intended for the same table and meet the requirements of the filtering condition.

This example updates the Advance and Royalty values to 0 and 10, respectively, for the title Pride and Predicates:

```
UPDATE title
SET Advance = 0.00,
    Royalty = 10.00
WHERE TitleName = 'Pride and Predicates';
```

Although we're using the TitleName in our filtering condition, it's more common to use key values or some other unique identifier for UPDATE statements to ensure that we're updating the precise row or rows intended. Let's change our UPDATE statement to use the identifier TitleID, which for Pride and Predicates is 101:

```
UPDATE title
SET Advance = 0.00,
    Royalty = 10.00
WHERE TitleID = 101;
```

NOTE   If you executed the preceding two statements, you noticed that both of them succeeded but displayed different messages in the Output panel. Whereas the former statement displays "1 row(s) affected" and "Changed: 1," the latter statement displays "0 row(s) affected" and "Changed: 0." There was nothing to change with the second UPDATE statement because the Advance and Royalty values were already set to the intended values with the execution of the first UPDATE statement.

We can also use variables to create repeatable code as we did in chapter 16 with INSERT statements. In this example, we set all the values back to what they originally were for Pride and Predicates, using TitleID as the filter condition:

```
SET
    @TitleID = 101,
    @Price = 9.95,
    @Advance = 5000.00,
    @Royalty = 15.00;

UPDATE title
SET Price = @Price,
    Advance = @Advance,
    Royalty = @Royalty
WHERE TitleID = @TitleID;
```

> **Try it now**
>
> If you haven't already done so, execute the UPDATE statements you've seen so far in this chapter. Use a query such as SELECT * from title WHERE TitleID = 101; between the statements to verify that the changes occurred.

We can make one other change with an update: remove a value. Recall that every column for every row of a table in an RDBMS must have some representation of a value, so the only option we have to remove a value is to set it to NULL, which indicates the absence of a value.

Not every column allows null values, but we know at least one column in our database that does: the MiddleName column in the author table. If we want to set the Middle-Name for the first author to NULL, we'd write an UPDATE statement like this:

```
UPDATE author
SET MiddleName = NULL
WHERE AuthorID = 1;
```

These are our options for updating values with a basic UPDATE statement. Next, let's look at how to use an UPDATE statement to query multiple tables as part of our filtering condition.

17.1.4 *Updating values with a multitable query*

In chapter 8, I noted that a *predicate* is any part of a SQL statement that evaluates whether something is true, false, or unknown. Since that chapter, we've used predicates for filtering conditions, which included conditions in the FROM, WHERE, and HAVING clauses.

As you work with SQL, you'll likely need to write an UPDATE statement that requires filtering with a predicate that uses more than one table. This kind of SQL statement can be tricky because we can update values in only one table in an UPDATE statement, and we want to make sure that we do it correctly. We need a FROM clause to identify the filtering conditions, and we need to put it in the correct place in our SQL statement.

Unfortunately, we can put this predicate in multiple places in an UPDATE statement, depending on which RDBMS we're using. Although many uses of keywords are standardized for all RDBMSes, no standard exists for updating values in a query with multiple tables.

> **WARNING** Although this section contains examples of updating values in some popular RDBMSes other than MySQL, these examples are not comprehensive. Be sure to check the documentation of the RDBMS you use to confirm the correct syntax for these kinds of UPDATE statements.

Suppose that we want to update the price of any titles by a particular author in our sql-novel database in MySQL. We know the AuthorID, which is 12, but we don't have the TitleName or TitleID of any particular title. We also want to update the price to $8.95. To complete this update, we need to join at least two tables.

As a refresher, the relationship between the title and author tables is established through the titleauthor table. Rows are uniquely identified in the title table by TitleID and in the author table by AuthorID. The titleauthor table contains both TitleID and AuthorID columns in a many-to-many relationship because any author could write more than one title and any title could have more than one author.

Before we dive into the UPDATE statement, let's start with a SELECT query to see the value we intend to update. If we want to write a query that shows the Price for any titles by the author with the AuthorID of 12, we might write a query using joins in the FROM clause like this:

```
SELECT title.Price
FROM title
INNER JOIN titleauthor
    ON title.TitleID = titleauthor.TitleID
INNER JOIN author
    ON titleauthor.AuthorID = author.AuthorID
WHERE author.AuthorID = 12;
```

This query returns the value we intend to change, but we can make it a bit more readable by using table aliases, as discussed in chapter 8. Let's use some table aliases to reduce the wordiness of our query:

```
SELECT t.Price
FROM title t
INNER JOIN titleauthor ta
    ON t.TitleID = ta.TitleID
INNER JOIN author a
    ON ta.AuthorID = a.AuthorID
WHERE a.AuthorID = 12;
```

There—that's a bit easier to read. Savvy readers may also note that we don't need the author table in this query because the AuthorID value is also included in the title-author table. We can make our query simpler by removing any reference to the author table and filtering on AuthorID in the titleauthor table:

```
SELECT t.Price
FROM title t
INNER JOIN titleauthor ta
    ON t.TitleID = ta.TitleID
WHERE ta.AuthorID = 12;
```

Now that we have the foundation of a SELECT statement, we can easily change it to our desired UPDATE statement by removing the SELECT clause and replacing the FROM keyword with UPDATE. Then, after the UPDATE, we can use SET to set the values before the WHERE clause. Because we established table aliases in the preceding FROM clause, we can use the same table aliases in our query to indicate which table in our query is having data updated. Here's what our UPDATE statement will look like:

```
UPDATE title t
INNER JOIN titleauthor ta
    ON t.TitleID = ta.TitleID
SET t.Price = 8.95
WHERE ta.AuthorID = 12;
```

This example may be a bit confusing because we split the predicate into two separate parts of our query, with the joining of tables in the update before the SET and the rest of the filtering after the SET in the WHERE clause. Again, this method of updating is specific to MySQL.

> **NOTE** The following examples are for common RDBMSes other than MySQL. These examples are provided to show differences and are not intended to be executed in MySQL. If you attempt to execute them, they'll result in failed queries and error messages.

If our database used PostgreSQL, we'd still indicate the table to be updated and any alias in the UPDATE portion of our query, but we'd use the FROM clause to join any additional tables. The following query works in PostgreSQL but not MySQL:

```
UPDATE title t
SET t.Price = 8.95
FROM titleauthor ta
WHERE t.TitleID = ta.TitleID
    AND ta.AuthorID = 12;
```

If our database was in a SQL Server instance, the logic might make a bit more sense compared with the SELECT query. In SQL Server, we'd simply replace the SELECT with the UPDATE and SET parts and leave the FROM and WHERE clauses unchanged. The following query works in SQL Server but not in MySQL:

```
UPDATE title t
SET t.Price = 8.95
FROM title t
INNER JOIN titleauthor ta
```

```
    ON t.TitleID = ta.TitleID
WHERE ta.AuthorID = 12;
```

The point is that although you can use joins for filtering in an UPDATE statement, each RDBMS has its own syntax for these kinds of queries. Unfortunately, this example is one of those rare parts of learning SQL that require you to venture beyond this book to learn the syntax of the RDBMS you're using.

17.2 Deleting rows

When we delete data using SQL, we're effectively doing the opposite of what an INSERT statement does. Whereas INSERT adds one or more rows to a table, DELETE removes one or more rows. Also, as with INSERT and UPDATE statements, we can change data in only one table per DELETE statement.

17.2.1 Deleting one or more rows

As we've done so many times, let's start with a verbal declaration. Suppose that we want to delete the row from the title table in which TitleID = 110. We might start with a verbal declaration like this: "I would like to delete any rows from the title table where the TitleID is 110." Our SQL statement is very close to this statement, using a new keyword, DELETE:

```
DELETE
FROM title
WHERE TitleID = 110;
```

As with INSERT and UPDATE statements, we're starting our statement with a data-manipulation keyword, which in this case is DELETE. Next, we identify the table from which we intend to delete data. Finally, we indicate the filtering to be used so that we delete only the intended rows.

> **WARNING** As with UPDATE statements, the WHERE clause isn't required but is perhaps the most critical part of our query. If you don't write *and execute* this filtering condition, you'll delete every row in the table. As you can imagine, this result can be catastrophic. Because these changes occur in real time, always take the utmost care to write and execute the filter to delete only the intended rows.

We can also use variables, of course, to make repeatable SQL statements for a query like this example. Here's how we'd do this for the preceding query:

```
SET @TitleID = 110;

DELETE
FROM title
WHERE TitleID = @TitleID;
```

> **TIP** Some RDBMSes allow the omission of the FROM keyword in DELETE statements like these, but you should use it anyway. Although it's best to reduce

the wordiness of queries whenever possible, omitting one word doesn't reduce wordiness significantly. Moreover, if you migrate your query from one RDBMS to another later, omitting the word FROM could result in a query that doesn't work.

17.2.2   *Deleting a row with a multitable query*

As discussed in section 17.1.4, the syntax for an UPDATE statement that joins multiple tables in the predicate varies depending on the RDBMS you're using. Unfortunately, the syntax for a DELETE statement can also vary from one RDBMS to another. The good news is that the syntax doesn't vary quite as much because MySQL, SQL Server, and MariaDB have the same syntax.

Even better news: this syntax is remarkably similar to a SELECT statement. In section 17.1.4, we created this SELECT statement before writing SQL for an UPDATE statement for a title that related to AuthorID 12:

```
SELECT t.Price
FROM title t
INNER JOIN titleauthor ta
    ON t.TitleID = ta.TitleID
WHERE ta.AuthorID = 12;
```

If we want to delete the row in the title table instead of updating the value for Price, we'd simply replace the SELECT clause with a DELETE that noted the table with rows to be deleted, like this:

```
DELETE t
FROM title t
INNER JOIN titleauthor ta
    ON t.TitleID = ta.TitleID
WHERE ta.AuthorID = 12;
```

Again, this syntax works in MySQL and a few other RDBMSes, but not all. Please refer to the documentation of the particular RDBMS you're using for the correct syntax to delete rows using a predicate that joins multiple tables.

17.2.3   *Deleting all rows in a table*

As noted in the warning in section 17.2.1, if a DELETE statement is executed without a WHERE clause, it can remove all the rows from a table. I say "can" because as mentioned in chapter 16, databases are often designed with certain constraints, including those that allow or prevent the insertion of certain values into a table. Those constraints can allow or prevent the deletion of rows as well.

If we don't have these constraints, and the tables in our database currently don't, we can remove all the rows in a table by executing a DELETE statement that has no filtering condition. We don't want to delete all the rows from the tables in our database, but for the sake of practice, we can execute this query on the myfirstquery table we used in chapter 2 with minimal effect on any future exercises. Here's what that query would look like:

```
DELETE
FROM myfirstquery;
```

As expected, executing this query results in the deletion of all rows in the myfirstquery table. We also have a more efficient way to remove all rows from a table, a way that's available in nearly every RDBMS: TRUNCATE TABLE.

Unlike removing all rows with a DELETE statement, which scans every row in a table and deletes them one at a time, TRUNCATE TABLE deletes rows without scanning them individually. This statement is designed for speed.

The syntax for TRUNCATE TABLE is simple. If we want to truncate the myfirstquery table, our SQL statement would look like this:

```
TRUNCATE TABLE myfirstquery;
```

The TRUNCATE TABLE statement has a lot less flexibility than a DELETE statement because it's designed for the single purpose of removing all rows from a table quickly. It can't be used to remove one row or some rows. Also, the same problems with constraints that can prevent a DELETE statement from deleting rows can prevent TRUNCATE TABLE from executing successfully.

> **Try it now**
>
> Use the preceding DELETE and TRUNCATE TABLE statements to remove all the rows from the myfirstquery table. If you want to test deleting multiple rows, try executing one or more INSERT statements to add rows to the myfirstquery table.

17.3 One big tip for data manipulation

In section 17.1.4, we wrote a SELECT statement to find the data to update. Although we did this to compare the basic structure of the SELECT statement with our UPDATE statement, we could just as easily have used this SELECT statement to validate which rows were going to be updated.

Two warnings in this chapter caution against accidentally updating or deleting all data in a table. I could have included even more warnings about updating the wrong data through incorrect logic for filtering contained in the predicates of UPDATE and DELETE statements. Remember that all changes occur in real time, so use caution when updating and deleting data.

One significant and common way to exercise caution is to write and execute a SELECT statement that uses the same logic contained in an UPDATE or DELETE statement. Doing this allows you to see what data will be affected before you execute your data-manipulation statement. I can tell you from experience that this approach—selecting data through a query first—has saved me and countless others from catastrophic results.

Although there's no way to undo an executed query, you can always proactively review the affected rows using a SELECT. I highly recommend selecting data with your filtering conditions, no matter how experienced you become in writing SQL.

17.4   Lab

1   Using what you learned in chapter 16, write and execute a query to add your name and address to the customer table. Use the value 22 for CustomerID. (Hint: You can drag and drop column names from the Navigator panel in MySQL Workbench.)

2   Write and execute a query to update the address of the row you just added to an address at which you previously resided (or any other address).

3   Write and execute a query to delete the row you inserted and updated in the customer table, but use a SELECT first to confirm that your SQL statement will produce the correct results.

17.5   Lab answers

1   Your query to insert a row into the customer table might look something like this:

```
INSERT customer (
    CustomerID,
    FirstName,
    LastName,
    Address,
    City,
    State,
    Zip,
    Country
)
VALUES (
    22,
    'Jeff',
    'Iannucci',
    '1600 Pennsylvania Ave NW',
    'Washington',
    'DC',
    '20500',
    'USA'
    );
```

2   Your query to update your address in the customer table might look something like this:

```
UPDATE customer
SET Address = '1700 W Washington St',
    City = 'Phoenix',
```

```
      State = 'AZ',
      Zip = '85007'
WHERE CustomerID = 22;
```

3 Your query to delete your row from the customer table might look something like this:

```
DELETE
FROM customer
WHERE CustomerID = 22;
```

Storing data in tables

18

In chapters 16 and 17, we started creating and manipulating data, and in this chapter, we'll examine ways to create and manipulate the tables themselves. In many ways, we'll be getting to the core of SQL language and its use because how the data is stored in tables is at the very heart of any relational database management system (RDBMS). Choosing how data is stored is one of the most important—perhaps *the* most important decision—that is made in any database.

Don't worry; this chapter won't be overly technical. It will still be easy enough for anyone to understand, and because you've been querying data with SQL statements that often mirror the English language for a while now, I'm confident that you'll find the concepts and commands easy to comprehend. This chapter should also reinforce your understanding of things like primary keys and data types.

18.1 Creating a table

As you'll soon see, creating a table in SQL can be very simple. First, though, you must consider a few things about the table before you write the SQL that creates the table.

18.1.1 Considerations before creating a table

The first step in creating a table is answering three basic questions about the table:

- What is the name of the table?

- What are the names of the columns that will be included in the table?
- What are the data types of those columns?

We'll have to put some thought into these names and data types, especially as they relate to existing tables in the database. We want the names to be explanatory, but we can't use a table name if there's already a table with that name.

We can reuse column names from other tables, however, as we've seen with the sql-novel database: OrderID, TitleID, and other column names appear in more than one table. But we usually want to do that only if some relationship exists between similarly named columns.

> **TIP** The idea of having similar names is one reason why I've used names such as OrderID and TitleID in the sqlnovel database. One day, you may work with a database containing many tables that have columns named ID or Name, which can be a bit confusing due to ambiguity. As you create tables, try to make column names meaningful, clear, obvious, and easy to understand for anyone else who may have to query the data.

As an exercise, we want to create a table for categories of the titles. Although we could avoid creating a new table by adding a Category column in the title table for a string of characters such as "Mystery" or "Romance," we know from the discussion of table relationships in chapter 8 that this approach isn't the best one to take in an RDBMS. (Later in this chapter, we'll add a column to the title table, but that column will relate to the primary key of a new table.)

For our new table of categories, we need to have only two columns: an ID column to serve as the primary key and a column to define the name of each category. We can keep the table name and columns consistent with the rest of our database by naming the table category and the columns CategoryID and CategoryName.

The ID column of a table is often defined as an integer data type, which is known as `int`. The `int` data type allows us to use a unique number for each row—usually up to numbers in the billions. I don't think this table will have billions of categories, so an integer data type should accommodate CategoryID. We could use some other integer data types—such as `tinyint`, `smallint`, `mediumint`, and `bigint`—but because they aren't included in every RDBMS, we'll use the universal `int` data type.

Columns with name values of varying length, such as CategoryName, are typically defined as a variable character type, known as `varchar`. This data type accounts for the fact that not every value will be the same length (number of characters). When we use this data type, our data is stored more efficiently than it would be if we'd used a `char` (character) data type because that data type stores the data using the entire defined length.

Although defining the maximum length isn't required for `varchar` data types, we typically want to do this to avoid using an inefficient default value, which will vary depending on our RDBMS. The values in our CategoryName column won't be more than 20 characters, so we'll define the data type as `varchar(20)`.

NOTE As you converse with other people about SQL, you'll discover that there's no common way to pronounce *varchar*. Pronunciations vary from "var-char" to "var-kar" to "vair-kair." The last option is most likely to be correct because the vowels match the pronunciation of the first syllables in *variable character*, but I've found that it's also the least likely to be used. Try not to get too confused by this situation. As the French say, *vive la différence*.

18.1.2 Creating a table

Now that we've defined our table name, column names, and column data types, let's say in English what we intend to do: "I would like to create a table named category. I would like the table to have a column named CategoryID that is an int data type. I would like the table to also have a column named CategoryName that is a varchar(20) data type." After all that, here's what the SQL to create our category table will look like:

```
CREATE TABLE category (
    CategoryID int,
    CategoryName varchar(20)
    );
```

Notice that after we define the table name with CREATE TABLE, we include all columns with a comma separating the names and data types of each column. This format should be a bit intuitive now that we've used commas to separate columns in SELECT and ORDER BY clauses. Also notice that the columns are enclosed in parentheses. Omitting the parentheses when using CREATE TABLE can be a common mistake for beginners, so remember to include them when creating a table.

Executing the preceding SQL won't return any results in the Results panel, but in the Output panel, you should see a green circle with a white check mark and the message "0 rows(s) affected." Although the panel doesn't show a lot of detail, it tells you that the table was created successfully.

Creating a table in this way is just a basic starting point. As we'll see later in this chapter and in subsequent chapters, the CREATE TABLE statement gives us quite a few options for adding more properties to a table. For now, we'll move to the next step, using what we learned about the INSERT keyword in chapter 16.

18.1.3 Adding values to an empty table

Our customer table is empty, so next, we want to insert the CategoryID and CategoryName values for the following categories:

1 Romance
2 Humor
3 Mystery
4 Fantasy
5 Science Fiction

Chapter 16 discussed adding multiple values to a table by using the INSERT and VALUES keywords. Let's use similar logic to insert these listed values into our new category table:

```
INSERT INTO category (CategoryID, CategoryName)
VALUES
    (1, 'Romance'),
    (2, 'Humor'),
    (3, 'Mystery'),
    (4, 'Fantasy'),
    (5, 'Science Fiction');
```

Executing the preceding SQL won't return anything in the Results panel, but if the execution is successful, we should see "5 row(s) affected" in the Message column of the Output panel. This message indicates that we added five rows to our category table, which was our intention.

> **Try it now**
>
> If you haven't created and populated the category table yet, execute the SQL in sections 18.1.2 and 18.1.3 to do so. You'll be using this table in this chapter and in subsequent chapters.

We can verify that we added the desired values to the category table by running a simple SELECT query to see the values in the table (results shown in figure 18.1):

```
SELECT
    CategoryID,
    CategoryName
FROM category;
```

CategoryID	CategoryName
1	Romance
2	Humor
3	Mystery
4	Fantasy
5	Science Fiction

Figure 18.1   All rows in the new category table

18.2   Altering a table

The next step in adding a category for each title is adding a new column to the title table that relates to the values in our new category table. Specifically, we want to relate the CategoryID values from the title table to those in the category table. We'll do this by adding a CategoryID column to our title table.

18.2.1   Adding a column to a table

Just as we had to consider three questions before creating a table, we need to consider three questions before adding a column:

- What is the name of the table we are adding the new column to?
- What are the names of the columns that will be added to the table?
- What are the data types of those columns?

We know that the answer to the first question is the title table. Because we want consistency in names and data types, the answers to the second and third questions are related to the CategoryID column in the category table: CategoryID and int, respectively.

To make these and other changes in a table in SQL, we'll use a new command: ALTER TABLE. Although the syntax of this command is similar to that of CREATE TABLE, it doesn't require us to use parentheses. Here's the SQL to add the column to the title table:

```
ALTER TABLE title
ADD CategoryID int;
```

As with our CREATE TABLE statement in section 18.1.2, we won't have any results from this query. The success of this query is noted in the Output panel only by a white check mark in a green circle and the message "0 row(s) affected."

Let's run a quick query to validate that the column was created, noting the results in figure 18.2 that show the column was created after all the other columns:

```
SELECT *
FROM title;
```

TitleID	TitleName	Price	Advance	Royalty	PublicationDate	CategoryID
101	Pride and Predicates	9.95	5000.00	15.00	2015-04-30 00:00:00	NULL
102	The Join Luck Club	9.95	6000.00	12.00	2016-02-06 00:00:00	NULL
103	Catcher in the Try	8.95	5000.00	10.00	2017-04-03 00:00:00	NULL
104	Anne of Fact Tables	12.95	10000.00	15.00	2018-01-12 00:00:00	NULL
105	The DateTime Machine	7.95	5500.00	15.00	2019-02-04 00:00:00	NULL
106	The Great GroupBy	10.95	0.00	20.00	2019-12-23 00:00:00	NULL
107	The Call of the While	8.95	2500.00	15.00	2020-03-14 00:00:00	NULL
108	The Sum Also Rises	7.95	5000.00	12.00	2021-11-12 00:00:00	NULL
109	David Emptyfield	9.95	0.00	10.00	2022-01-16 00:00:00	NULL
110	Red Badge of Cursors	7.95	0.00	15.00	2022-03-29 00:00:00	NULL
111	Of Mice and Metadata	8.95	0.00	12.00	2022-05-17 00:00:00	NULL
112	A Table of Two Cities	9.95	0.00	15.00	2022-08-07 00:00:00	NULL

Figure 18.2   The title table with the new CategoryID column at far right

Our new column doesn't contain any values yet, so the results of our query show NULL for every row. To add the values, we'll use UPDATE statements. Although we used INSERT to add values to our category table, INSERT adds a new row to a table. We don't want to do that here; we want to add a value for a single column to the existing rows, which UPDATE allows.

Let's add these values for all rows based on the category of each title. In case you didn't memorize all the CategoryID and CategoryName values or don't feel like flipping back a few pages, the following SQL has comments to remind you:

```
/* 1 - Romance */
UPDATE title
SET CategoryID = 1
WHERE TitleID IN (101, 104);

/* 2 - Humor */
UPDATE title
SET CategoryID = 2
WHERE TitleID IN (106, 109);

/* 3 - Mystery */
UPDATE title
SET CategoryID = 3
WHERE TitleID IN (102, 103, 110);

/* 4 - Fantasy */
UPDATE title
SET CategoryID = 4
WHERE TitleID IN (107, 112);

/* 5 - Science Fiction */
UPDATE title
SET CategoryID = 5
WHERE TitleID IN (105, 108, 111);
```

After we execute all the preceding UPDATE statements, we should see values for the CategoryID column in all rows. Let's execute our query to return all rows of the title table, verifying in figure 18.3 that all values for CategoryID are now populated:

```
SELECT *
FROM title;
```

TitleID	TitleName	Price	Advance	Royalty	PublicationDate	CategoryID
101	Pride and Predicates	9.95	5000.00	15.00	2015-04-30 00:00:00	1
102	The Join Luck Club	9.95	6000.00	12.00	2016-02-06 00:00:00	3
103	Catcher in the Try	8.95	5000.00	10.00	2017-04-03 00:00:00	3
104	Anne of Fact Tables	12.95	10000.00	15.00	2018-01-12 00:00:00	1
105	The DateTime Machine	7.95	5500.00	15.00	2019-02-04 00:00:00	5
106	The Great GroupBy	10.95	0.00	20.00	2019-12-23 00:00:00	2
107	The Call of the While	8.95	2500.00	15.00	2020-03-14 00:00:00	4
108	The Sum Also Rises	7.95	5000.00	12.00	2021-11-12 00:00:00	5
109	David Emptyfield	9.95	0.00	10.00	2022-01-16 00:00:00	2
110	Red Badge of Cursors	7.95	0.00	15.00	2022-03-29 00:00:00	3
111	Of Mice and Metadata	8.95	0.00	12.00	2022-05-17 00:00:00	5
112	A Table of Two Cities	9.95	0.00	15.00	2022-08-07 00:00:00	4

Figure 18.3   The title table with the CategoryID populated with values for all rows

We've confirmed that we added the values for CategoryID, but those values don't tell us directly what the category names for each title are. Let's show the CategoryName for each TitleName by writing a query that relates the title and category tables by CategoryID. This relationship is established with an INNER JOIN (discussed in chapter 8). The results in figure 18.4 confirm the category for each title, ordered by TitleID:

```
SELECT
    t.TitleID,
    t.TitleName,
    c.CategoryName
FROM title t
INNER JOIN category c
    ON t.CategoryID = c.CategoryID
ORDER BY t.TitleID;
```

TitleID	TitleName	CategoryName
101	Pride and Predicates	Romance
102	The Join Luck Club	Mystery
103	Catcher in the Try	Mystery
104	Anne of Fact Tables	Romance
105	The DateTime Machine	Science Fiction
106	The Great GroupBy	Humor
107	The Call of the While	Fantasy
108	The Sum Also Rises	Science Fiction
109	David Emptyfield	Humor
110	Red Badge of Cursors	Mystery
111	Of Mice and Metadata	Science Fiction
112	A Table of Two Cities	Fantasy

Figure 18.4   The CategoryName for every TitleName in the title table, related by CategoryID

18.2.2 Considerations before adding a column

Adding a category for each title can be relatively simple, but as with creating a table, we have a few things to consider before adding new columns to tables.

When a column is added to a table, a SQL novice may be bothered by the fact that the new column is added at the end of all the other columns. A new column is always added at the end, although some RDBMSes (such as MySQL) allow us to change the order of the columns. This change, however, is generally discouraged for tables that already contain data.

There are two main reasons for adding columns only at the end of all other columns:

- Adding a new column before any other columns requires a lot of extra activity to rearrange the data, using more resources than adding the column at the end. When we add the column at the end, we minimize the amount of activity and resources that will be required.

- Generally, it's unnecessary to position columns in a certain order for a table. As we've already seen, we can order columns for display however we like in our SQL queries.

The one exception to adding a column at the end occurs when we create a new column to be used in the primary key of a table. We generally want that column to come first because the primary key often defines the way that data is ordered in a table. Although I've referred to primary keys since chapter 8, section 18.3 takes a deeper look at how to create and use them.

18.3 Primary keys

This book is designed to get you up to speed gradually with writing SQL queries, so I haven't discussed primary keys much. But because now I'm talking about designing tables and relating data, it's time to revisit that topic.

18.3.1 *Considerations for primary keys*

The primary key is the backbone of any RDBMS because it ensures that the data in tables is relatable. With primary keys, we have to adhere to a few rules:

- *A primary key must be unique.* This rule is the most important one. If the primary key isn't unique, we'll never know which row in a relationship is the correct one. Suppose that we assigned a value of 1 to the CategoryID column for each of the five rows in our new category table. If all five rows had the same value, we couldn't possibly determine the correct CategoryName for any relationship in which the CategoryID is 1.

- *Every row must have a value for the primary key.* As we've seen, we can't join a value of NULL to any value, including other values of NULL. For this reason, if any row in a table has NULL as a primary-key value, that row can never be related to any other data.

- *The primary key's values can never change.* We use primary key values to relate to other tables, much as we used CategoryID values to relate to the title table. If we changed the CategoryID values in the category table in any way, such as by adding 10 to the existing value, the values in the two tables wouldn't match, and the relationship between the two tables would no longer exist.

Adhering to these three rules allows relationships that use primary keys to maintain *referential integrity*, which means that any value from one table that refers to the primary key value in another table will always refer to the same value in the table that contains the primary key. Although the values for other columns in our table can change (we could change a CategoryName from Mystery to Mystery Thriller, for example), the values for the primary key can never change.

18.3.2 *Adding a primary key*

Now that we know the rules for any primary key, we can create one for our category table. To do this, we can use the same ALTER TABLE statement that we used to add a column, with some slight differences:

```
ALTER TABLE category
ADD CONSTRAINT PRIMARY KEY (CategoryID);
```

There are two notable differences between adding a column and adding a primary key with ALTER TABLE. First, we used the word CONSTRAINT when noting that we were adding a primary key. I haven't explicitly said it before, but a primary key is a kind of *constraint*—an object designed to enforce a rule of some sort. Therefore, we can't break the rules of the constraint after it's created. With this new PRIMARY KEY constraint, we must adhere to the rules concerning the category table outlined in section 18.3.1.

Although doing so isn't required, it's common to give a primary key a logical name. The reason is that you may create other objects in your table that have different constraints, and you'll want the names of these objects to indicate their purpose. Just as we give tables obvious names for their data, such as customer and author, we want to give our primary keys obvious names. Moreover, as you'll see later in this chapter, assigning a name to a primary key (or any other kind of constraint) makes it much easier to manipulate if you have to change or delete it later.

A common way to name primary keys is to use the naming convention PK_, which is the PK prefix followed by an underscore and the table name. Even if you know nothing about a particular database, if you saw any reference to an object named PK_category, you'd understand it to be the PRIMARY KEY constraint of a table named category. For this reason, it's desirable to create our primary key with a name:

```
ALTER TABLE category
ADD CONSTRAINT PK_category PRIMARY KEY (CategoryID);
```

Try it now

Create the PRIMARY KEY constraint for the category table with the preceding SQL statement.

Although here, you're adding the primary key to an existing table, most of the time, you'll add the primary key when you create the table. You can accomplish this task easily by defining the primary key in the CREATE TABLE statement after defining the columns, almost as though you were adding another column. You could have created the category table with the primary key defined by using the following SQL:

```
CREATE TABLE category (
    CategoryID int,
    CategoryName varchar(20),
    CONSTRAINT PK_category PRIMARY KEY (CategoryID)
    );
```

TIP Although it isn't necessary to create a primary key for every table in every database, a primary key belongs in any table that has (for lack of a better phrase) a group of unique entities. Tables with rows that represent unique entities such as products, orders, and customers should always have a primary key to ensure that those rows are unique.

One final note about primary keys: they can consist of more than one column. Our orderitem table, for example, should have a primary key that includes both OrderID and ItemID because together, these columns form a unique key. Multiple rows may have the same OrderID, but each of those rows should also have a unique ItemID for every row that includes the same OrderID.

To create a primary key with multiple columns in a table such as orderitem, we'd use a comma separator when specifying the columns, like this:

```
ALTER TABLE orderitem
ADD CONSTRAINT PK_orderitem PRIMARY KEY (OrderID, OrderItem);
```

Using primary keys allows us to ensure that we can identify each row in a table as unique. Because these rows are often referred to by other tables in relationships, we can explicitly define these relationships with another kind of constraint: the foreign key.

18.4 Foreign keys and constraints

Foreign keys are established to enforce the rules of any relationship between two tables with respect to a common column. Any foreign-key relationship involves a *parent table*, where the key values originate, and *child tables*, which contain values that refer to the parent table. Put simply, we create a foreign key on a child table to enforce the rule that the values in the child table must exist in the parent table.

18.4.1 Data diagrams

Data diagrams can help us understand the relationships between tables in our database by depicting these relationships visually. Figure 18.5 is a data diagram of all the tables in the sqlnovel database, including our new category table.

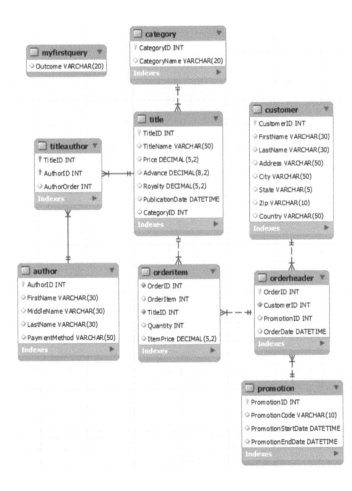

Figure 18.5 A data diagram that shows all tables in the sqlnovel database and their relationships to other tables

Each box in this diagram represents a table, and each box contains a list of all columns and data types for that table. We want to focus on the lines between the boxes, which represent the relationships. If a line between two tables exists, a foreign key from one table to another exists.

Although the data diagram in figure 18.5 doesn't show the specific columns involved in the relationships, you can find out what they are by examining the tables closely. If you follow through and execute the prescribed exercises throughout this chapter and in the lab section, you'll see how to create your own data diagram.

One other thing to note: the myfirstquery table has no lines connecting it to other tables. That table has no relationship to any other tables in the database because it was used only to get you started with your first query in chapter 2. You've come a long way since then!

18.4.2 Adding a foreign-key constraint

Because a functional foreign key requires another type of constraint, we'll use an ALTER TABLE statement similar to the one we used to create the PRIMARY KEY constraint. As with the primary key, we want to give our FOREIGN KEY constraint a logical name. A common approach is to use a name in the format FK_, which is the FK prefix followed by an underscore, the name of the child table, another underscore, and the name of the parent table. This format ensures that the name of our FOREIGN KEY constraint will be unique in the database. Using this naming convention, we can create our FOREIGN KEY constraint with the following statement:

```
ALTER TABLE title
ADD CONSTRAINT FK_title_category
FOREIGN KEY (CategoryID) REFERENCES category(CategoryID);
```

> **Try it now**
>
> Create the FOREIGN KEY constraint on the title table with the preceding SQL statement.

This statement is a bit different from the one we used to create the PRIMARY KEY constraint because we're creating a key relationship between two columns in different tables. The first column, after the keywords FOREIGN KEY, indicates the column on the child table that will reference another column in the parent table, which is why we use the REFERENCES keyword.

We want to be careful when we create constraints—PRIMARY KEY, FOREIGN KEY, or otherwise—on tables that already contain data because if the current values don't meet the rules of our constraint, we'll get an error. For this reason, it's best to create constraints on tables when we create the table and before we insert any rows of data.

TIP Although this chapter uses common conventions to name constraints, these aren't the only ways to name constraints. When you work outside the sqlnovel database, consider whether the database you're working with already uses defined naming conventions. If so, create your objects using the existing naming conventions so that your object names are consistent with the names of other objects in the database.

18.5 Deleting a table, column, or constraint

Although we want to keep the objects we've created in this chapter, if we want to undo our work, we can do so with statements that use the DROP keyword.

WARNING The SQL in this section is provided for informational purposes only. You don't want to drop the category table or any of its related columns and constraints because you'll be using this data throughout the remainder of the book. If you decide that you want to practice dropping these objects despite this warning, you'll have to go back through this chapter to re-create them.

With that warning out of the way, here's how we could remove the objects we have created in this chapter.

18.5.1 Deleting a constraint

As with adding a constraint, deleting any constraint involves the ALTER TABLE statement. Because we're dropping our constraint, not defining anything, we need only the names of the table and the constraint that we're dropping. In this case, we'd use the following SQL:

```
ALTER TABLE title
DROP FOREIGN KEY FK_title_category;
```

If we want to delete the PK_category primary key of our category table, we could do that in either of two ways. The first way is to remove it as a constraint, like this:

```
ALTER TABLE category
DROP CONSTRAINT PK_category;
```

Because the primary key is a special kind of constraint, however, we could use ALTER TABLE to say that we want to remove the primary key without supplying the name of the constraint:

```
ALTER TABLE category
DROP PRIMARY KEY;
```

NOTE We don't need to specify the name of the primary key in the statement because the table can have only one primary key.

18.5.2 Deleting a column

In this chapter, we created a column in the title table. To remove that column, we'd use ALTER TABLE and DROP:

```
ALTER TABLE title
DROP COLUMN CategoryID;
```

As with dropping constraints, we typically don't need more than the names of the table and column to remove a column.

18.5.3 Deleting a table

Deleting a table involves the least SQL of any of our object-removal scripts. We use DROP TABLE with the table name:

```
DROP TABLE category;
```

> **NOTE**   If we want to remove all these objects, we'd need to do it in the order in section 18.5, removing the constraints first. If we want to drop the table or column first, most RDBMSes (including MySQL) would return an error message saying that the object can't be dropped because of these constraints.

That's enough discussion of removing objects. Let's start the lab, where we can practice creating constraints such as primary keys and foreign keys.

18.6   Lab

1 The sqlnovel database is missing a few primary keys. Using the data diagram in section 18.4.1 and the naming conventions in section 18.3.2, write and execute SQL statements to add PRIMARY KEY constraints for the following tables:

- author
- customer
- orderheader
- promotion
- title
- titleauthor

2 The orderitem table isn't included in the preceding list. What happen if you try to create a PRIMARY KEY constraint on the OrderID and OrderItem columns? How can you resolve this problem?

3 The sqlnovel database is also missing a few FOREIGN KEY constraints. Using the data diagram in section 18.4.1 and the naming conventions in section 18.4.2, write and execute SQL statements to add FOREIGN KEY constraints for the following tables and columns:

- The CustomerID column of the orderheader table
- The PromotionID column of the orderheader table
- The OrderID column of the orderitem table
- The TitleID column of the orderitem table
- The TitleID column of the titleauthor table
- The AuthorID column of the titleauthor table

4 If you've successfully completed all the preceding tasks, now is your chance to enjoy your work. Create a data diagram. In MySQL Workbench, choose Database > Reverse Engineer. Click Next in all the following screens, and be sure to select the sqlnovel check box in the Select Schemas screen. When you're done, you should have a data diagram of the sqlnovel database.

18.7   Lab answers

1 You can create PRIMARY KEY constraints for these tables with the following SQL statements:

```
ALTER TABLE author
    ADD CONSTRAINT PK_author PRIMARY KEY (AuthorID);
ALTER TABLE customer
    ADD CONSTRAINT PK_customer PRIMARY KEY (CustomerID);
ALTER TABLE orderheader
    ADD CONSTRAINT PK_orderheader PRIMARY KEY (OrderID);
ALTER TABLE promotion
    ADD CONSTRAINT PK_promotion PRIMARY KEY (PromotionID);
ALTER TABLE title
    ADD CONSTRAINT PK_title PRIMARY KEY (TitleID);
ALTER TABLE titleauthor
    ADD CONSTRAINT PK_titleauthor PRIMARY KEY (TitleID, AuthorID);
```

2 The statement that creates the PRIMARY KEY constraint on orderitem looks like this:

```
ALTER TABLE orderitem
    ADD CONSTRAINT PK_orderitem PRIMARY KEY (OrderID, ItemID);
```

If you execute this statement, however, the Output window displays the error message "Error Code: 1062. Duplicate entry '1022-1' for key 'orderitem.PRIMARY'." This error message indicates a data inconsistency in what would be your primary key, and it tells you where that error is. The error is for OrderID 1022 and OrderItem 1. You can see the problem by executing the following query, which should return one row but instead returns two rows (figure 18.6):

OrderID	OrderItem	TitleID	Quantity	ItemPrice
1022	1	101	1	7.95
1022	1	103	1	6.95

Figure 18.6   The two rows that prevent the primary key from being created for the orderitem table

```
SELECT *
FROM orderitem
WHERE OrderID = 1022
    AND OrderItem = 1;
```

There are two rows that would result in duplicate values for our primary key, which isn't allowed. All key values must be unique. Fortunately, these rows don't appear to be actual duplicates because they have different TitleID values. You can safely correct this data error with an UPDATE statement, changing the OrderItem value from 1 to 2 for one of the rows:

```
UPDATE orderitem
SET OrderItem = 2
WHERE OrderID = 1022
    AND OrderItem = 1
    AND TitleID = 103;
```

After executing the preceding UPDATE statement, you should be able to create the primary key for the orderitem table. Create that PRIMARY KEY constraint.

3   You can create the FOREIGN KEY constraints for these tables and columns with the following SQL statements:

```
ALTER TABLE orderheader
    ADD CONSTRAINT FK_orderheader_customer FOREIGN KEY (CustomerID)
    REFERENCES customer(CustomerID);
ALTER TABLE orderheader
    ADD CONSTRAINT FK_orderheader_promotion FOREIGN KEY (PromotionID)
    REFERENCES promotion(PromotionID);
ALTER TABLE orderitem
    ADD CONSTRAINT FK_orderitem_orderheader FOREIGN KEY (OrderID)
    REFERENCES orderheader(OrderID);
ALTER TABLE orderitem
    ADD CONSTRAINT FK_orderitem_title FOREIGN KEY (TitleID)
    REFERENCES title(TitleID);
ALTER TABLE titleauthor
    ADD CONSTRAINT FK_titleauthor_title FOREIGN KEY (TitleID)
    REFERENCES title(TitleID);
ALTER TABLE titleauthor
    ADD CONSTRAINT FK_titleauthor_author FOREIGN KEY (AuthorID)
    REFERENCES author(AuthorID);
```

4   There's no correct answer if you created the data diagram successfully. Have fun moving around the tables to make the lines representing the relationships clearer, and be sure to hover over the lines to see how they highlight the columns represented in the relationships.

Creating constraints and indexes

We talked about two important constraints in chapter 18: PRIMARY KEY and FOREIGN KEY constraints. This chapter looks at a few more constraints that help us ensure the integrity of the data in our tables.

We'll also discuss *indexes*, which are table-related objects that help with the performance of our queries. Just as indexes in books like this one can help you quickly find the subject you're looking for, indexes in a database can reduce the time it takes queries to find specific data.

I hope that you've enjoyed creating tables and associated constraints because you're about to create more.

19.1 Constraints

By completing the examples in chapter 18, you learned that you can create constraints in two ways: by creating them for an existing table using ALTER TABLE or by creating a new table using CREATE TABLE.

You have two ways to create a constraint using CREATE TABLE. First, you can create the constraint after all columns are declared, as you did in chapter 18. Here's an example of the PRIMARY KEY constraint you created for the category table:

```
CREATE TABLE category (
    CategoryID int,
    CategoryName varchar(20),
    CONSTRAINT PK_category PRIMARY KEY (CategoryID)
    );
```

You can also create a constraint as part of the declaration of the column after the data type has been declared. Here's an example of how you could have done that for the primary key of the category table:

```
CREATE TABLE category (
   CategoryID int PRIMARY KEY,
   CategoryName varchar(20)
   );
```

Although this approach is simpler, creating a constraint this way doesn't allow us to name the constraint. If we create the constraint this way, the name of the constraint is generated automatically by our relational database management system (RDBMS). This name will likely be some series of letters and numbers that doesn't indicate our intentions for the constraint.

That said, you don't necessarily need a name for every constraint. Although I highly recommend using the first method to create PRIMARY KEY and FOREIGN KEY constraints, other constraints in this chapter are typically created with the second method.

19.1.1 *NOT NULL constraints*

The NOT NULL constraint enforces a requirement that there cannot be null values in a column—which, if we think about it, is probably the case for most columns in any table. Tables are made to contain data, and we'll require many, if not all, columns in a table to have values.

Suppose that we want a table in our sqlnovel database that tracks shipments of novels to customers. We'll name the table shipment and add the following six columns:

- *ShipmentID*—Identifies each unique row in the table
- *OrderID*—Identifies the order to which the shipment is related
- *ShipmentCost*—Identifies the cost of the shipment in U.S. dollars
- *ShipmentMethod*—Identifies whether the order was sent via parcel post (P) or express (E)
- *TrackingNumber*—Identifies the tracking number provided by the shipment carrier
- *ShipmentDate*—Identifies the date when the shipment was sent

The data types for our columns will be

- *ShipmentID*—int, a unique integer value
- *OrderID*—int, the same as in the orderheader table
- *ShipmentCost*—decimal(5,2) to accommodate numbers from 0.00 to 999.99
- *ShipmentMethod*—char(1) because the value will be either P or E
- *TrackingNumber*—varchar(20) for whatever value the shipment carrier provides
- *ShipmentDate*—datetime, a data value

We also want to create a PRIMARY KEY constraint named PK_shipment on the ShipmentID column, and a FOREIGN KEY constraint named FK_shipment_orderheader on the OrderID column that references the OrderID values in orderheader. With all this information, we can create the shipment table using the following SQL statement:

```
CREATE TABLE shipment (
    ShipmentID int,
    OrderID int,
    ShipmentCost decimal(5,2),
    ShipmentMethod char(1),
    TrackingNumber varchar(20),
    ShipmentDate datetime,
    CONSTRAINT PK_shipment PRIMARY KEY (ShipmentID),
    CONSTRAINT FK_shipment_orderheader FOREIGN KEY (OrderID)
        REFERENCES orderheader(OrderID)
    );
```

NOTE Don't execute this SQL yet. You'll modify it quite a bit in this chapter.

The next thing we want to determine is which of these columns will be *nullable*, which means that these columns can contain null values. For every column we determine to be not nullable, we want to add a NOT NULL constraint to ensure that all rows contain values for those columns. An example of a nullable column is the MiddleName column in the author table; some authors have a middle name and others don't. Consider each column in the shipment table:

- ShipmentID is not nullable because we can't have null values in a primary key.
- OrderID is not nullable because every shipment must relate to an order.
- ShipmentCost is not nullable because every shipment has a cost of $0.00 or more.
- ShipmentMethod is not nullable because we need to know how every shipment was sent.
- TrackingNumber is not nullable because each shipment has a tracking number.
- ShipmentDate is not nullable because we need to know when a shipment was sent.

After careful review, it looks as though none of these columns is nullable, so we should add a NOT NULL constraint to each column. We can do that by modifying our SQL to indicate which columns are NOT NULL after their data types are declared:

```
CREATE TABLE shipment (
    ShipmentID int NOT NULL,
    OrderID int NOT NULL,
    ShipmentCost decimal(5,2) NOT NULL,
    ShipmentMethod char(1) NOT NULL,
    TrackingNumber varchar(20) NOT NULL,
    ShipmentDate datetime NOT NULL,
    CONSTRAINT PK_shipment PRIMARY KEY (ShipmentID),
    CONSTRAINT FK_shipment_orderheader FOREIGN KEY (OrderID)
```

```
        REFERENCES orderheader(OrderID)
    );
```

By doing this, we ensure that every row will have a value for every column, which is what we want. If someone tries to enter a row that doesn't have a value for every column, they'll get an error message. This message will vary from one RDBMS to another, but in MySQL, it says that one of the columns doesn't have a default value.

What does this mean? Well, *default values* involve another kind of constraint.

19.1.2 *DEFAULT constraints*

DEFAULT constraints allow us to use a set default value for a column if no value is specified. Default values established by these constraints will be used whenever an INSERT statement doesn't indicate a value for columns with a DEFAULT constraint.

The DEFAULT constraint must be a *literal constant*, meaning that it will be the same expression for each row that's inserted. An *expression* is some combination of values, operators, or functions that are evaluated to another value. This expression could be a number, a date, or a string of characters, although in MySQL and most other RDBMSes, we can also use some date and time functions as the default.

Our shipment table can benefit from this kind of constraint with one of these functions. In chapter 14, we learned about the CURRENT_DATE() function, which returns the date and time for the immediate moment. We can use this function to make sure that whenever a row is inserted into our shipment table, it records the value for CURRENT_DATE() in the ShipmentDate column at the time the row is created.

> **WARNING**   Although it's fairly common, the CURRENT_DATE() function isn't available in every RDBMS. For SQL Server, use GETDATE(); for Oracle, use SYSDATE; and for SQLite, use date('now').

For a DEFAULT constraint, we'll declare the keyword DEFAULT; then we'll declare the default value after declaring the data types for our column. Here's what our CREATE TABLE statement with this new default for ShipmentDate looks like:

```
CREATE TABLE shipment (
    ShipmentID int NOT NULL,
    OrderID int NOT NULL,
    ShipmentCost decimal(5,2) NOT NULL,
    ShipmentMethod char(1) NOT NULL,
    TrackingNumber varchar(20) NOT NULL,
    ShipmentDate datetime NOT NULL DEFAULT (CURRENT_DATE()),
    CONSTRAINT PK_shipment PRIMARY KEY (ShipmentID),
    CONSTRAINT FK_shipment_orderheader FOREIGN KEY (OrderID)
        REFERENCES orderheader(OrderID)
    );
```

Notice two points about this new constraint:

- *You need to put parentheses around the default value of* CURRENT_DATE() *in your* CREATE TABLE *statement.* The use of parentheses isn't required for most RDBMSes, but it is in MySQL. Consult the documentation for any RDBMS you're using to make sure that the syntax of your SQL statement is correct.

- *You can create more than one constraint on a column, as you're doing with the Shipment-Date column.* You don't even need to use a comma separator between columns, and you don't want to because the comma separator would indicate a new column, not a second constraint on the ShipmentDate column. Now this column has both a NOT NULL and a DEFAULT constraint, which is not uncommon for columns that automatically indicate the time when a row was added.

NOTE Having a DEFAULT constraint on a column doesn't mean that we don't also need the NOT NULL constraint. The DEFAULT constraint guarantees that a value will be inserted if one is not specified, but we also need the NOT NULL constraint to ensure that we don't have NULL specified as a value at the time when the row is inserted.

19.1.3 *UNIQUE constraints*

Now let's look at another kind of constraint for a different column: the UNIQUE constraint. UNIQUE constraints enforce the requirement that any value in a column be unique in that column. If we insert or update a value for a column with a UNIQUE constraint and that value already exists in another row, an error will occur.

UNIQUE constraints are a bit like the PRIMARY KEY constraints we've already used, but there are a few exceptions. The main difference is that a table can contain only one PRIMARY KEY constraint, but it can contain multiple UNIQUE constraints on columns if necessary.

Unlike PRIMARY KEY constraints, UNIQUE constraints can include null values. The maximum number of null values in a column with a UNIQUE constraint depends on the RDBMS you're using; MySQL allows multiple null values, for example, whereas SQL Server and Oracle allow only one null value. If this restriction is a concern for you, consult the documentation for your RDBMS, although it's rare to have a column that requires a UNIQUE constraint and is still nullable.

Because tracking numbers are UNIQUE for the shipment carrier, we want to create a UNIQUE constraint on the TrackingNumber column to ensure that a duplicate value is never used for this column. Adding this constraint is as simple as adding the word UNIQUE to the column declaration, similar to what we did with other constraints in this chapter:

```
CREATE TABLE shipment (
    ShipmentID int NOT NULL,
    OrderID int NOT NULL,
    ShipmentCost decimal(5,2) NOT NULL,
    ShipmentMethod char(1) NOT NULL,
    TrackingNumber varchar(20) NOT NULL UNIQUE,
    ShipmentDate datetime NOT NULL DEFAULT (CURRENT_DATE()),
```

```
    CONSTRAINT PK_shipment PRIMARY KEY (ShipmentID),
    CONSTRAINT FK_shipment_orderheader FOREIGN KEY (OrderID)
        REFERENCES orderheader(OrderID)
    );
```

19.1.4 CHECK constraints

We want to use one final constraint in our table: the CHECK constraint. A CHECK constraint allows us to limit the values used in a column by comparing them to some kind of expression. Being able to use an expression in the CHECK constraint gives us quite a bit of flexibility in evaluating the validity of values for any given column.

For the shipment table, we want to add CHECK constraints to the ShipmentCost and ShipmentMethod columns. The ShipmentMethod column requires a value that's either E or P, so we'll write the expression to be used in our constraint as `Shipment-Method IN ('P', 'E')`.

> **WARNING**   The expressions we use in CHECK constraints can include multiple columns, so we must state the column (or columns) used in our expressions.

For the CHECK constraint on ShipmentCost, we want the value to be between 0.00 and 999.99, so we'll write our expression as `ShipmentCost BETWEEN 0.00 AND 999.99`. Remember that BETWEEN includes the beginning and end values, so values of 0.00 and 999.99 are valid. We'll add our CHECK constraints much the same way that we added the DEFAULT constraint, with our constraint expression included in parentheses:

```
CREATE TABLE shipment (
    ShipmentID int NOT NULL,
    OrderID int NOT NULL,
    ShipmentCost decimal(5,2) NOT NULL
        CHECK (ShipmentCost BETWEEN 0.00 AND 999.99),
    ShipmentMethod char(1) NOT NULL CHECK (ShipmentMethod IN ('P', 'E')),
    TrackingNumber varchar(20) NOT NULL UNIQUE,
    ShipmentDate datetime NOT NULL DEFAULT (CURRENT_DATE()),
    CONSTRAINT PK_shipment PRIMARY KEY (ShipmentID),
    CONSTRAINT FK_shipment_orderheader FOREIGN KEY (OrderID)
        REFERENCES orderheader(OrderID)
    );
```

Although the CHECK constraints we're creating for the shipment table are fairly simple, as noted earlier, these kinds of constraints can involve multiple columns. We could have written a single constraint with a larger expression to validate that the Shipment-Cost was in the stated range of numeric values and that the ShipmentMethod was one of the two acceptable values. When we use multiple columns in the expression of our constraint, we typically want to create the constraint after all the columns, as we did with the PRIMARY KEY and FOREIGN KEY constraints.

19.2 *Automatically incrementing values for a column*

We want to make one final change in our table—a very common change that's a bit like a DEFAULT constraint. We've established that we want the ShipmentID column to be the primary key of our new shipment table. The primary key values need to be unique so that we can identify individual rows in this table.

In chapter 18, we inserted explicit values for the primary key (CategoryID) of the category table. For many tables, we won't want to use explicit values for the column determined to be the primary key. Instead, we'll want to take advantage of a feature that every RDBMS has—a feature that automatically increments values.

In MySQL, this feature uses the AUTO_INCREMENT keyword. Although it's technically not a constraint, it behaves a bit like a DEFAULT constraint in that it allows us to insert rows into the table without specifying a value for a column with AUTO_INCREMENT enabled.

When we INSERT rows into the shipment table with AUTO_INCREMENT enabled, we will omit specifying values for the ShipmentID column. The first row inserted this way automatically has a value of 1 for ShipmentID, the second row inserted has a value of 2, and so on. Setting this value to populate the column with incremental values automatically ensures that the primary key will be unique and not NULL.

Also, we'll declare AUTO_INCREMENT in our SQL the same way that we've been declaring our constraints. Here's our CREATE TABLE statement, now with the ShipmentID column set to AUTO_INCREMENT:

```
CREATE TABLE shipment (
    ShipmentID int NOT NULL AUTO_INCREMENT,
    OrderID int NOT NULL,
    ShipmentCost decimal(5,2) NOT NULL
        CHECK (ShipmentCost BETWEEN 0.00 AND 999.99),
    ShipmentMethod char(1) NOT NULL CHECK (ShipmentMethod IN ('P', 'E')),
    TrackingNumber varchar(20) NOT NULL UNIQUE,
    ShipmentDate datetime NOT NULL DEFAULT (CURRENT_DATE()),
    CONSTRAINT PK_shipment PRIMARY KEY (ShipmentID),
    CONSTRAINT FK_shipment_orderheader FOREIGN KEY (OrderID)
        REFERENCES orderheader(OrderID)
    );
```

Our shipment table, with all the desired constraints, is ready to be created.

Try it now

Create the shipment table with the preceding SQL script. You'll practice using this table in the lab exercises at the end of this chapter.

19.3   Indexes

Every constraint we've created is intended to ensure the integrity of our data, but in MySQL, some of those constraints also created objects that we haven't looked at yet: indexes. Indexes exist in every RDBMS, so let's take a closer look at them.

An *index* is an object that logically sorts data to make it more readable in commonly used queries, allowing those queries to return data faster. Indexes come in two forms: clustered and nonclustered. We'll look at clustered indexes first.

19.3.1   Clustered indexes

Clustered indexes are data structures that control the physical order of the rows in a table, which means that their order is how the data will be stored on disks or other storage media. When a table is created without any defined indexes or constraints, the rows of data are stored in no particular order, so any query that uses that table has to read every row to determine whether the values contained should be retrieved, filtered, joined, and so on.

To better understand clustered indexes, think of a telephone book containing the names and telephone numbers of folks who live in your hometown. This telephone book is typically sorted by surname and then the first name of each person, with related telephone numbers and perhaps address information included in each row on any given page. If this telephone book were a table, the clustered index would be on surname and then first name because that order is how the rows are organized.

We want to sort rows based on the most commonly used columns in our table, so we should be thoughtful about the way we create our clustered index. Because the rows in our table can be sorted in only one way, it's important to note that any table can include only one clustered index. After it's created, the clustered index effectively is the table, not a separate object.

If you executed the SQL script in section 19.2, you've already created a clustered index for the shipment table because MySQL created one automatically when you created your PRIMARY KEY constraint. This situation usually isn't a problem because the clustered index is most often created on the column (or columns) that make up the primary key.

As you may have noticed, when you joined tables in queries, you joined them with related primary and foreign keys. Because the RDBMS needs to read those key values to join rows in different tables, it makes sense to create clustered indexes on the primary-key columns in your tables.

> **NOTE** Even if you don't define a primary key on a table, the RDBMS creates a hidden column, often called a *row identifier*, that contains a unique value for every row. If you had two or more rows with identical values, the row identifier would allow the RDBMS to know that these rows were different. Because the column is hidden, though, users typically wouldn't see it, so we generally want

to create `PRIMARY KEY` constraints and clustered indexes for tables that require unique values for each row.

As I said earlier, we already have a clustered index in our table. In MySQL, we can see the indexes in a table in MySQL Workbench. In the Navigator panel, we can expand our sqlnovel database, expand Tables, expand our shipment table, and finally expand Indexes. As shown in figure 19.1, we have three indexes in our shipment table.

We can see even more information about each index by highlighting it and viewing the Information panel, which should be below the Navigator panel. If we highlight the index named PRIMARY, we see the information about this index (figure 19.2).

Figure 19.1   The three indexes of the shipment table in the sqlnovel database, viewed in MySQL Workbench

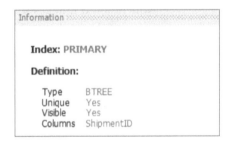

Figure 19.2   Information about the PRIMARY index of the shipment table, viewed in MySQL Workbench

Although it doesn't explicitly say "clustered index," in MySQL, the index labeled PRIMARY is the clustered index. Admittedly, there isn't much information in the Information panel, but the main consideration for us is the Columns value. This value tells us that ShipmentID is the column used for the clustered index of our table, which is the column we used to define the `PRIMARY KEY` constraint.

WARNING   Because clustered indexes aren't separate objects and are more like properties of a table that are often related to the primary key, every RDBMS has a different way of handling the way they're created. In some RDBMSes, such as SQL Server and DB2, you can create them explicitly using an `ALTER TABLE` or `CREATE INDEX` statement, but in others, such as MySQL and PostgreSQL, you can't. Refer to the documentation for your specific RDBMS to see what options you have for creating clustered indexes.

19.3.2 Nonclustered indexes

Although clustered indexes are common and highly beneficial to performance, non-clustered indexes are also helpful in speeding our queries. A *nonclustered* index is different from a clustered index in two main ways:

- Unlike clustered indexes, nonclustered indexes are separate objects from the tables they relate to.
- Because nonclustered indexes are separate objects, a table can contain more than one of them.

A good analogy for a nonclustered index is a catalog system for books in a library. Nonfiction books in a library are stored under a numeric catalog system, such as the Dewey Decimal System. Most of us don't look for a book by its numeric value in this system, however; rather, we use the title. We use the catalog to look up the title of our desired book, which gives us the numeric value of the book we want. Then we go through the shelves of the library that are ordered by the numeric system and find our book.

Nonclustered indexes work like the catalog system in a library. They're a separate ordering of the books, in this case by title, which allows us to quickly find the title and numeric value and then use that value to go to the place in the library where the book exists. In this analogy, the numeric value would be the primary key and clustered index of the nonfiction books in the library.

As you can see from this analogy, the catalog system (the nonclustered index) greatly speeds the search for the book we're looking for. If we didn't have the catalog, we'd have to scan the entire library until we found the book. We create nonclustered indexes for the same reason: to improve performance in finding rows of data in a table without reading the entire table.

Although we can put all the columns we want in a nonclustered index, we generally have only a few columns or even a single column. Typically, we're searching only on one or two columns, so we don't want to make our nonclustered indexes larger than necessary. The more columns the indexes have, the more storage space they take up and the more resources they require for any INSERT, UPDATE, and DELETE statements involving the table they relate to.

We saw in figure 19.1 that we have two nonclustered indexes in our shipment table, so let's examine them. To look at them, we can click them in the Navigator panel and review their information in the Information panel. Let's look at the TrackingNumber index information, shown in figure 19.3.

Because we created a UNIQUE constraint on the TrackingNumber column, MySQL automatically created a nonclustered index on this column. As figure 19.3 indicates, this index has a value of Yes for the Unique property.

MySQL is unusual in that it created the index for this column automatically; many other RDBMSes wouldn't do that. Because this column is required to contain unique values, we likely would want to create a nonclustered index for the column anyway.

If we think about the nature of this column, which contains tracking numbers for shipments, we expect queries to look for shipment information related to one specific TrackingNumber. Rather than scan the entire shipment table every time we want to find data related to a specific TrackingNumber, our queries can use this nonclustered index. This is exactly the kind of column we would want a nonclustered index on.

Information

Index: TrackingNumber

Definition:

Type	BTREE
Unique	Yes
Visible	Yes
Columns	TrackingNumber

Figure 19.3   Information about the TrackingNumber index of the shipment table, viewed in MySQL Workbench

The analogy earlier in this chapter discusses a library catalog that works as a sort of nonclustered index for all nonfiction books, and here, the TrackingNumber would serve the same purpose for the tracking numbers of our shipments. If this index on TrackingNumber hadn't been created automatically (and it won't be in many other RDBMSes), we could create it with the following SQL statement:

```
CREATE INDEX IX_shipment_TrackingNumber ON shipment (TrackingNumber);
```

This syntax is common to just about every RDBMS, so I don't have to add any qualifiers about its use.

TIP   The preceding SQL statement that creates the nonclustered index on the shipment table uses a common but specific naming convention: IX to indicate an index, an underscore, the table name, another underscore, and the name of the column of the index. As always, be intentional about the names of objects in your database, and follow a consistent naming convention to make objects that other people can easily understand.

Figure 19.1 indicates we have a third index in our table: FK_shipment_orderheader. This index was created automatically by our FOREIGN KEY constraint, which is a behavior of MySQL but not necessarily a behavior of other RDBMSes. It's common to create nonclustered indexes on the columns contained in FOREIGN KEY constraints, however, because these columns are used to link tables via the relationships in the keys. Having the nonclustered indexes on the foreign key columns can reduce the need to read all the data in a table to join with other tables. We can see the properties of this index by clicking FK_shipment_orderheader in the Navigator panel and then viewing the Information panel (figure 19.4).

One thing to note about this index: the value of the Unique property is No, which is different from the other two indexes of our shipment table. Although the UNIQUE constraint we made also created an index that requires unique values, it's important to note that nonclustered indexes aren't required to have unique values. In the case of the FK_shipment_orderheader index, unique values aren't required because we might have a one-to-many relationship between the orderheader and shipment tables as far as OrderID values are concerned.

This chapter covered a lot of database design concepts. Let's briefly summarize the main points about constraints and indexes:

Information

Index: FK_shipment_orderheader

Definition:

Type	BTREE
Unique	No
Visible	Yes
Columns	OrderID

Figure 19.4   Information about the FK_shipment_orderheader index of the shipment table, viewed in MySQL Workbench

- Constraints are properties on one or more columns that enforce data integrity.
- NOT NULL constraints ensure that no NULL values are contained in a column.
- DEFAULT constraints enter a default value if no value is specified for a column on INSERT.
- UNIQUE constraints enforce that all values in a column are different.
- CHECK constraints are used to limit the range of values that can be contained in a column.
- A clustered index defines the physical sort order of a table, typically on the primary key.
- A table can have only one clustered index.
- A nonclustered index is a separate object from the table.
- A table can have many nonclustered indexes, although every additional nonclustered index negatively affects the performance of INSERT, UPDATE, and DELETE statements.
- In MySQL (but not every RDBMS), a clustered index is created automatically when we define a PRIMARY KEY constraint.
- In MySQL (but not every RDBMS), a nonclustered index is created for every UNIQUE or FOREIGN KEY constraint we create.

If you're feeling up to it, try to flex your new skills with constraints and indexes in the lab exercises.

19.4   Lab

1 Using the following values, write a SQL statement to insert rows into the new shipment table:

- OrderID = 1001
- ShipmentCost = 0.00
- ShipmentMethod = 'P'
- TrackingNumber = '1A2C3M4E'

2 Because the shipment table currently doesn't have a row for every order, how would you write a query to see the OrderID, OrderDate, and ShipmentDate for every order?

3 Could you have written the expression in section 19.1.4 differently? If so, how?

4 You want to create a report that shows the count of all orders shipped on a particular date. What constraint or index could you create to improve the performance of this report?

19.5 Lab answers

1 You don't have to specify a value for ShipmentID because it's an AUTO_INCREMENT column, and you don't have to specify a value for ShipmentDate because it has a default constraint. Therefore, your SQL should look something like this:

```
INSERT shipment (
    OrderId,
    ShipmentCost,
    ShipmentMethod,
    TrackingNumber
    )
VALUES (
    1001,
    0.00,
    'P',
    '1A2C3M4E'
    );
```

2 Because you have values for every OrderID in orderheader but don't have values for every OrderID in shipment, you need to use a LEFT OUTER JOIN, like this:

```
SELECT
    oh.OrderID,
    oh.OrderDate,
    s.ShipmentDate
FROM orderheader oh
LEFT OUTER JOIN shipment s
    ON oh.OrderID = s.OrderID;
```

If you used an INNER JOIN instead, your result set would include only orders that have a value in the OrderID column of both tables.

3 You could write this expression in a few ways, including this way:

```
ShipmentCost >= 0.00 AND ShipmentCost <= 999.99.
```

4 The SQL used in your report would look something like this:

```
SELECT
    ShipmentDate,
```

```
        COUNT(ShipmentDate)
FROM shipment
WHERE ShipmentDate = @ShipmentDate
GROUP BY ShipmentDate;
```

To support this query, you'd create a nonclustered index on the ShipmentDate column:

```
CREATE INDEX IX_shipment_ShipmentDate ON shipment (ShipmentDate);
```

This nonclustered index would help keep you from having to read the entire table to determine the total of what would be a fraction of the orders shipped on any given day.

Reusing queries with views and stored procedures

Through 19 chapters, we've written a lot of SQL queries. We've used filters, functions, aggregations, and more to find specific data. We've even added, updated, and removed data, and we've used variables to enable our scripts to do the same things over and over with different values.

In this chapter, we'll bring a lot of that work together by moving from executing SQL scripts to saving scripts as objects in the database—scripts that anyone who has the necessary permissions can execute. Depending on the relational database management system (RDBMS) we're using, we can use a few objects to store these scripts. For now, we'll focus on two nearly universal objects: views and stored procedures.

A *view* stores a SELECT statement and provides a single result set that can be used like a table. A *stored procedure* stores one or more queries that can be executed at the same time to perform nearly any required task in a database.

20.1 Views

Views are database objects we create based on a SELECT statement. Views provide a single result set that resembles a table, which is why they're often referred to as *virtual tables*. The term *virtual tables* indicates that we can use views like tables in our queries.

Referring to views as *virtual tables* is a bit misleading, though, because views aren't tables and don't contain data. It may be more helpful to think of them as SELECT statements with a name, although that description doesn't fully describe their usefulness.

Views allow us to reuse a query easily; they also enable us to reduce a complex query to a simple, accessible object. We can take that object and assign users permissions to enable them to use the view (or not).

20.1.1 Creating views

Any view starts with a SELECT statement. If we want to create a view that shows the names of titles and their category names, we could write a query like this (results shown in figure 20.1):

TitleName	CategoryName
Pride and Predicates	Romance
The Join Luck Club	Mystery
Catcher in the Try	Mystery
Anne of Fact Tables	Romance
The DateTime Machine	Science Fiction
The Great GroupBy	Humor
The Call of the While	Fantasy
The Sum Also Rises	Science Fiction
David Emptyfield	Humor
Red Badge of Cursors	Mystery
Of Mice and Metadata	Science Fiction
A Table of Two Cities	Fantasy

Figure 20.1   All TitleName values from the title table and the related CategoryName values in the category table

```
SELECT
    t.TitleName,
    c.CategoryName
 FROM title t
INNER JOIN category c
    ON t.CategoryID = c.CategoryID;
```

To create a view with this query, we need to create a SQL statement in the following order:

1 CREATE VIEW

2 View name

3 AS

4 SELECT statement

Using this easy syntax, we can create a view named vw_TitleCategory like this:

```
CREATE VIEW vw_TitleCategory
AS
SELECT
    t.TitleName,
    c.CategoryName
FROM title t
INNER JOIN category c
    ON t.CategoryID = c.CategoryID;
```

When we create the view, it saves our SELECT statement to be executed whenever we want. To see the results of our view, we select it from the view as though it were a table:

```
SELECT *
FROM vw_TitleCategory;
```

The results of executing the preceding query, shown in figure 20.1, are the same as those of executing our original SQL statement.

For queries that you have to write over and over, views can save you coding time because the desired result set is ready to execute. Again, this view doesn't contain data; it simply calls the data via the underlying SQL statement when it's executed. But executing isn't all we can do with views.

20.1.2 *Filtering with views*

Just as we can filter the results of a table, we can filter the results in a WHERE clause, as we've done many times in other queries. If we want to see only the titles in our view that are in the Mystery category, as shown in figure 20.2, we modify our SELECT from the view to have the appropriate filtering in a WHERE clause, like this:

TitleName	CategoryName
The Join Luck Club	Mystery
Catcher in the Try	Mystery
Red Badge of Cursors	Mystery

Figure 20.2 The results of selecting all rows from vw_TitleCategory with a CategoryName value of Mystery

```
SELECT *
FROM vw_TitleCategory
WHERE CategoryName = 'Mystery';
```

With views, we can do nearly everything we've done with tables. We can filter results, order results, and aggregate data. We can even join views to other tables and views, but to do that with our view, we have to make some changes.

20.1.3 *Joining views*

As you may recall from the many times you've joined tables, you must define relationships to make joins successful. The vw_TitleCategory view contains two columns, but neither is related to any key values that form relationships with other tables. No tables in the database have any relationship that uses the TitleName or CategoryName column as a key value.

To use our view with other tables, we need to add the key values from the underlying tables. For our view, that means adding the TitleID from the title table and the CategoryID from the category table. Now, we could add the CategoryID from the title table instead of from the category table, but it's good practice to use primary keys instead of foreign keys in views whenever possible.

> **WARNING** Just as column names in tables must be unique, column names in views must be unique as well. If you attempt to create a view with column names that aren't unique, most RDBMSes, including MySQL, return an error message telling you that duplicate column names exist.

We'll modify our view using syntax similar to what we used to create our view. But we'll use the ALTER keyword instead of CREATE, as we did when we modified a table in chapter 18:

- ALTER VIEW
- View name
- AS
- Modified SQL query

Using this syntax, we can modify our vw_TitleCategory view to include the two additional columns:

```
ALTER VIEW vw_TitleCategory
AS
SELECT
    t.TitleID,
    t.TitleName,
    c.CategoryID,
    c.CategoryName
 FROM title t
INNER JOIN category c
    ON t.CategoryID = c.CategoryID;
```

Try it now

If you haven't created and altered the vw_TitleCategory yet, modify the preceding query from ALTER VIEW to CREATE VIEW to create it. You'll use it again later in this chapter.

After executing our ALTER VIEW statement, we can examine the results of our view with the following query (results shown in figure 20.3):

```
SELECT *
FROM vw_TitleCategory;
```

Notice that the results aren't in any particular order. This is fine because we don't want to order the values in our view unless we have to. As with a SELECT statement, adding an ORDER BY clause to a view can make query performance much worse when we're dealing with millions of rows of data.

TitleID	TitleName	CategoryID	CategoryName
101	Pride and Predicates	1	Romance
102	The Join Luck Club	3	Mystery
103	Catcher in the Try	3	Mystery
104	Anne of Fact Tables	1	Romance
105	The DateTime Machine	5	Science Fiction
106	The Great GroupBy	2	Humor
107	The Call of the While	4	Fantasy
108	The Sum Also Rises	5	Science Fiction
109	David Emptyfield	2	Humor
110	Red Badge of Cursors	3	Mystery
111	Of Mice and Metadata	5	Science Fiction
112	A Table of Two Cities	4	Fantasy

Figure 20.3   The results of selecting all rows and columns from vw_TtileCategoryID, which now includes the TitleID and CategoryID columns

Now we can not only join this view to other tables and view, but also create calculated columns. If we want to see how many titles were sold in each category, for example, we can join our view in a query to the orderitem table by using the relationship of the TitleID columns. Here's what that query looks like (results shown in figure 20.4):

```
SELECT
    tc.CategoryName,
    SUM(oi.Quantity) AS TitlesOrdered
FROM vw_TitleCategory tc
LEFT OUTER JOIN orderitem oi
    ON tc.TitleID = oi.TitleID
GROUP BY tc.CategoryName;
```

CategoryName	TitlesOrdered
Romance	27
Mystery	24
Science Fiction	16
Humor	1
Fantasy	2

Figure 20.4   The results of the number of titles ordered in each category

20.1.4 Considerations for views

Views are incredibly useful, but some rules and caveats apply. Here are some of the main factors you should consider when you create and use views:

- A view can't have the same name as any other view or table. Keep this rule in mind when naming your views.
- When you name views, try to use a naming convention that identifies them as views, not tables. Our example uses the prefix vw_ in the view name. A consistent naming convention becomes important when other users use views you created to look at queries; you want them to be able to distinguish tables from views easily.
- It's a good idea to add columns for the primary key and foreign key values to the SELECT clause of the SQL statement used by the view. This approach allows you to relate the results of your view to other tables and views.
- Chapter 11 examined using *subqueries*—queries contained in other queries—to find the data you want with SQL. Similarly, views can call other views via subqueries or joins. These views used within other views are referred to as *nested views*. Avoid using them, though, because they dramatically degrade query performance.
- If your view contains a calculated column, as the preceding query does, always create an alias for the column name. Most RDBMSes require every column in a view to have a defined name.
- Although it may seem improbable, many RDBMSes allow data to be updated or even inserted into views. Doing so can be problematic because these changes can affect data in multiple tables, so in general, you should avoid this practice.

NOTE In light of that last point, views aren't the right tool for modifying data in SQL, but stored procedures can be wonderful tools for that purpose. They're also a better tool for selecting data.

20.2 Stored procedures

Like views, stored procedures allow us to store a SQL statement in our database so we can easily reuse it. We can also assign users permissions to determine whether they can use the stored procedures. Unlike views, stored procedures allow for even more complexity, such as executing multiple queries and passing values through variables.

20.2.1 Creating stored procedures

Let's start by turning our SQL statement from section 20.1.1 into a stored procedure. Nearly every RDBMS has a basic syntax for creating stored procedures, which looks like this:

```
1  CREATE PROCEDURE
```

2 Name of the stored procedure

3 SQL for the stored procedure to execute

NOTE Unfortunately, each RDBMS has its own subtle syntax differences for handling the creation of a stored procedure. But don't let that fact keep you from learning about them, because despite these differences, the use of stored procedures is similar across RDBMSes except SQLite, which doesn't support stored procedures.

To create our stored procedure in MySQL, first we must change the delimiter. When we wrote our first query in chapter 2, we learned to add a semicolon (a *statement terminator*) to the end of a query to tell the RDBMS where the SQL in our query stops. MySQL is rigid about the statement terminator, which can be a concern when writing stored procedures. Because these procedures can contain multiple statements, the first semicolon our code encounters would look like the end of the stored procedure to the RDBMS.

To work around this situation, we'll briefly change the statement terminator to a value other than a semicolon. In our SQL, we'll change the statement terminator to double slashes (//) by using the MySQL-specific keyword DELIMITER, create our stored procedure with the standard semicolon delimiter, and then use DELIMITER to change the statement terminator back to a semicolon. We'll name the procedure GetTitle-Category. Here's the SQL to create our stored procedure that gets all TitleName values and the associated CategoryName values, followed by notes that explain what the code does:

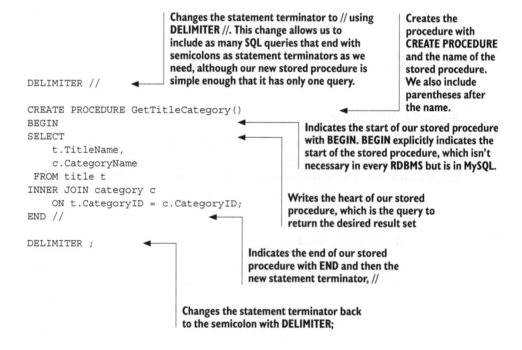

Changes the statement terminator to // using **DELIMITER //.** This change allows us to include as many SQL queries that end with semicolons as statement terminators as we need, although our new stored procedure is simple enough that it has only one query.

Creates the procedure with **CREATE PROCEDURE** and the name of the stored procedure. We also include parentheses after the name.

```
DELIMITER //

CREATE PROCEDURE GetTitleCategory()
BEGIN
SELECT
    t.TitleName,
    c.CategoryName
 FROM title t
INNER JOIN category c
    ON t.CategoryID = c.CategoryID;
END //

DELIMITER ;
```

Indicates the start of our stored procedure with **BEGIN. BEGIN** explicitly indicates the start of the stored procedure, which isn't necessary in every RDBMS but is in MySQL.

Writes the heart of our stored procedure, which is the query to return the desired result set

Indicates the end of our stored procedure with **END** and then the new statement terminator, //

Changes the statement terminator back to the semicolon with **DELIMITER;**

Now that we have created our stored procedure, we can put it to use. To execute our stored procedure, we'll use the CALL keyword (results shown in figure 20.5):

```
CALL GetTitleCategory;
```

This stored procedure is a basic one. We can do much more with stored procedures, so in section 20.2.2, we'll add functionality to pass a variable and filter our results.

> **NOTE** The writing of a stored procedure is specific to an RDBMS, and so is the execution. Although MySQL, PostgreSQL, and MariaDB use the CALL keyword, SQL Server and Oracle use EXEC.

TitleName	CategoryName
Pride and Predicates	Romance
The Join Luck Club	Mystery
Catcher in the Try	Mystery
Anne of Fact Tables	Romance
The DateTime Machine	Science Fiction
The Great GroupBy	Humor
The Call of the While	Fantasy
The Sum Also Rises	Science Fiction
David Emptyfield	Humor
Red Badge of Cursors	Mystery
Of Mice and Metadata	Science Fiction
A Table of Two Cities	Fantasy

Figure 20.5 The results of all TitleName values from the title table and their related CategoryName values in the category table, as returned by the stored procedure GetTitleCategory

20.2.2 *Using variables with stored procedures*

One of the biggest advantages of stored procedures over views is the fact that stored procedures have parameters. A *parameter* is a variable that can be passed into or out of a stored procedure. Any stored procedure can have multiple parameters that we can use for anything from filtering data to changing values in tables to determining the output results of a stored procedure. When we use parameters with a stored procedure, each parameter must have three properties defined:

- The name
- The data type
- Whether the parameter is used for input or output

The final property gives us choices on how to use a parameter. If a parameter is defined for *input*, a value is passed into the stored procedure for use. If a parameter is defined for *output*, the value of the parameter is determined during the execution of the stored procedure and returned.

> **NOTE** MySQL offers a third option for parameters: INOUT. This option allows a parameter to be passed in, modified if necessary, and then passed back out. This option isn't available in every RDBMS.

We can modify our GetTitleCategory stored procedure to have an input parameter that filters on TitleName. To modify a stored procedure in MySQL, however, first we have to drop it, similar to the way we dropped tables in chapter 18:

```
DROP PROCEDURE GetTitleCategory;
```

Now we can re-create our stored procedure with an input parameter. We'll name our parameter _TitleName so it won't be confused with the column named TitleName, and we'll define the data type as the one defined for the TitleName column in the title table. We can see the data type of columns for any table in MySQL by using SHOW COLUMNS. This statement is how we'd use SHOW COLUMNS to find the data types of the columns in the title table (results shown in figure 20.6):

```
SHOW COLUMNS FROM title;
```

Field	Type	Null	Key	Default	Extra
TitleID	int	NO	PRI	NULL	
TitleName	varchar(50)	NO		NULL	
Price	decimal(5,2)	NO		NULL	
Advance	decimal(8,2)	NO		NULL	
Royalty	decimal(5,2)	YES		NULL	
PublicationDate	datetime	NO		NULL	
CategoryID	int	YES	MUL	NULL	

Figure 20.6   The data types of all columns in the title table, returned by SHOW COLUMNS

We can see that the data type for the TitleName column is varchar(50), so we'll define that data type for our input parameter. The last thing we have to do is use the parameter for filtering within the stored procedure. To accomplish this task, we'll add WHERE t.TitleName = _TitleName. The following SQL creates our new stored procedure:

```
DROP PROCEDURE GetTitleCategory;

DELIMITER //

CREATE PROCEDURE GetTitleCategory(
    IN _TitleName varchar(50)
    )
BEGIN
SELECT
    t.TitleName,
    c.CategoryName
 FROM title t
INNER JOIN category c
    ON t.CategoryID = c.CategoryID
WHERE t.TitleName = _TitleName;
END //

DELIMITER ;
```

Now we can declare a variable and pass it to the stored procedure to return only the results for the desired TitleName value. Using the value The Sum Also Rises, we can execute the stored procedure with the following SQL (results shown in figure 20.7):

```
SET @TitleName = 'The Sum Also Rises';
CALL GetTitleCategory (@TitleName);
```

Now that we've added the input parameter _TitleName to GetTitleCategory, every execution of the stored procedure will require a value for that parameter. If we try to execute GetTitleCategory without a value for _TitleName, we'll get the error message "Incorrect number of arguments." In the

TitleName	CategoryName
The Sum Also Rises	Science Fiction

Figure 20.7 The results of executing GetTitleCategory using the value The Sum Also Rises with the input parameter _TitleName

context of a stored procedure, an *argument* is the value being passed to the parameter. Now GetTitleCategory expects a value for every execution, and if we don't pass one, we're passing zero arguments. As the error correctly calculates, zero is the incorrect number when one argument is expected.

When writing a stored procedure, we may want to account for the fact that we may not have a value for an argument, so instead of not passing an argument, we can pass one that has NULL as the value. This approach isn't uncommon. As we've seen throughout this book, NULL can be a value that has to be accounted for.

One way to handle passing a value of NULL to the _TitleName parameter is to return all rows in a result set, which we can do by using the COALESCE function (see chapter 15). We can change the filtering in our stored procedure to WHERE t.TitleName = COALESCE(_TitleName, t.TitleName) to account for a value of NULL used as an argument for the _TitleName parameter.

With this logic, we can execute our stored procedure with an argument of NULL. If a specific value is passed, our result set is still filtered on that value, but if NULL is passed, we return every row in which TitleName equals itself, which is every row.

Let's drop our stored procedure and re-create it with the new filtering logic that uses COALESCE. We can do all of this at the same time with the following SQL:

```
DROP PROCEDURE GetTitleCategory;

DELIMITER //

CREATE PROCEDURE GetTitleCategory(
IN _TitleName varchar(50)
    )
BEGIN
SELECT
    t.TitleName,
    c.CategoryName
FROM title t
INNER JOIN category c
    ON t.CategoryID = c.CategoryID
WHERE t.TitleName = COALESCE(_TitleName, t.TitleName);
END //

DELIMITER ;
```

With this new change, we can execute our stored procedure with or without a NULL value as an argument. Using a value of NULL returns values for all TitleNames, as shown in figure 20.8:

```
SET @TitleName = NULL;
CALL GetTitleCategory (@TitleName);
```

If we execute GetTitleName with an argument that isn't NULL, like The Sum Also Rises, we get the filtered results for only that TitleName, as shown in figure 20.9:

```
SET @TitleName = 'The Sum Also Rises';
CALL GetTitleCategory (@TitleName);
```

TitleName	CategoryName
Pride and Predicates	Romance
The Join Luck Club	Mystery
Catcher in the Try	Mystery
Anne of Fact Tables	Romance
The DateTime Machine	Science Fiction
The Great GroupBy	Humor
The Call of the While	Fantasy
The Sum Also Rises	Science Fiction
David Emptyfield	Humor
Red Badge of Cursors	Mystery
Of Mice and Metadata	Science Fiction
A Table of Two Cities	Fantasy

Figure 20.8   The results of all TitleName values from the title table and the related CategoryName values in the category table, returned by the stored procedure GetTitleCategory with an argument of NULL for the `_TitleName` **parameter**

TitleName	CategoryName
The Sum Also Rises	Science Fiction

Figure 20.9   The results of TitleName values from the title table and the related CategoryName values in the category table, returned by the stored procedure GetTitleCategory with an argument of The Sum Also Rises for the `_TitleName` **parameter**

> **Try it now**
>
> Create the final version of the GetTitleCategory stored procedure, and try executing it with different values as arguments for `_TitleName`, including NULL.

20.2.3   *Considerations for stored procedures*

I hope you see why stored procedures are popular ways to store our SQL statements in an RDBMS. Before you run out and change all your queries to stored procedures, however, you have a few significant factors to consider:

- Stored procedures can call other stored procedures and even pass variable values back and forth. Be careful about nesting stored procedures, which can become a headache to troubleshoot.

- As you do for views and other objects, use a consistent naming convention for your stored procedures so they're clearly identified as stored procedures and so other people will understand their purposes.

- If you're writing a stored procedure with parameters, always verify that the data types of the parameters match the data types of any columns they'll be evaluated against.

- If you're using variables to pass values to the parameters of a stored procedure, make sure that the data type of your variables matches that of the stored procedure.

- Because stored procedures can contain multiple queries, use lots of clear, descriptive comments in complex stored procedures to indicate what each part of your stored procedure is meant to do.

20.3 Differences between views and stored procedures

In this chapter, we've looked at two of the most popular ways to store SQL for reuse. As we've seen, views and stored procedures have different attributes. Let's review the main differences to help you better decide when to use either of them, as shown in table 20.1.

Table 20.1 Some main differences between views and stored procedures

Attributes	View	Stored procedure
Input	Doesn't use parameters	Can use parameters
Output	Can return only a single result set	Can return zero, one, or multiple result sets or output parameters
Multiple queries	Can contain only a single query	Can contain multiple queries
Relationships	Can be joined to other views or tables via relationships	Can't be joined to other objects
Dependencies	Can contain a query using tables or views but not stored procedures	Can contain queries using tables, views, or other stored procedures

Although this chapter covers most of what you need to know about views, it only scratches the surface of the capabilities of stored procedures. As you'll see in chapter 21, you can create stored procedures to read data and write data, with logic determined by various conditions.

20.4 Lab

1 Create a view named vw_Order that contains all the columns from the orderheader and orderitem tables except the OrderID column from the orderitem table. Recall that these tables are related by their OrderID columns.

2 Why do you think you should exclude the OrderID column from the orderitem table?

3 Create a stored procedure named GetOrder with the following specifications:

- Uses the vw_Order view you just created

- Has a parameter named _OrderID and filters the results based on matching the value of that parameter to the OrderID column of vw_Order

- Joins the title table using the relationship of the TitleID columns

- Returns the following columns: OrderID, OrderDate, TitleName, Quantity, and ItemPrice

4 What kind of data type did you define for the `_OrderID` parameter in GetOrder, and why?

5 After you create GetOrder, what happens if you execute the following code?

```
CALL GetOrder(1049)
```

20.5 *Lab answers*

1 The SQL for your view should look something like this:

```
CREATE VIEW vw_Order
AS
SELECT
    oh.OrderID,
    oh.CustomerID,
    oh.PromotionID,
    oh.OrderDate,
    oi.OrderItem,
    oi.TitleID,
    oi.Quantity,
    oi.ItemPrice
  FROM orderheader oh
INNER JOIN orderitem oi
    ON oh.OrderID = oi.OrderID;
```

2 If you hadn't excluded the OrderID column from the orderitem table in your view, there'd be two columns named OrderID. If you tried to create this view with two OrderID columns, the RDBMS would return an error because it wouldn't know which column to use.

3 The SQL to create the GetOrder stored procedure should look something like this:

```
DELIMITER //

CREATE PROCEDURE GetOrder(
    IN _OrderID int
    )
BEGIN
SELECT
    o.OrderID,
    o.OrderDate,
    t.TitleName,
    o.Quantity,
    o.ItemPrice
FROM vw_Order o
INNER JOIN title t
    ON o.TitleID = t.TitleID
```

```
WHERE o.OrderID = _OrderID;
END //

DELIMITER ;
```

4 You should have used an integer(int) data type for the _OrderID parameter because that's the data type of the OrderID column you'll be evaluating with the parameter. If you didn't know the data type, you could have discovered it using the following query in MySQL:

```
SHOW COLUMNS FROM orderheader;
```

5 The command should execute, returning the results shown in figure 20.10. Executing the stored procedure this way shows that you can use either variables or literal values, such as 1049, when passing arguments to a parameter.

OrderID	OrderDate	TitleName	Quantity	ItemPrice
1049	2021-03-05 00:00:00	Pride and Predicates	1	6.95
1049	2021-03-05 00:00:00	The Join Luck Club	1	6.95
1049	2021-03-05 00:00:00	Catcher in the Try	1	5.95

Figure 20.10 The results of executing your new GetOrder stored procedure with an argument of the literal value 1049 passed to the _OrderID **parameter**

Making decisions in queries

Now that you know how to add, update, or remove data from a table, let's look at some of the tools SQL provides for making decisions in queries and stored procedures. What if you want to group data and return a value of 0 if a value of the SUM is NULL, for example? What if you want to make the output of a query dependent on some condition or to evaluate parameters in a stored procedure and provide conditional feedback in the output? This chapter looks at all these scenarios and more.

21.1 Conditional functions and expressions

Do you recall that you've already used one function in a conditional expression a few times? That function is COALESCE. You used it in chapter 15 to concatenate the full names of authors and in chapter 20 to handle NULL values for TitleName. In the first example, COALESCE allowed you to avoid a result of NULL for concatenated full names in cases when there were null values for the MiddleName of any authors.

21.1.1 COALESCE function

In chapter 15, we used the following query, which provided two values to COALESCE to evaluate:

```
SELECT CONCAT(FirstName, ' ', COALESCE(MiddleName, ''), ' ', LastName)
    AS AuthorName
FROM author;
```

The COALESCE function evaluates any number of expressions from left to right, returning the first non-null values it finds. Because the MiddleName column of the author table was the first value provided, the COALESCE function evaluated the MiddleName value for each author and then determined whether the MiddleName value was NULL. For each row in which the value was not NULL, the MiddleName value was used in the context of the query. For each row in which the value was NULL, the second value—an empty string represented by two single quotes (' ')—was used for concatenation.

The COALESCE function has more functionality than we used in the preceding query because we can give it more than two expressions to evaluate for NULL values. Here's a simple example that uses three expressions, of which the first two are NULL:

```
SELECT COALESCE(NULL, NULL, 'I am not null!') AS CoalesceTest;
```

The COALESCE function evaluated the first two expressions, determined them to be NULL values, and returned the third expression—the string 'I am not null!'—as the first non-NULL expression. We could have had the COALESCE function evaluate more than three expressions, but as soon as one expression is determined to be not NULL, all subsequent expressions are ignored.

Try it now

Execute the following query using the COALESCE function:

```
SELECT COALESCE(NULL, NULL, 'I am not null!', 'I am ignored!')
   AS CoalesceTest;
```

21.1.2 *IFNULL function*

Another common function is used for evaluating nulls: IFNULL. The IFNULL function is nearly identical in use to the COALESCE function, the main exception being that it's limited to evaluating only two expressions. The first expression is evaluated for null values, and if the value is determined to be NULL, the second expression is returned. Here's an example:

```
SELECT IFNULL(NULL, 'I am not null!') AS IfNullTest;
```

> **NOTE** The IFNULL function doesn't exist in all relational database management systems (RDBMSes). In Microsoft Access and SQL Server, you'll use the ISNULL function instead, and in Oracle, you'll use the NVL function. Although these functions have different names, you use them the same way as IFNULL.

Although we've used literal values in these examples, COALESCE and IFNULL are often used with calculations that might include null values. Let's consider a common scenario in which we want to see a list of all title names and determine whether they're included in any orders.

First, we'll consider the tables we need to use in this query. We need the title table because it has TitleNames. We also need the orderitem table, which contains the Quantity column, representing the quantity of each item ordered in each row. Finally, we need the orderheader table because it relates to both the title and orderitem tables with the TitleID and OrderID columns, respectively.

The way we join these tables is crucial to our output. We want to start with the title table because we want the total quantity sold for each title, but we need to use LEFT JOINs to join the other tables because some titles may not have been included in any orders. If we used INNER JOINs to join all the tables, we'd get a result set that included only titles that were included in orders—not what we wanted from this query.

TitleName	TotalQuantity
A Table of Two Cities	NULL
Anne of Fact Tables	2
Catcher in the Try	11
David Emptyfield	NULL
Of Mice and Metadata	NULL
Pride and Predicates	25
Red Badge of Cursors	NULL
The Call of the While	2
The DateTime Machine	13
The Great GroupBy	1
The Join Luck Club	13
The Sum Also Rises	3

Figure 21.1   The TitleName and the total quantity of TitleName included in orders. TitleName values that weren't included in orders are represented by NULL.

We also want to group by TitleName from the title table and use a SUM function to get the sum of the Quantity column from orderitem for each TitleName. Our query will look something like the following code snippet (results shown in figure 21.1):

```
SELECT
    t.TitleName,
    SUM(oi.Quantity) AS TotalQuantity
FROM title t
LEFT JOIN orderitem oi
    ON t.TitleID = oi.TitleID
LEFT JOIN orderheader oh
    ON oh.OrderID = oi.OrderID
GROUP BY t.TitleName
ORDER BY t.TitleName;
```

If you executed the queries in chapter 16 that added the extra titles, some rows in your results should have NULL for TotalQuantity. In a sales report, NULL typically isn't what readers expect, so make a minor adjustment to your query to add IFNULL, which returns a value of 0 for any title that isn't included in an order (results shown in figure 21.2):

```
SELECT
    t.TitleName,
    IFNULL(SUM(oi.Quantity),0) AS TotalQuantity
FROM title t
LEFT JOIN orderitem oi
    ON t.TitleID = oi.TitleID
LEFT JOIN orderheader oh
```

```
      ON oh.OrderID = oi.OrderID
GROUP BY t.TitleName
ORDER BY t.TitleName;
```

TitleName	TotalQuantity
A Table of Two Cities	0
Anne of Fact Tables	2
Catcher in the Try	11
David Emptyfield	0
Of Mice and Metadata	0
Pride and Predicates	25
Red Badge of Cursors	0
The Call of the While	2
The DateTime Machine	13
The Great GroupBy	1
The Join Luck Club	13
The Sum Also Rises	3

Now our results have a value of 0 instead of NULL for any title that wasn't included in any order, which is a more useful indicator of titles included in orders.

> **TIP** Because COALESCE has more functionality and is supported by every RDBMS, use this function instead of IFNULL or ISNULL to evaluate nulls. We'll be using COALESCE throughout this book instead of IFNULL.

Figure 21.2 The TitleName and the total quantity of TitleName included in orders. TitleName values that weren't included in orders are represented by a value of 0 instead of NULL, due to the use of the IFNULL function.

21.1.3 CASE expression

COALESCE and IFNULL help us evaluate expressions for null values. But what if we need to evaluate for something other than null values or evaluate for different conditions? In these situations, we can use the CASE expression.

The CASE expression, often referred to in queries as a CASE statement, is a more powerful tool than COALESCE and IFNULL because it allows us to evaluate conditions and return different values based on those conditions. CASE lets us make choices on the values that are returned, using logic that emulates the English language. If we want to find titles with prices that are $7.95 and return a value that confirms whether they are $7.95, for example, we might say something like this: "I would like title name and price from the title table. When the price is $7.95, I want to say, 'This title is $7.95.' Otherwise, I want to say, 'This title is not $7.95.' "

We can use a CASE expression to accomplish the intention of the last two sentences. The structure of our CASE expression has a few rules:

- It must start with the keyword CASE.
- It must contain one or more conditions for equality that say WHEN (some value or expression) THEN (the desired value). Because this test is for equality, it won't evaluate NULL values.
- We can use ELSE to account for any value that doesn't meet the WHEN conditions, but ELSE can be used only after all WHEN conditions. Most CASE expressions include ELSE to account for unknown or NULL values.
- The CASE expression must conclude with the keyword END. If the CASE expression is used in the SELECT part of our query, we typically want to use an alias for the column name for readability.

This expression may sound a little complicated, but its use is intuitive. Here's what our SQL from the preceding example looks like when we use CASE (results shown in figure 21.3):

```
SELECT
    TitleName,
    Price,
    CASE Price
        WHEN 7.95 THEN 'This title is $7.95.'
        ELSE 'This title is not $7.95.'
        END AS IsPrice795
FROM title;
```

As I mentioned, the evaluation in a CASE expression can be for another expression, which may not necessarily be a value like values in a column. An expression could be the result of anything from concatenating two or more columns to performing a mathematical calculation. We can evaluate either of those examples or any other expression with a CASE expression.

Let's look at an example using the ROUND function (first discussed in chapter 15). If we want an expression to represent the integer values of a number such as the price of a title, we use the expression ROUND(Price, 0) to find the nearest integer value.

We can modify the preceding query to look for books with a price of about $8 by using the expression ROUND(Price, 0) and then use a CASE expression to return a factual statement about the price (results shown in figure 21.4):

```
SELECT
    TitleName,
    Price,
    CASE ROUND(Price, 0)
        WHEN 8 THEN 'This title is around $8.'
        ELSE 'This title is not around $8.'
        END AS IsPriceAround8Dollars
FROM title;
```

The preceding two queries are examples of using simple CASE expressions, which means that we're evaluating possible values to match a single expression. We can also use a searched CASE expression for more

TitleName	Price	IsPrice795
Pride and Predicates	9.95	This title is not $7.95.
The Join Luck Club	9.95	This title is not $7.95.
Catcher in the Try	8.95	This title is not $7.95.
Anne of Fact Tables	12.95	This title is not $7.95.
The DateTime Machine	7.95	This title is $7.95.
The Great GroupBy	10.95	This title is not $7.95.
The Call of the While	8.95	This title is not $7.95.
The Sum Also Rises	7.95	This title is $7.95.
David Emptyfield	9.95	This title is not $7.95.
Red Badge of Cursors	7.95	This title is $7.95.
Of Mice and Metadata	8.95	This title is not $7.95.
A Table of Two Cities	9.95	This title is not $7.95.

Figure 21.3   The TitleName and Price for all titles, as well as a column aliased as IsPrice795. The values in column IsPrice795 are the results of an evaluation of the price by a CASE expression.

TitleName	Price	IsPriceAround8Dollars
Pride and Predicates	9.95	This title is not around $8.
The Join Luck Club	9.95	This title is not around $8.
Catcher in the Try	8.95	This title is not around $8.
Anne of Fact Tables	12.95	This title is not around $8.
The DateTime Machine	7.95	This title is around $8.
The Great GroupBy	10.95	This title is not around $8.
The Call of the While	8.95	This title is not around $8.
The Sum Also Rises	7.95	This title is around $8.
David Emptyfield	9.95	This title is not around $8.
Red Badge of Cursors	7.95	This title is around $8.
Of Mice and Metadata	8.95	This title is not around $8.
A Table of Two Cities	9.95	This title is not around $8.

Figure 21.4   The TitleName and Price for all titles, as well as a column aliased as IsPriceAround8Dollars. The values in column IsPriceAround8Dollars are the result of an evaluation of the expression ROUND(Price, 0) using a CASE expression.

comprehensive evaluations, such as ranges of data values. With a searched CASE expression, we'll evaluate one or more other expressions to see whether they're true or false.

We can modify the preceding query to search for ranges of price values and see whether a price is less than, equal to, or more than $8 by using a searched CASE statement with the following query (results shown in figure 21.5):

```
SELECT
    TitleName,
    Price,
    CASE
        WHEN Price < 8.00 THEN 'This title is less than $8.00.'
        WHEN Price = 8.00 THEN 'This title is $8.00.'
        WHEN Price > 8.00 THEN 'This title is more than $8.00.'
        END AS IsPriceAround8Dollars
FROM title;
```

The searched CASE expressions evaluated for being true or false are known as *Boolean expressions*. I realize that this chapter has talked about several kinds of expressions, complicated by CASE expressions evaluating other expressions. Please remember that those expressions evaluated in the WHEN parts of the preceding query are Boolean; we'll use them again later in this chapter.

> **NOTE** Although we've used CASE expressions only in the SELECT clause, if you need this kind of decision-making logic elsewhere in your queries, you can use CASE expressions in other clauses, including WHERE, HAVING, and ORDER BY.

TitleName	Price	IsPriceAround8Dollars
Pride and Predicates	9.95	This title is more than $8.00.
The Join Luck Club	9.95	This title is more than $8.00.
Catcher in the Try	8.95	This title is more than $8.00.
Anne of Fact Tables	12.95	This title is more than $8.00.
The DateTime Machine	7.95	This title is less than $8.00.
The Great GroupBy	10.95	This title is more than $8.00.
The Call of the While	8.95	This title is more than $8.00.
The Sum Also Rises	7.95	This title is less than $8.00.
David Emptyfield	9.95	This title is more than $8.00.
Red Badge of Cursors	7.95	This title is less than $8.00.
Of Mice and Metadata	8.95	This title is more than $8.00.
A Table of Two Cities	9.95	This title is more than $8.00.

Figure 21.5   The TitleName and Price for all titles, as well as a column aliased as `IsPriceAround8Dollars`**. The values in column** `IsPriceAround8Dollars` **are the result of a searched CASE expression evaluating whether the Price value is less than, equal to, or more than $8.00.**

21.2   Decision structures

Functions and expressions aren't the only tools we have in SQL for evaluation and decision-making. We can also use several keywords to decide whether we'll even execute SQL statements.

Nearly every RDBMS has keywords you can use to control decision-making. If you've ever used a programming language, the good news is that those keywords should be familiar. If you're new to programming, don't worry; the keywords are very intuitive.

21.2.1   IF and THEN

First, we'll look at the one keyword necessary to start any decision-making: IF . This keyword is the starting point for any *decision structure*, which is how we refer to any SQL we write that involves deciding whether we want to execute a statement. We'll base our decisions on the same Boolean conditions we used in section 21.1.3. This means that if a condition is true, we want the included SQL to execute, and if that condition is false, we don't want it to execute.

Decision structures are commonly used within stored procedures, so let's look at a simple example of using the IF keyword to make a decision inside a stored procedure that adds a row to the promotion table. We can write a stored procedure to add a row for a new PromotionCode, but we can create a decision structure to avoid writing the row if a value for PromotionCode isn't provided.

Before we look at the entire stored procedure, let's look at the individual parts of the SQL we'll use inside the stored procedure to determine whether a PromotionCode value exists. Here's the first part of the stored procedure:

```
CREATE PROCEDURE AddPromotion (
    IN _PromotionID int,
    IN _PromotionCode varchar(10),
    IN _PromotionStartDate datetime,
    IN _PromotionEndDate datetime
)
BEGIN
```

Looking at this part of the stored procedure, we see a name (AddPromotion) and four input parameters: _PromotionID, _PromotionCode, _PromotionStartDate, and _PromotionEndDate. The data types used for these parameters are the same as the corresponding columns in the promotion table. We also have the BEGIN keyword after we declare the parameters to indicate where the stored procedure begins doing what we want it to do.

> **TIP** Always create parameters with the same data types as any columns they'll read or write values to. Using a different data type will cause the RDBMS to do more work and negatively affect query performance. If you don't know the data types of the columns, you can always use SHOW COLUMNS (discussed in chapter 20) to determine column data types. Although SHOW COLUMNS exists only in MySQL, every RDBMS has similar keywords to help you view the data types of the columns of any table.

Next, let's look at the SQL for the rest of the stored procedure:

```
IF _PromotionCode IS NOT NULL THEN
    INSERT INTO promotion (
    PromotionID,
    PromotionCode,
    PromotionStartDate,
    PromotionEndDate
    )
    SELECT
        _PromotionID,
        _PromotionCode,
```

```
    _PromotionStartDate,
    _PromotionEndDate
    ;
END IF;
END
```

Here, we have the IF keyword, which says we want to determine whether the condition of _PromotionCode IS NOT NULL is true. If a value other than NULL was provided for _PromotionCode, the INSERT statement executes. If the value for _PromotionCode is NULL, the subsequent INSERT statement doesn't execute.

We end our conditional statement with END IF, and we end the stored procedure with END. Let's put everything together as a single statement that we can use to create our stored procedure and create it so we can test the conditional logic of our decision structure. We'll use the same DELIMITER commands in MySQL to change the delimiter from a semicolon so we can execute the entire stored procedure:

```
DELIMITER //

CREATE PROCEDURE AddPromotion (
    IN _PromotionID int,
    IN _PromotionCode varchar(10),
    IN _PromotionStartDate datetime,
    IN _PromotionEndDate datetime
  )
 BEGIN

IF _PromotionCode IS NOT NULL THEN
    INSERT INTO promotion (
    PromotionID,
    PromotionCode,
    PromotionStartDate,
    PromotionEndDate
    )
    SELECT
        _PromotionID,
        _PromotionCode,
        _PromotionStartDate,
        _PromotionEndDate
        ;
END IF;
END //

DELIMITER ;
```

If we execute this SQL, we should have our stored procedure AddPromotion ready to execute. First, let's try executing the code with the following arguments for the parameters:

```
CALL AddPromotion (14, '2OFF2023', '2023-01-04', '2023-02-11');
```

Executing this command should result in the message "1 row(s) affected" in the Output panel. We can verify that the row was inserted with the following query (results shown in figure 21.6):

```
SELECT *
FROM promotion
WHERE PromotionID = 14;
```

PromotionID	PromotionCode	PromotionStartDate	PromotionEndDate
14	2OFF2023	2023-01-04 00:00:00	2023-02-11 00:00:00

Figure 21.6   The results of selecting any rows from the promotion table in which the PromotionID is 14. We inserted that row with the AddPromotion stored procedure.

Now that we've verified that our stored procedure works correctly when the result of our IF condition is true, let's try it when the result is false. We'll execute the following SQL, which uses an argument of NULL for the _PromotionCode parameter:

```
CALL AddPromotion (15, NULL, '2023-07-04', '2023-07-11');
```

Executing this command should result in the error message "0 row(s) affected" in the Output panel. We can use a similar query to the one we used to confirm that no row was inserted. Executing the following query returns no results:

```
SELECT *
FROM promotion
WHERE PromotionID = 15;
```

You've written the stored procedure AddPromotion, and you've examined the decision structure it uses to determine whether a row should be inserted into the promotion table. But what if you aren't familiar with the internal workings of this stored procedure? Suppose that you executed the CALL of the stored procedure that returned no results. Wouldn't you want to know why executing the stored procedure didn't work as expected?

When you're writing stored procedures, especially when you're using any kind of decision structure, you usually want the procedure to provide some sort of feedback on the results of the decisions made. To add functionality to your stored procedure that provides feedback or takes some other action if the condition of the evaluation is false, or even if you want to add more conditions, we can use some other keywords.

21.2.2 *ELSE*

Just as IF evaluates whether a condition is true, ELSE provides an alternative action to take if an evaluated condition is determined to be false or NULL. We can use ELSE the same way that we used IF, except that it comes *after* the IF statement.

WARNING   Although the use of ELSE is optional, any statement with ELSE can follow only an IF statement. If you write an ELSE statement without a preceding IF statement, you'll get a syntax error.

Let's review the decision structure we want to have in AddPromotion:

1   If _PromotionCode is not NULL, we insert the values provided in the promotion table.

2   Otherwise, we don't want to insert the values; we want to return a message explaining why the insert was skipped.

Think of ELSE as a shorter version of the word *otherwise*, meaning that after the IF condition isn't met, this is the last thing we do. To accomplish the goal stated in point 2, we need to add this bit of SQL before the END IF:

```
ELSE
    SELECT 'No PromotionCode, INSERT skipped.' AS Message;
```

This code says that if a condition of false or NULL exists for the IF condition, we'll select a literal value of No PromotionCode, INSERT skipped. that will be returned as Message. It's about as straightforward as can be. Let's execute the following SQL to DROP AddPromotion and then re-create the AddPromotion stored procedure with our new logic:

```
DROP PROCEDURE AddPromotion;

DELIMITER //

CREATE PROCEDURE AddPromotion (
    IN _PromotionID int,
    IN _PromotionCode varchar(10),
    IN _PromotionStartDate datetime,
    IN _PromotionEndDate datetime
)
BEGIN

IF _PromotionCode IS NOT NULL THEN
    INSERT INTO promotion (
    PromotionID,
    PromotionCode,
    PromotionStartDate,
    PromotionEndDate
    )
    SELECT
        _PromotionID,
        _PromotionCode,
        _PromotionStartDate,
        _PromotionEndDate
        ;
ELSE
    SELECT 'No PromotionCode, INSERT skipped.' AS Message;
END IF;
```

```
END //

DELIMITER ;
```

After executing the preceding SQL, we can try executing the previous call of Add-Promotion with an argument of NULL for _PromotionCode. The results in figure 21.7 show that we received the message included in the ELSE statement:

Message
No PromotionCode, INSERT skipped.

Figure 21.7 The output from the ELSE statement we added to AddPromotion, which provides a helpful message about why an insert was skipped

```
CALL AddPromotion (15, NULL, '2023-07-04', '2023-07-11');
```

So far, we've used a simple decision structure that evaluates one particular condition, but we can also evaluate multiple conditions using IF and ELSE.

21.2.3 *Multiple conditions*

Our previous decision structure evaluated the value for _PromotionCode for being NOT NULL, but if we want AddPromotion to be a useful stored procedure, we probably should account for possible null values in the other parameters as well. To do so, we have to change our decision structure to reflect several options for evaluation. Let's consider the new decision structure we want to have in AddPromotion:

1 If _PromotionID is null, we want to return a message explaining why the insert was skipped.

2 If _PromotionCode is null, we want to return a message explaining why the insert was skipped.

3 If _PromotionStartDate is null, we want to return a message explaining why the insert was skipped.

4 If _PromotionEndDate is null, we want to return a message explaining why the insert was skipped.

5 Otherwise, we want to insert the values provided in the promotion table.

The SQL inside AddPromotion that handles this decision structure needs a new keyword. This keyword is ELSEIF, which is an additional IF - to handle all these additional evaluations. We use it like this:

```
IF _PromotionID IS NULL THEN
    SELECT 'No PromotionID, INSERT skipped.' AS Message;
ELSEIF _PromotionCode IS NULL THEN
    SELECT 'No PromotionCode, INSERT skipped.' AS Message;
ELSEIF _PromotionStartDate IS NULL THEN
    SELECT 'No PromotionStartDate, INSERT skipped.' AS Message;
ELSEIF _PromotionEndDate IS NULL THEN
    SELECT 'No PromotionEndDate, INSERT skipped.' AS Message;
ELSE
    INSERT INTO promotion (
```

```
    PromotionID,
    PromotionCode,
    PromotionStartDate,
    PromotionEndDate
    )
    SELECT
        _PromotionID,
        _PromotionCode,
        _PromotionStartDate,
        _PromotionEndDate
        ;
END IF;
```

If we modify AddPromotion to include this logic using ELSEIF, we have a message for every possible reason for failure to insert the values.

NOTE   In SQL Server, the keyword ELSEIF is represented by two words: ELSE IF.

Unfortunately, we don't get any message if the query inserts the values successfully. To add that functionality, we need to add another statement to our ELSE statement. Because we now have multiple statements to execute after ELSE, we need to group those statements in a single block with the BEGIN and END keywords. Let's look at the ELSE statement to add the message INSERT successful.:

```
ELSE BEGIN
    INSERT INTO promotion (
    PromotionID,
    PromotionCode,
    PromotionStartDate,
    PromotionEndDate
    )
    SELECT
        _PromotionID,
        _PromotionCode,
        _PromotionStartDate,
        _PromotionEndDate
        ;

    SELECT 'INSERT successful.' AS Message;
    END;
```

The BEGIN and END keywords allow you to group multiple statements in a single block, much as your entire stored procedure has a BEGIN and END. As your SQL becomes more complex, you'll use these keywords frequently, especially in stored procedures.

Try it now

DROP and CREATE the AddPromotion stored procedure, using the decision structure changes discussed in section 21.2.3. Then try executing it with arguments of NULL for the various parameters and verifying that the correct message is returned.

You've made a lot of decisions today, so you have a wealth of options for making decisions in your queries. In chapter 22, you'll learn to use these decision-making options to evaluate individual rows of data.

21.3 Lab

1 Using CASE, write a query that returns the following three columns from the promotion table:

- The PromotionCode column
- The first character of the PromotionCode column with the alias PromotionCodeLeft1
- The sentence This promotion is $X off. with the alias PromotionDiscount and the literal value of X replaced by the value of the second column

2 This query uses a CASE statement to attempt to replace NULL values for MiddleName with an empty string. Why doesn't it work as expected?

```
SELECT
    FirstName,
    CASE MiddleName
        WHEN NULL THEN ''
        ELSE MiddleName
        END AS MiddleName,
    LastName
FROM author;
```

3 If you want to add logic to AddPromotion to skip an insert if the argument for _PromotionCode exists in the promotion table, what might that code look like? (This question is a bit tricky, but try to use what you've learned to answer it.)

21.4 Lab answers

1 You can use the LEFT function (mentioned in chapter 14) to help with the query, which might look something like this:

```
SELECT
    PromotionCode,
    LEFT(PromotionCode, 1) AS PromotionCodeLeft1,
    CASE LEFT(PromotionCode, 1)
        WHEN 1 THEN 'This promotion is for $1 off.'
        WHEN 2 THEN 'This promotion is for $2 off.'
        WHEN 3 THEN 'This promotion is for $3 off.'
        END AS PromotionDiscount
FROM promotion;
```

2 You cannot evaluate for equality with NULL because NULL can never equal NULL. To work as intended, the CASE statement has to evaluate an expression like this:

```
SELECT
    FirstName,
    CASE WHEN MiddleName IS NULL THEN ''
        ELSE MiddleName
        END AS MiddleName,
    LastName
FROM author;
```

3 You might add this logic by using an additional `ELSEIF` statement like this:

```
ELSEIF NOT EXISTS (SELECT PromotionCode FROM promotion WHERE
PromotionCode = _PromotionEndDate) THEN
    SELECT 'Duplicate PromotionCode, INSERT skipped.' AS Message;
```

This example is a little more advanced than the ones covered in this chapter, but it shows that you can do more than check for a NULL value in a Boolean expression. You can even use `EXISTS` and `NOT EXISTS` to evaluate entire queries.

Using cursors 22

In chapter 21, we explored making decisions in queries and learned how to make conditional evaluations. Using IF and THEN keywords allowed us to evaluate one or more values and then decide whether to do something else, such as insert a row of values into a table.

In this chapter, we'll look at other ways to evaluate data and make decisions in SQL, focusing primarily on cursors. Cursors enable us to evaluate a set of data one row or value at a time. Also, as we'll see, they have a bit of complexity, and there are important considerations regarding their use.

The use of cursors in MySQL is restricted to database objects containing prepared SQL, such as stored procedures. Because of this restriction, we'll look at some previously undiscussed features of variables and parameters before we dive into creating and using cursors.

22.1 Reviewing variables and parameters

We've used variables since chapter 13 and parameters since chapter 20. Although variables and parameters are similar in that they're placeholders for values, they have different properties relative to their use. The following sections show how we can use some of these properties.

22.1.1 *Variables inside stored procedures*

Chapter 13 briefly mentioned the way variables are declared in MySQL and how they differ in other relational database management systems (RDBMSes). In case you don't remember, here's the warning from that chapter:

> **WARNING** This method of declaring variables in MySQL isn't universal. When you use a different RDBMS, such as SQL Server or PostgreSQL, first you have to declare a user-defined variable using the DECLARE keyword; then you assign it a specified data type.

Interestingly, in MySQL we have to use the more common method (with the DECLARE keyword noted in the warning) of operating inside a stored procedure. Let's look at an example. If we want to declare a variable to hold a value for TitleID from the title table outside a stored procedure, we'd do so like this:

```
SET @TitleID = 101;
```

Inside a stored procedure, however, we'd have to declare the variable and its data type using the DECLARE keyword, like this:

```
DECLARE _TitleID int;
```

Now we have a few options for assigning a value (such as 101) to our variable inside the stored procedure. The first option is using the SET keyword like this:

```
SET _TitleID = 101;
```

The SET keyword gives us some options for setting this value dynamically via a sub-query. Here's an example:

```
SET _TitleID =
    (SELECT TitleID
    FROM title
    WHERE TitleName = 'Pride and Predicates');
```

We have another option for assigning a specific value to our variable. We can use a default value using the DEFAULT keyword:

```
DECLARE _TitleID int DEFAULT 101;
```

This final option is what we'll use in cursor examples for the rest of this chapter.

22.1.2 *Output parameters*

Chapter 20 noted that parameters in stored procedures can be used for either input or output. So far, we've used only input parameters, which allow us to pass a value into a stored procedure, by declaring them with the IN keyword:

```
CREATE PROCEDURE GetSomeData(
   IN _TitleName varchar(50)
   )
```

Declaring a parameter for output lets us take a value determined inside the stored procedure and its SQL and pass it to a script or even another stored procedure. We do this fairly intuitively with the OUT keyword, as in this example:

```
CREATE PROCEDURE GetSomeData(
   OUT _TitleName varchar(50)
   )
```

The cursor examples in this chapter use output parameters, so you'll have several chances to get comfortable with them and their use.

22.2 Cursors

At its most basic level, a *cursor* is a database object that steps through the results of a SELECT query, allowing you to retrieve and, if you desire, manipulate data one row at a time. Much as a cursor in an electronic document tells you where you're working, a cursor is a row pointer that enables you to loop through the result set of a query, processing individual rows for whatever intended reason.

Although cursors are simple to explain, they can be intimidating to use due to the complexity of their parts relative to other objects we've used, such as views and stored procedures. By that, I mean we can create simple views and stored procedures but not simple cursors. Even the most basic cursors may look a bit intimidating at first. To make cursors more understandable, let's examine their four core components.

22.2.1 Anatomy of a cursor

No matter how simple or complex they are, every cursor has four parts that include these descriptive keywords:

- DECLARE—Just as we used DECLARE earlier in this chapter to create a variable inside a stored procedure, we'll use it to create our cursor. The DECLARE part will contain the SELECT query that defines the set of data our cursor will use.
- OPEN—After we create the cursor, we must open it. Although the DECLARE part defined the data set for the cursor to use, that SELECT query won't execute until we open the query in this part. Here, the cursor gets the results of our SELECT query and holds them in server memory while we use the cursor.
- FETCH—The FETCH keyword retrieves rows from the data set one row at a time. This part is the main part of the cursor, where we populate variables, modify data, and do whatever else we intend to do with it. We work with that single row until the next time we FETCH another row as we loop through the result set, and we stop fetching rows when we reach the end of the data set.

- CLOSE—When we determine that we're done fetching and evaluating rows in our data set, we CLOSE the cursor, which releases the contents of the cursor from server memory.

NOTE These four parts must exist for a cursor to work, and they must be in this order.

WARNING Although MySQL doesn't, other RDBMSes may require you to deallocate a cursor when you finish using it. Please refer to the documentation of your specific RDBMS to see whether this step is required for any cursors you write outside MySQL.

22.2.2 *Creating a cursor*

Suppose that we want to determine the quantity of titles sold at the price listed in the title table, with no promotional discounts applied. We could write a stored procedure that uses a cursor to step through each order, checking it for any titles sold at the price listed in the title table. As our cursor goes through each order, it can keep a running total of the quantity of titles sold at the list price in an output parameter, which is returned to us with the final quantity of titles sold at the list price.

I'll go through the parts of this cursor later in this section. For now, when you take your first look at this stored procedure, try to see whether you can identify the four main parts of the cursor:

```
DELIMITER //

CREATE PROCEDURE GetTitleTotalQuantitySoldListPrice(
    OUT _TotalQuantitySold int
    )
BEGIN

DECLARE _Done boolean DEFAULT FALSE;

DECLARE _OrderID int;

DECLARE AllOrders CURSOR FOR

SELECT OrderID
FROM orderheader;

DECLARE CONTINUE HANDLER FOR NOT FOUND SET _Done = TRUE;

SET _TotalQuantitySold = 0;

OPEN AllOrders;

GetOrders: LOOP

    FETCH AllOrders INTO _OrderID;
```

```
        SET _TotalQuantitySold = _TotalQuantitySold +

            (SELECT COALESCE(SUM(Quantity),0)
            FROM title t
            INNER JOIN orderitem oi
                ON t.TitleID = oi.TitleID
                AND t.Price = oi.ItemPrice
            WHERE oi.OrderID = _OrderID
            );

        IF _Done = TRUE THEN

            LEAVE GetOrders;
        END IF;

    END LOOP GetOrders;

    CLOSE AllOrders;

END //

DELIMITER ;
```

That's a lot of SQL to evaluate, so we'll examine it one bit at a time. We start by changing the delimiter to two forward slashes so we can use semicolons inside our stored procedure:

```
DELIMITER //
```

Next, we will use CREATE PROCEDURE to say we want to make a procedure named GetTitleTotalQuantitySoldListPrice. Note that our procedure has a parameter called _TotalQuantitySold, which not only has a data type of int but also is used as an output parameter. We know this because the word OUT precedes the parameter name:

```
CREATE PROCEDURE GetTitleTotalQuantitySoldListPrice(
    OUT _TotalQuantitySold int
    )
BEGIN
```

Then we declare two variables: one for _Done and one for _OrderID. The _OrderID variable will be used for the OrderIDs that we'll evaluate one by one in the cursor. The _Done variable will determine whether we've finished evaluating all rows. This variable uses a new data type called boolean, which means that its value is either TRUE or FALSE. We assign a default value of FALSE at the start of the stored procedure because we haven't finished (or even started) evaluating a data set in our cursor:

```
DECLARE _Done boolean DEFAULT FALSE;
DECLARE _OrderID int;
```

Now we have the first part of our cursor: the DECLARE part. We declared our cursor with the name AllOrders, and our data set will include every OrderID in the orderheader table:

```
DECLARE AllOrders CURSOR FOR

SELECT OrderID
FROM orderheader;
```

Then we use another DECLARE statement to tell the RDBMS that it should handle the condition of no more rows to evaluate (NOT FOUND SET) by setting our _Done variable, which indicates that we're done using the cursor, to TRUE. This allows us to break out of the loop and stop fetching rows:

```
DECLARE CONTINUE HANDLER FOR NOT FOUND SET _Done = TRUE;
```

Because MySQL doesn't allow us to set a default value for parameters, we're setting the value of _TotalQuantitySold to 0 as a starting value. Later, we'll increase this value incrementally as we find titles that were sold at the list price:

```
SET _TotalQuantitySold = 0;
```

Now we get to the second part of the cursor, where we OPEN the cursor. The query used in the DECLARE part executes, and the resulting data set is stored in memory for use by the cursor:

```
OPEN AllOrders;
```

Next, we use a LOOP statement named GetOrders to loop through the data set. This LOOP statement is a requirement for cursors in MySQL:

```
GetOrders: LOOP
```

> **NOTE** Not all RDBMSes require you to use LOOP with a cursor, so this part may be unnecessary in another RDBMS. Consult the documentation of the RDBMS you're using to understand the various requirements for any cursor.

With the cursor open, we retrieve the first row of values with the FETCH part of our query. In the case of our cursor, we're selecting only the OrderID column of values, so we're fetching the first value for OrderID and assigning it to the _OrderID variable:

```
    FETCH AllOrders INTO _OrderID;
```

Now that we have a value for _OrderID, we can evaluate the order to see whether it includes any titles that were sold for the price listed in the title table. If it does, we'll increase the value of _TotalQuantitySold by the quantity of titles that were sold for the list price in the order. If it doesn't, using COALESCE will allow us to increment the value for _TotalQuantitySold by zero. Remember that the query used by the cursor is evaluated in a loop, so we'll repeat it for every OrderID in the set from the DECLARE part of our cursor:

```
SET _TotalQuantitySold = _TotalQuantitySold +

    (SELECT COALESCE(SUM(Quantity),0)
    FROM title t
    INNER JOIN orderitem oi
        ON t.TitleID = oi.TitleID
        AND t.Price = oi.ItemPrice
    WHERE oi.OrderID = _OrderID
    );
```

Remember when we declared our handler to set the value of _Done to TRUE if it reached the end of the results in the cursor? Well, if that's the case here, we'll use an IF statement to exit the loop with the LEAVE keyword:

```
IF _Done = TRUE THEN

    LEAVE GetOrders;
END IF;
```

NOTE LEAVE is another keyword used in MySQL, but it's not used to exit cursor loops in other RDBMSes. Again, consult the documentation for any RDBMS you're using to determine how to exit a cursor loop.

Our loop process can't go on forever, so here, we define the end of the loop. If we haven't exited the loop via the preceding statement, we fetch another value for OrderID at the beginning of the loop:

```
END LOOP GetOrders;
```

If we've reached this point, we've exited the loop, so we're done using our cursor. If we're done using our cursor, we need to close it and release the contents from memory. To do this, we use the CLOSE keyword, which is the fourth and final part of our cursor:

```
CLOSE AllOrders;
```

All the work with the cursor is done now, so we need to note the end of the stored procedure with the END keyword and the nonstandard statement delimiter noted at the beginning of our script:

```
END //
```

Finally, we change the statement delimiter back to the standard semicolon:

```
DELIMITER ;
```

If we execute all that SQL, we can call the stored procedure with the output parameter, which we can capture in a variable named `@TotalQuantitySold`. Then we can select the value of the variable to see the total quantity of titles sold at list price, with the value shown in figure 22.1:

```
CALL GetTitleTotalQuantitySoldListPrice(@TotalQuantitySold);
SELECT @TotalQuantitySold AS TotalQuantitySold;
```

TotalQuantitySold
27

Figure 22.1 The TotalQuantity of titles sold at list price, determined by the stored procedure we wrote, which uses a cursor to determine this value

> **Try it now**
>
> Create the stored procedure GetTitleTotalQuantitySoldListPrice and execute the preceding query to verify the total quantity of titles sold at list price.

Even the most basic cursors can appear to be complicated, but I hope that this walkthrough of a cursor used inside a stored procedure cleared up any confusion. If you're still a bit confused, you may be encouraged to know that less-complicated alternatives can give you much of the same functionality you'd get from a cursor.

22.3 *Alternatives to cursors*

A common replacement for a cursor in SQL is a WHILE loop, which requires a lot less language to do the same row-by-row evaluation while looping through a set of data.

22.3.1 *Using WHILE*

What makes the WHILE loop simpler is the fact that we don't have to open or close our data set. We don't even need a data set for a WHILE loop—only a condition for the WHILE statement that must be met to determine whether to continue the loop. Here's how we'd rewrite our GetTitleTotalQuantitySoldListPrice stored procedure to use a WHILE loop instead of a cursor:

```
DROP PROCEDURE GetTitleTotalQuantitySoldListPrice;

DELIMITER //

CREATE PROCEDURE GetTitleTotalQuantitySoldListPrice(
    OUT _TotalQuantitySold int
    )
BEGIN
```

```
DECLARE _OrderID int;

SET _TotalQuantitySold = 0;
SET _OrderID = (SELECT MIN(OrderID) FROM orderheader);

WHILE _OrderID IS NOT NULL DO
    SET _TotalQuantitySold = _TotalQuantitySold +

        (SELECT COALESCE(SUM(Quantity),0)
        FROM title t
        INNER JOIN orderitem oi
            ON t.TitleID = oi.TitleID
            AND t.Price = oi.ItemPrice
        WHERE oi.OrderID = _OrderID
        );

    SET _OrderID =
        (SELECT MIN(OrderID)
        FROM orderheader
        WHERE OrderID > _OrderID);

    END WHILE;

END //

DELIMITER ;
```

Let's examine the new parts so that we understand what we're doing. First, instead of fetching the first value into our _OrderID, variable, we used a SET statement, which uses the MIN function to select the minimum value from the orderheader table. That value is effectively the same as the first value chosen by the preceding cursor:

```
SET _OrderID = (SELECT MIN(OrderID) FROM orderheader);
```

Then we declare our WHILE statement, which says to keep looping through the SQL contained in the loop until _OrderID is NULL. We start the loop with a new keyword, DO:

```
WHILE _OrderID IS NOT NULL DO
```

> **NOTE** Although the DO keyword is used in MySQL, other RDBMSes often start with BEGIN. I know it may be frustrating to keep being warned about the differences in SQL use among RDBMSes, but consult the appropriate documentation to avoid syntax errors.

This next part should look familiar. It's the same logic we used in our cursor to incrementally add to the _TotalQuantitySold parameter that we used in our cursor:

```
SET _TotalQuantitySold = _TotalQuantitySold +

    (SELECT COALESCE(SUM(Quantity),0)
```

```
FROM title t
INNER JOIN orderitem oi
    ON t.TitleID = oi.TitleID
    AND t.Price = oi.ItemPrice
WHERE oi.OrderID = _OrderID
);
```

Next, we'll increment the value of _OrderID to the next-highest value, using logic similar to what we used to grab the first minimum value. The difference is that now we're grabbing the minimum value that's higher than the current value, which is the next value for OrderID in the orderheader table:

```
SET _OrderID =
    (SELECT MIN(OrderID)
    FROM orderheader
    WHERE OrderID > _OrderID);
```

Finally, we end the SQL included in the WHILE loop with END WHILE:

```
END WHILE;
```

This code is less SQL than we used for our cursor, but it effectively does the same thing. Because the cursor and the WHILE loop do the same thing, however, they could create the same problem: blocking. *Blocking* happens when a query locks resources such as rows in a table, causing other queries that require the same resources to wait until the first query completes its execution.

Although all the SQL we've written and executed so far has been for our MySQL database, of which we're the only users, the SQL you write outside this book will be for a database with tens, hundreds, or even thousands of users. Depending on database settings that you may not control, your cursor or WHILE loop in a database with more connections could cause blocking for other users, making their queries take longer or even fail if the connection has to wait too long. One way to work around this problem is to use temporary tables.

> **TIP** Many RDBMSes have options for cursors beyond what we've used to reduce the chance of blocking. But the default options for cursors often result in blocking.

22.3.2 *Temporary tables*

Temporary tables are useful because they allow us to copy a data set that might be heavily used to a separate table that exists only as long as our connection to the database exists. When the connection is closed, the temporary tables are dropped from the database. More pertinent to cursors and WHILE loops, we can use them with no chance of blocking because they can be used only by the queries in our connection.

The syntax for creating a temporary table in MySQL is almost identical to the syntax we used to create tables in chapter 18. The only difference is that we add the word TEMPORARY between CREATE and TABLE.

NOTE   Although temporary tables exist for nearly every RDBMS, the syntax for creating them isn't universal. I hope you aren't tired of seeing this message, but consult the relevant documentation.

To prevent blocking, we could create a temporary table inside our stored procedure, populate the table with the range of values we plan to use, and then direct our WHILE loop (or cursor) to loop through the temporary table.

For the preceding version of GetTitleTotalQuantitySoldListPrice, here's how we could drop the existing stored procedure and then re-create it using a temporary table named orderheadertemp that replaces our use of the orderheader table:

```
DROP PROCEDURE GetTitleTotalQuantitySoldListPrice;

DELIMITER //

CREATE PROCEDURE GetTitleTotalQuantitySoldListPrice(
    OUT _TotalQuantitySold int
    )
BEGIN
DECLARE _OrderID int;

SET _TotalQuantitySold = 0;

CREATE TEMPORARY TABLE orderheadertemp (OrderID int);

INSERT orderheadertemp (OrderID)
SELECT OrderID
FROM orderheader;

SET _OrderID = (SELECT MIN(OrderID) FROM orderheadertemp);

WHILE _OrderID IS NOT NULL DO
    SET _TotalQuantitySold = _TotalQuantitySold +

        (SELECT COALESCE(SUM(Quantity),0)
        FROM title t
        INNER JOIN orderitem oi
            ON t.TitleID = oi.TitleID
            AND t.Price = oi.ItemPrice
        WHERE oi.OrderID = _OrderID
        );

    SET _OrderID =
        (SELECT MIN(OrderID)
        FROM orderheadertemp
        WHERE OrderID > _OrderID);
```

```
    END WHILE;

END //

DELIMITER ;
```

Temporary tables are wonderful tools to use for more than preventing blocking. We can use them to hold data sets that are used repeatedly in a SQL script, and we can use them to simplify complex queries by separating them into smaller, more efficient queries. But after all this talk of cursors, WHILE loops, and temporary tables, we should take a moment to ask a question: Is all this even necessary?

22.4 Considerations for using cursors

If you've read all the preceding chapters and completed the exercises, there's a good chance that you've thought of a better way to find the total quantity of titles sold at list price. In that case, you're correct. You could have handled this request much more simply without using a cursor or a WHILE loop:

```
SELECT COALESCE(SUM(Quantity),0) AS TotalQuantitySold
FROM title t
INNER JOIN orderitem oi
    ON t.TitleID = oi.TitleID
    AND t.Price = oi.ItemPrice;
```

Unfortunately, cursors and WHILE loops have a common problem: they are usually inferior to other options in SQL. Cursors and WHILE loops are inferior solutions for most query requests because the nature of evaluating data sets row by row is the opposite of the way that an RDBMS is designed to evaluate data, which is to use data sets.

22.4.1 Thinking in sets

Starting with our first query, everything we've seen in this book up to the last part of chapter 21 involves set-based programming. *Set-based programming* tells the RDBMS what data set or data sets we want to evaluate; from there, we let the RDBMS figure out the best way to complete the query.

We used set-based programming with our SQL queries over and over until we started working with the IF, THEN, and ELSE keywords, along with cursors and WHILE loops. That type of programming is called *procedural programming*, which gives the RDBMS specific instructions about what to do and how to do it. Procedural programming is quite common for programming languages other than SQL.

One reason why cursors are so long and wordy is that we need to tell the RDBMS every step to take to get a cursor to evaluate data. Unfortunately, because we're telling the RDBMS what to do, taking a procedural approach in SQL often results in slow performance, extensive blocking, and the consumption of more server resources than a query with a set-based approach would use.

22.4.2 *Thinking about cursor use*

I don't mean to say that you should *never* use cursors, although it's possible to solve nearly every query request without using them. But as you near the final chapters of this book, I want to encourage you to use your total knowledge of SQL and look at cursors with a bit of skepticism.

Knowing how to construct a cursor can be useful when you have a request with no other solution than to evaluate each row in a set individually. But those cases are rare, so even when you think you need to use a cursor, take a moment to ask whether a set-based solution exists.

In terms of evaluating existing code, look at any cursor you encounter as a potential opportunity to improve performance by replacing it with set-based programming. You'll likely encounter cursors frequently in existing stored procedures, as many folks with experience doing procedural programming in other languages often lean on cursors in SQL instead of the set-based methods you've learned throughout this book. Use your knowledge not only to reduce the complexity involved in cursors but also to improve the performance of stored procedures and reduce the resources they require from the server.

I hope you're excited about the prospect of reviewing someone else's SQL, because that's exactly what you'll do in chapter 23.

22.5 Lab

This lab is a bit different from earlier labs. Here, you'll consider a few scenarios and try to determine whether you need to use a cursor to retrieve the data:

1. Evaluate every TitleName in the title table to determine the quantity of each title ordered by customers in California. This query should include customers with a value of CA for the State column in the customer table.

2. Evaluate every CustomerID in the customer table to determine whether the customer purchased the title Pride and Predicates. Return Yes if they did and No if they didn't in a column named OrderedPrideAndPredicates.

3. Evaluate each order to determine whether it was the first that a customer placed. Return the OrderID, CustomerID, and OrderDate of all orders that were the first by any customer.

4. Evaluate every CustomerID in the customer table to see whether the customer placed an order in the past year. If a customer placed such an order, execute a stored procedure named CreateThankYouMessage. This stored procedure, which contains a single CustomerID parameter, creates a message to be sent to the customer.

22.6 Lab answers

1. You don't need a cursor to determine this information. You can find the requested data set with a query like this one, which uses a subquery to collect the quantity of titles ordered by customers in California:

```
SELECT
    t.TitleName,
    COALESCE(SUM(x.Quantity),0) AS QuantityFromCA
FROM title t
LEFT JOIN (
    SELECT
        oi.TitleID,
        oi.Quantity
    FROM orderitem oi
    INNER JOIN orderheader oh
        ON oi.OrderID = oh.OrderID
    INNER JOIN customer c
        ON oh.CustomerID = c.CustomerID
    WHERE c.State = 'CA'
    ) x
    ON t.TitleID = x.TitleID
GROUP BY t.TitleName;
```

2 You don't need a cursor for this task either. You can use a subquery and a CASE
   statement to determine the presence of data in the subquery. Be careful to use
   COALESCE or some other way to evaluate something other than NULL, because
   NULL can't be evaluated in a CASE statement. The following example defaults
   NULL values to 0 because no CustomerID of 0 exists:

```
SELECT
    c.CustomerID,
    CASE COALESCE(x.CustomerID,0)
        WHEN 0 THEN 'No'
        ELSE 'Yes'
        END AS OrderedPrideAndPredicates
FROM customer c
LEFT JOIN (
    SELECT oh.CustomerID
    FROM orderheader oh
    INNER JOIN orderitem oi
        ON oh.OrderID = oi.OrderID
    INNER JOIN title t
        ON oi.TitleID = t.TitleID
    WHERE t.TitleName = 'Pride and Predicates'
    GROUP BY oh.CustomerID
    )x
    ON c.CustomerID = x.CustomerID
ORDER BY c.CustomerID;
```

3 Again, you don't need a cursor. You can use another subquery to determine the
   first OrderID for each CustomerID and then select the desired rows from the
   subquery with an INNER JOIN:

```
SELECT
    oh.OrderID,
    oh.CustomerID,
    oh.OrderDate
```

```
FROM orderheader oh
INNER JOIN (
    SELECT
        ohf.CustomerID,
        MIN(ohf.OrderID) AS FirstOrderID
    FROM orderheader ohf
    GROUP BY ohf.CustomerID
    ) x
ON oh.OrderID = x.FirstOrderID;
```

Also, in each of these three exercises, you could use the SQL in the subqueries to populate a temporary table and then join that temporary table instead of joining the subquery. The point is that you have choices beyond using a cursor to achieve the desired results.

4 This case is one of the few times you'd need to use a cursor. You have a data set of CustomerID values, but you can't use set-based programming to complete the request because you can provide only one value at a time to the CreateThank-YouMessage stored procedure.

Using someone else's script 23

I hope you're feeling confident about all the SQL you've learned in this book. I've covered the most basic and frequently used keywords and statements, so you should be well prepared to fulfill requests to retrieve and even manipulate data in a relational database.

As with a foreign language, though, you need to be able to listen and read as well as speak or write. You need to be able to read existing SQL in stored procedures and elsewhere in whatever databases your organization has. Because this book is an introduction to the SQL language, you'll likely even find yourself looking on the internet for examples of SQL scripts that use keywords and concepts you haven't been exposed to yet.

To practice these vital skills and apply what you've learned, in this chapter, you'll review SQL examples written by someone else. Know that the examples will work, but you have to look at them closely to determine what the author intended. Also, these scripts go against the best practices you've learned, so you'll also be considering how to improve the SQL in the scripts.

There's no lab section at the end of the chapter because this chapter is like one large review. There aren't even any "Try it now" sidebars, but you're welcome to try these scripts if you want. Your main task here is to walk through the scripts, understand what they're meant to do, and improve them based on everything you've learned in this book.

23.1   Someone else's script: Creating a table

All these examples involve a new table named authorpayment that tracks royalty payments to authors. The rows in the table reflect the amount paid to each author by title and year. The presumption is that authors will be paid annually based on the sales of the titles.

23.1.1   The CREATE TABLE script

Let's start with the first script, which creates the table:

```
CREATE TABLE authorpayment (
    ID int,
    Author int,
    Title int,
    PaymentYear char(4),
    PaymentAmount decimal(7,2)
    );
```

Although this script isn't particularly verbose, I'm sure that if you recall the concepts and examples discussed in chapters 18 and 19, you'll immediately spot a few things that could be corrected. Take a moment to consider the script and make some notes about what you'd change. When you're ready, continue reading, and I'll share my thoughts.

23.1.2   Reviewing the CREATE TABLE script

The first thing you may notice is the column named ID, which is ambiguous. Unfortunately, naming the first column in a table ID is common when people design database tables in a hurry and without clear intentions. You always want to be clear about a column's purpose in case the column is used in other queries, so you should rename this column AuthorPaymentID.

Also, if this AuthorPaymentID column is intended to contain unique values that form the primary key of the table, you should add a PRIMARY KEY constraint to the column and even consider adding an AUTO_INCREMENT property to populate the column with values that increment automatically.

Next, the Author column appears not to have been fully thought out. It has the same data type as the AuthorID column used in several tables in the sqlnovel database, so for consistency, you should change the name to AuthorID. For the sake of data integrity, the column should also contain a foreign key reference to the author table so that AuthorID in the authorpayment table is populated only with values from the author table. Further, because every payment has to go to an author, you want to put a NOT NULL constraint on this column.

All these same points apply to the Title column. You should rename it TitleID for consistency, create a FOREIGN KEY constraint that references the TitleID values in the title table, and add a NOT NULL constraint to force a TitleID to be included in every row.

The PaymentYear column is a little odd because it has a data type of char(4). This data type means that the values will be stored as a string of characters, even though years are numeric values. You don't need to worry about any non-numeric characters occurring in years when the authors will be paid, so you should use an integer (int) data type instead.

> **NOTE** You may want to use a character data type to store numeric values in one case: when you have leading zeros. U.S. zip codes used for mailing addresses are good examples because many zip codes start with at least one zero. If you entered the zip code 03872 into a column with an integer data type, it would be stored as 3872. For this reason, U.S. zip codes are typically stored as character (char) data types.

You should also place a NOT NULL constraint on the PaymentYear column because every row needs to reflect a particular year. Also, although it's not necessary to do so, you might want to put a CHECK constraint on the PaymentYear column to allow only values that fall within a certain range of years. This constraint would limit the data that could be entered, preventing many potential typos that could affect the integrity of the data. A good range for this constraint would be 2000 to 2100 because frankly, if this database is still being used in 2100, it will be well past time to upgrade.

Finally, the PaymentAmount column looks good because the data type, decimal(7,2), means that you can accommodate payment values up to 99,999.99. You want to place a NOT NULL constraint on this column as well because every payment requires an amount. The only other addition you might consider is a CHECK constraint on the values to ensure that you have only positive values in this column; presumably, authors won't be paid negative amounts.

23.1.3 *Improving the CREATE TABLE script*

If you put everything together, the SQL to create the authorpayment table looks something like this:

```
CREATE TABLE authorpayment (
    AuthorPaymentID int NOT NULL AUTO_INCREMENT,
    AuthorID int NOT NULL,
    TitleID int NOT NULL,
    PaymentYear int NOT NULL CHECK (PaymentYear BETWEEN 2000 AND 2100),
    PaymentAmount decimal(7,2) NOT NULL CHECK (PaymentAmount BETWEEN 0.00 AND
      99999.99),
    CONSTRAINT PK_AuthorPayment PRIMARY KEY (AuthorPaymentID),
    CONSTRAINT FK_authorpayment_author FOREIGN KEY (AuthorID) REFERENCES
      author(AuthorID),
    CONSTRAINT FK_authorpayment_title FOREIGN KEY (TitleID) REFERENCES
      title(TitleID)
);
```

I hope that you see and understand how these changes will help enforce data integrity and make the table understandable and consistent with the other tables in the database. In the future, you might even consider adding a unique index to cover AuthorID, TitleID, and PaymentYear because it appears that these values should be unique for each row. In addition, you might consider changing the primary key to use that combination of columns instead of the AuthorPaymentID, which would mean you wouldn't need to create the unique index.

23.2   *Someone else's script: Inserting data*

Next, let's look at a script that inserts rows into this new table. This stored procedure should run for each year, collecting sales information and then determining the royalty payment to the author.

23.2.1   *The INSERT stored procedure*

Here's a stored procedure for you to review:

```
DELIMITER //

CREATE PROCEDURE InsertAnnualPayment(
    IN _PaymentYear int
    )
BEGIN

DECLARE _Done boolean DEFAULT FALSE;
DECLARE _TitleID int;
DECLARE _AuthorID int;
DECLARE _Royalty decimal(5,2);
DECLARE _AuthorCount int;
DECLARE _TotalSales decimal(7,2);
DECLARE _PaymentAmount decimal(7,2);

DECLARE AllTitles CURSOR FOR

SELECT TitleID, AuthorID
FROM titleauthor
ORDER BY
    TitleID,
    AuthorOrder;

DECLARE CONTINUE HANDLER FOR NOT FOUND SET _Done = TRUE;

OPEN AllTitles;

GetTitles: LOOP

    FETCH AllTitles INTO _TitleID, _AuthorID;

    SET _Royalty = (
        SELECT Royalty
        FROM title
        WHERE TitleID = _TitleID
        );

    SET _AuthorCount = (
        SELECT COUNT(AuthorID)
        FROM titleauthor
```

```
        WHERE TitleID = _TitleID
        );

    SET _TotalSales = (
        SELECT SUM(orderitem.Quantity * orderitem.ItemPrice)
        FROM orderheader
        INNER JOIN orderitem
            ON orderheader.OrderID = orderitem.OrderID
        WHERE orderitem.TitleID = _TitleID
            AND YEAR(orderheader.OrderDate) = _PaymentYear
        );

    SET _PaymentAmount =
        COALESCE(CONVERT(
            ((_TotalSales * (_Royalty/100))/_AuthorCount), decimal(7,2))
            , 0.00);

    IF _PaymentAmount > 0.00 THEN
        INSERT authorpayment (
            AuthorID,
            TitleID,
            PaymentYear,
            PaymentAmount
            )
        SELECT
            _AuthorID,
            _TitleID,
            _PaymentYear,
            _PaymentAmount;
        END IF;

        IF _Done = TRUE THEN

            LEAVE GetTitles;
        END IF;

    END LOOP GetTitles;

    CLOSE AllTitles;

END //

DELIMITER ;
```

Take a moment to review the stored procedure and maybe even take some notes before proceeding.

23.2.2 *Reviewing the INSERT stored procedure*

If you read chapter 22, the first thing to notice about this stored procedure is that it uses a cursor to determine the annual royalty payments. I hope that when you see this cursor, you start wondering whether you can turn this row-by-row evaluation into a set-based evaluation instead.

To determine whether you can replace the cursor, first look at what the stored procedure is doing with the cursor. Let's go through each section of the stored procedure.

The start of the stored procedure is fairly standard. It looks as though an int value is required for the input parameter _PaymentYear, which is the only parameter:

```
DELIMITER //

CREATE PROCEDURE InsertAnnualPayment(
    IN _PaymentYear int
    )
BEGIN
```

After that section, several variables are declared. Although all the variables seem to have sensible data types, on closer inspection, you see that the _Royalty value doesn't match the decimal(5,2) data type used for the Royalty column in the title table. Mismatched data types can lead to data errors or inconsistencies. Also, as you go through the cursor, you'll see that many, if not all, of these variables may be unnecessary:

```
DECLARE _Done boolean DEFAULT FALSE;
DECLARE _TitleID int;
DECLARE _AuthorID int;
DECLARE _Royalty int;
DECLARE _AuthorCount int;
DECLARE _TotalSales decimal(7,2);
DECLARE _PaymentAmount decimal(7,2);
```

The cursor with the name AllTitles is declared. Notice that unlike the cursors you used in chapter 22, this cursor uses two columns instead of one:

```
DECLARE AllTitles CURSOR FOR

SELECT TitleID, AuthorID
FROM titleauthor
ORDER BY
    TitleID,
    AuthorOrder;
```

The handler variable _Done is declared to determine when to exit the cursor loop:

```
DECLARE CONTINUE HANDLER FOR NOT FOUND SET _Done = TRUE;
```

Then comes the OPEN the cursor, where the results of the query used by the cursor are retrieved:

```
OPEN AllTitles;
```

Next is the LOOP used by the cursor, named GetTitles:

```
GetTitles: LOOP
```

The first results of the cursor are fetched, and the values are assigned to the variables _TitleID and _AuthorID:

```
FETCH AllTitles INTO _TitleID, _AuthorID;
```

After that, values are assigned to other variables. The first assignment is the value for _Royalty, which is assigned for the particular _TitleID value. You probably don't need the _Royalty variable. You could just as easily use the value in the title table instead of populating and using this variable:

```
SET _Royalty = (
    SELECT Royalty
    FROM title
    WHERE TitleID = _TitleID
    );
```

The value for _AuthorCount is determined for the particular _TitleID. Having a separate query determine this value may not be a bad idea, although if you use a GROUP BY on the titleauthor table and group by TitleID, you might be able to use an INNER JOIN to include the Royalty amount noted earlier as well. Because Royalty is a column in the title table, you know that a one-to-one relationship exists with the results grouped by TitleID in the titleauthor table:

```
SET _AuthorCount = (
    SELECT COUNT(AuthorID)
    FROM titleauthor
    WHERE TitleID = _TitleID
    );
```

The value for _TotalSales, which represents sales in terms of dollars, is determined by taking the SUM of the Quantity multiplied by the Price for the title for all orders placed in the _PaymentYear. The rows that match the _PaymentYear are calculated by using the YEAR function to determine the year of every value of the OrderDate column in the orderheader table. It makes sense to have this calculation as a separate query, but you probably should avoid using the YEAR function this way. Although they appear to be convenient, as noted in chapter 14, functions can be inefficient if you have millions of rows to evaluate in tables:

```
SET _TotalSales = (
    SELECT SUM(orderitem.Quantity * orderitem.ItemPrice)
    FROM orderheader
    INNER JOIN orderitem
        ON orderheader.OrderID = orderitem.OrderID
    WHERE orderitem.TitleID = _TitleID
        AND YEAR(orderheader.OrderDate) = _PaymentYear
    );
```

In the last variable assignment, the calculation to determine the value for
_PaymentAmount, which is the amount to be paid to the author based on their royalty, is
calculated using the _TotalSales, _Royalty, and _AuthorCount values. You're getting
to the heart of the cursor used by the stored procedure, and it seems that apart from
the values for _TotalSales and AuthorCount, a lot of unnecessary queries are being
used to determine values because the author wasn't thinking about a set-based solution:

```
SET _PaymentAmount =
    COALESCE(CONVERT(
        ((_TotalSales * (_Royalty/100))/_AuthorCount), decimal(7,2))
        , 0.00);
```

If the value for _PaymentAmount is greater than 0, a row representing the payment is
inserted into the authorpayment table. Although this approach is necessary with a cursor, if you used a set-based approach, you wouldn't need this IF…THEN statement. The
results from properly used INNER JOINs would exclude any titles and authors that did
not have any titles sold, and therefore would result in no payment:

```
IF _PaymentAmount > 0.00 THEN
    INSERT authorpayment (
        AuthorID,
        TitleID,
        PaymentYear,
        PaymentAmount
        )
    SELECT
        _AuthorID,
        _TitleID,
        _PaymentYear,
        _PaymentAmount;
    END IF;
```

If you've fetched all the values for the rows in your cursor, here is where you exit the loop:

```
IF _Done = TRUE THEN

    LEAVE GetTitles;
END IF;
```

At the end of the stored procedure, you end the LOOP, close the cursor, use END to represent the end of all actions in the stored procedure, and then change the delimiter
back to the standard semicolon:

```
END LOOP GetTitles;

CLOSE AllTitles;

END //

DELIMITER ;
```

After reviewing the entire stored procedure, you should be able to make improvements that eliminate the use of a cursor, which makes the relational database management system (RDBMS) do less work and also eliminates the need for any variables.

23.2.3 Improving the INSERT stored procedure

The first thing you want to do is rewrite the sections containing queries you want to keep. Your review noted that you could use a query to determine the count of authors for each title (used to calculate the royalty payment) and include the Royalty values from the title table as well. The query, which will be used in a subquery, might look like this:

```
SELECT
    t.TitleID,
    t.Royalty,
    COUNT(ta.AuthorID) AS AuthorCount
FROM title t
INNER JOIN titleauthor ta
    ON t.TitleID = ta.TitleID
GROUP BY
    t.TitleID,
    t.Royalty
```

The review also revealed that you could use the logic to determine the sales of a title per year in dollars in a subquery. You want to avoid using a function on the OrderDate column of the orderheader table, which would cause extra work for the RDBMS. You can use some different date functions to take the value for year and then calculate starting and ending dates for the value of the _PaymentYear parameter.

The first date function is MAKEDATE, which allows you to make a date of the first day of the year using only a value for the year. You'll set the date for the first day of the chosen year like this:

```
MAKEDATE(_PaymentYear, 1)
```

You could use MAKEDATE to select the last day of the year by replacing the value 1 with 365, but that doesn't work for every year. Leap years have 366 days, and because you don't know if the value passed for _PaymentYear is a leap year, it would be better to calculate the end of your date range as anything less than the start of the next year. To calculate that, use the DATE_ADD function like this:

```
DATE_ADD(MAKEDATE(@Year, 1), INTERVAL 1 YEAR)
```

> **NOTE** Although not all RDBMSs have these specific functions, they all have similar functions with different names that can help you determine a date from parts such as the year, as well as functions that help you make calculations with dates.

With the range of dates that will replace the YEAR function sorted, here's the query to determine total sales per title, which will also be used in a subquery:

```
SELECT
    oi.TitleID,
    SUM(oi.Quantity * oi.ItemPrice) AS TotalSales
FROM orderheader oh
INNER JOIN orderitem oi
    ON oh.OrderID = oi.OrderID
WHERE oh.OrderDate >= MAKEDATE(@Year, 1)
    AND oh.OrderDate < DATE_ADD(MAKEDATE(@Year, 1), INTERVAL 1 YEAR)
GROUP BY
    oi.TitleID
```

You need one more query that calculates the payment amount. Having the payment amount value for each AuthorID and TitleID in the chosen year allows you to populate the authorpayment table. Because both of the two preceding queries to be used for subqueries include TitleID, they should be easy to join.

Using the logic to calculate the payment amount from the original stored procedure, you can put all the logic together in a stored procedure with one query. Because a bit of complexity is involved, add a few comments to your stored procedure to explain your intentions:

```
DELIMITER //

CREATE PROCEDURE InsertAnnualPayment(
    IN _PaymentYear int
    )
BEGIN

INSERT authorpayment (
    AuthorID,
    TitleID,
    PaymentYear,
    PaymentAmount
    )
/* Calculate the total royalty per author */
SELECT
    ta.AuthorID,
    ta.TitleID,
    _PaymentYear,
    CONVERT((
        (sales.TotalSales * (royalty.Royalty/100))/royalty.AuthorCount),
        decimal(7,2)) AS RoyaltyPerAuthor
FROM titleauthor ta
INNER JOIN (
    /* Determine annual sales by title */
    SELECT
        oi.TitleID,
        SUM(oi.Quantity * oi.ItemPrice) AS TotalSales
    FROM orderheader oh
    INNER JOIN orderitem oi
        ON oh.OrderID = oi.OrderID
```

```
    WHERE oh.OrderDate >= MAKEDATE(@Year, 1)
        AND oh.OrderDate < DATE_ADD(MAKEDATE(@Year, 1), INTERVAL 1 YEAR)
    GROUP BY
        oi.TitleID
    ) sales
    ON ta.TitleID = sales.TitleID
INNER JOIN (
    /* Determine the royalty and count of authors */
    SELECT
        t.TitleID,
        t.Royalty,
        COUNT(ta2.AuthorID) AS AuthorCount
    FROM title t
    INNER JOIN titleauthor ta2
        ON t.TitleID = ta2.TitleID
    GROUP BY
        t.TitleID,
        t.Royalty
        ) royalty
    ON ta.TitleID = royalty.TitleID;

END //

DELIMITER ;
```

Now you have a stored procedure with no cursor, no variables, and no queries beyond what you need. You can populate the authorpayment table using set-based programming, which should be your goal whenever you write SQL. You don't have to worry about mismatched data types, and you aren't using functions in ways that could affect performance.

The stored procedure is greatly improved. But could you improve it even more?

23.2.4 *Improving the INSERT stored procedure even more*

You've learned a lot in 23 chapters, so don't be afraid to consider other keywords and techniques when you make further improvements in someone else's script. You may be able to improve a few more parts of this stored procedure, starting with the subqueries.

Although the two subqueries in this new version of the stored procedure perform better than the cursor, this solution might not be the best one if your orderheader and orderitem tables contain millions of records. It may be a good idea to replace the subquery that calculates the TotalSales for each title in a given year with a temporary table. Although this approach means writing more data to a temporary table, the subsequent INNER JOIN may read less data than all the data read in the subquery. Although using temporary tables isn't required for the current data set, which has only a few rows in each table, in many situations, a bit of testing will reveal that using temporary tables can help performance.

Another possible improvement is related to the _PaymentYear parameter. The single _PaymentYear parameter used by the stored procedure doesn't offer much flexibility, so you might consider replacing it with parameters for the start and end dates of a range of dates. This approach allows for annual, quarterly, monthly, and even custom ranges of values. Consider making any script more flexible if you can, anticipating that there'll be more diverse query requests in the future.

Finally, depending on the use of this data, it may be worthwhile to replace the Insert-AnnualPayment stored procedure and the authorpayment table with a view that calculates the author and title royalty for every sale. Remember that a view is simply a stored query to be called on whenever you want. If you remove the consideration for a specific date range, you could build a query to calculate the royalty of every orderitem with a query like this:

```
SELECT
    ta.AuthorID,
    ta.TitleID,
    oh.OrderID,
    oh.OrderDate,
    CONVERT((
        (SUM(oi.Quantity * oi.ItemPrice) * (t.Royalty/100))/ac.AuthorCount),
        decimal(7,2)) AS RoyaltyPerAuthor
FROM title t
INNER JOIN titleauthor ta
    ON t.TitleID = ta.TitleID
INNER JOIN orderitem oi
    ON ta.TitleID = oi.TitleID
INNER JOIN orderheader oh
    ON oi.OrderID = oh.OrderID
INNER JOIN (
    /* Determine the royalty and count of authors */
    SELECT
        TitleID,
        COUNT(AuthorID) AS AuthorCount
    FROM titleauthor
    GROUP BY
        TitleID
        ) ac
    ON ta.TitleID = ac.TitleID
 GROUP BY
    ta.AuthorID,
    ta.TitleID,
    oh.OrderID
    oh.OrderDate;
```

This view would eliminate the redundancy of all the data in the authorpayment table. It would also allow you to query the view for whatever values of AuthorID, TitleID, and OrderID you want, as well as query any range of OrderDate values. A view doesn't allow you to persist the data the way the authorpayment table does, but if you don't need the data to be persisted, a view is a great option.

The key idea that you should take away from this chapter is this: you have options. Throughout this month of lunches, you've learned dozens of keywords and concepts, and you've seen how to use them effectively. I hope that reviewing these scripts was helpful and that it gave you a higher level of confidence in your ability to use the SQL language.

24

Never the end

We've arrived at the final chapter of *Learn SQL in a Month of Lunches*. I hope that this book has been useful to you and convinced you that even with little or no programming experience, anyone can learn to write useful SQL queries.

Starting with chapter 1, the goal was for you to be immediately effective in writing SQL queries. With all the concepts and keywords discussed and used, you should feel confident enough to write queries that satisfy a wide range of requests. Now you know different ways to filter, join, and group data, as well as how to modify data and even create objects such as tables and stored procedures. I'm confident that you've learned enough to understand most examples of SQL that someone else wrote.

Still, the end of this book is hardly the end of your exploration of the SQL language. This is truly the beginning because the more you work with SQL, the more new, exciting keywords and objects you'll discover. Where do you go next? Well, here are a few ideas.

24.1 More SQL

As you must have noticed, the MySQL Workbench Navigator has a section named Functions that I never addressed. Although you worked with dozens of functions throughout this book, such as CONCAT and COALESCE, those functions aren't included because they're system functions, and the Functions section is for user-defined functions. That's right—you can create your own functions! As you progress

271

in your experience with SQL, you'll encounter requests that require evaluating values or expressions with a function that you need to create.

Another consideration for future learning is window functions. Although these functions aren't available in every relational database management system (RDBMS), when you're working with an RDBMS that includes them, you can perform powerful calculations such as running totals, rankings, and percentiles for each row. In some ways, these functions operate like a cursor but without the drawbacks of locking, blocking, and excessive resource use.

When you need to construct SQL based on unknown conditions, many RDBMSs offer you the option to use dynamic SQL. As strange as it sounds, *dynamic SQL* allows you to create a string of SQL to be executed later. Although it's somewhat unusual, this technique gives you another level of flexibility in your SQL, which can be useful when a query needs to dynamically change filtering clauses or even the names of tables being queried.

These are a few of the many tools and techniques yet to be discovered on your SQL journey. Where should you go next?

24.2   *Other SQL resources*

The best way to increase your skill level in any language, whether it's spoken to a computer or to another person, is to practice. I added labs in nearly every chapter to get you to practice thinking about SQL and using it to solve problems. You can continue to practice by using the sqlnovel database to write SQL to do things like insert new rows into the orderheader and orderitem tables and retrieve data for sales by category. The practice possibilities are limited only by your imagination.

Then again, your immediate need may be to work with an RDBMS other than MySQL, in which case you can install a tool that allows you to work with that RDBMS and find a sample database to use for practicing SQL queries. Free sample databases are available for every RDBMS, so use your favorite search engine to find them, and use these databases to write your own practice queries. The more you practice writing SQL, the easier it will be to respond to any request effectively.

If you found this book helpful, take a look at other RDBMS-specific books from Manning that can help you improve your SQL skills, such as *100 SQL Server Mistakes and How to Avoid Them*, by Peter Carter (https://www.manning.com/books/100-sql-server-mistakes-and-how-to-avoid-them), and *PostgreSQL Mistakes and How to Avoid Them*, by Jimmy Angelakos (https://www.manning.com/books/postgresql-mistakes-and-how-to-avoid-them). As I've noted throughout this book, every RDBMS is slightly different in terms of SQL syntax, and an RDBMS-specific book can increase your depth of knowledge in ways that can benefit your career. Although it's good to have broad knowledge of the SQL language in the ways I've discussed throughout this book, obtaining most of your experience in a particular RDBMS could allow you to showcase yourself as an expert in that particular flavor of SQL.

Perhaps you'll discover that you want to move beyond writing queries that retrieve data and learn about creating databases. If so, consider books such as *Understanding*

Databases, by David Clinton (https://www.manning.com/books/understanding -databases) and *Grokking Relational Database Design,* by Qiang Hao and Michail Tsikerdekis (https://www.manning.com/books/grokking-relational-database-design), that cover ways to design databases that perform well and scale with the massive amounts of data that modern databases contain. This book didn't discuss database design in depth, but understanding the capabilities and limitations of a database is also an important skill.

Above all, no matter what you choose to do next, be curious, and don't stop learning.

24.3 Farewell

It's been my pleasure to help you begin what I hope is a long-lasting journey using the SQL language. Whatever the future holds for you, I congratulate you on all the work you've done so far, and I wish you the best in whatever comes next!

index